# Oh My Goddess!

ああっ女神さまっ

**34**

STORY AND ART BY
## Kosuke Fujishima

**TRANSLATION BY**
Christopher Lewis

**LETTERING AND TOUCH-UP BY**
Susie Lee AND Betty Dong
WITH Tom2K

**DARK HORSE MANGA™**

CHAPTER 213
Triple-Speed Happiness........3

CHAPTER 214
Jubilation Engine.............27

CHAPTER 215
Happy Monkey
Generations....................47

CHAPTER 216
I'll Fly for You!...............67

CHAPTER 217
My Important Words,
Your Pure Future...............89

CHAPTER 218
A Goddess's Blessing.........111

Letters to the Enchantress....136

CHAPTER 213

# Triple-Speed Happiness

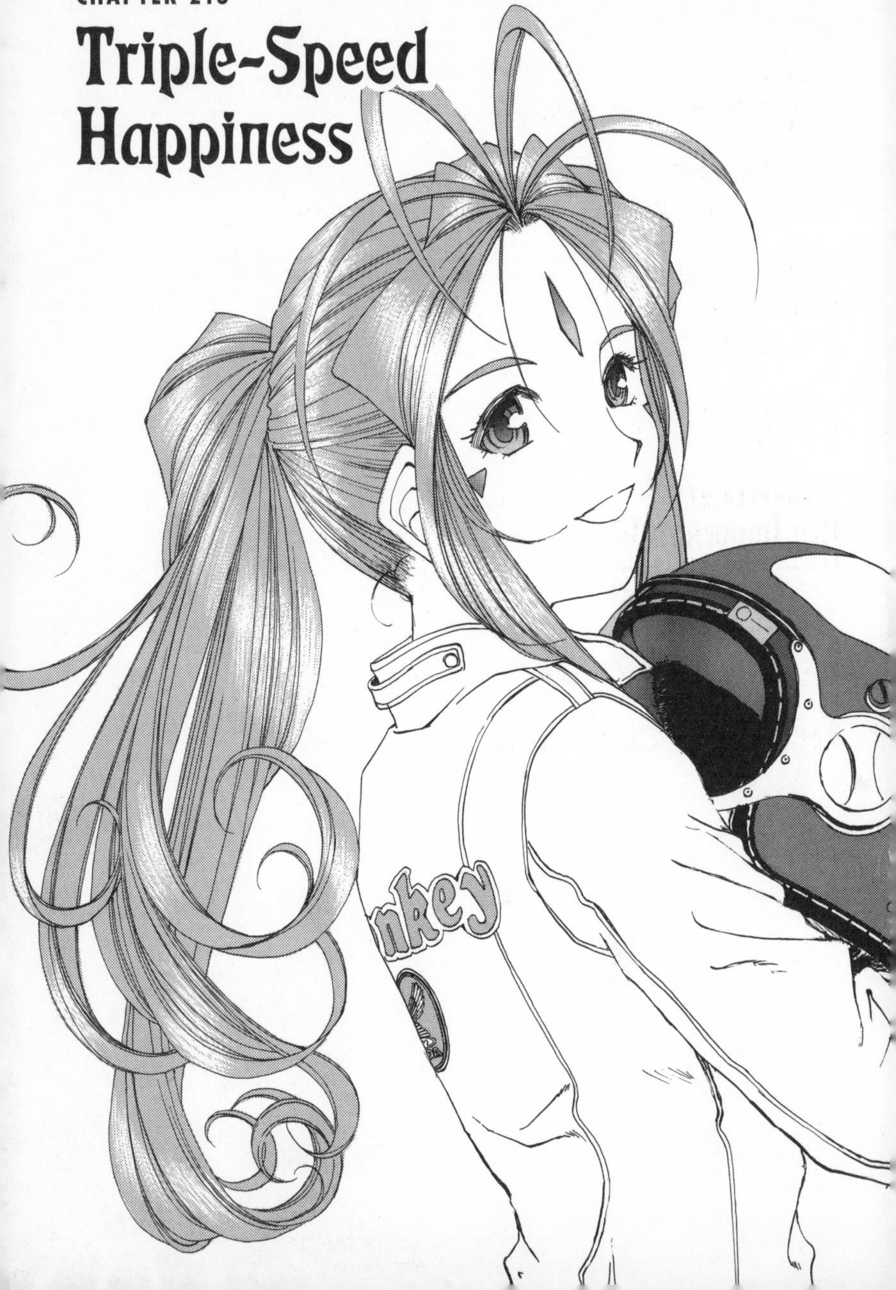

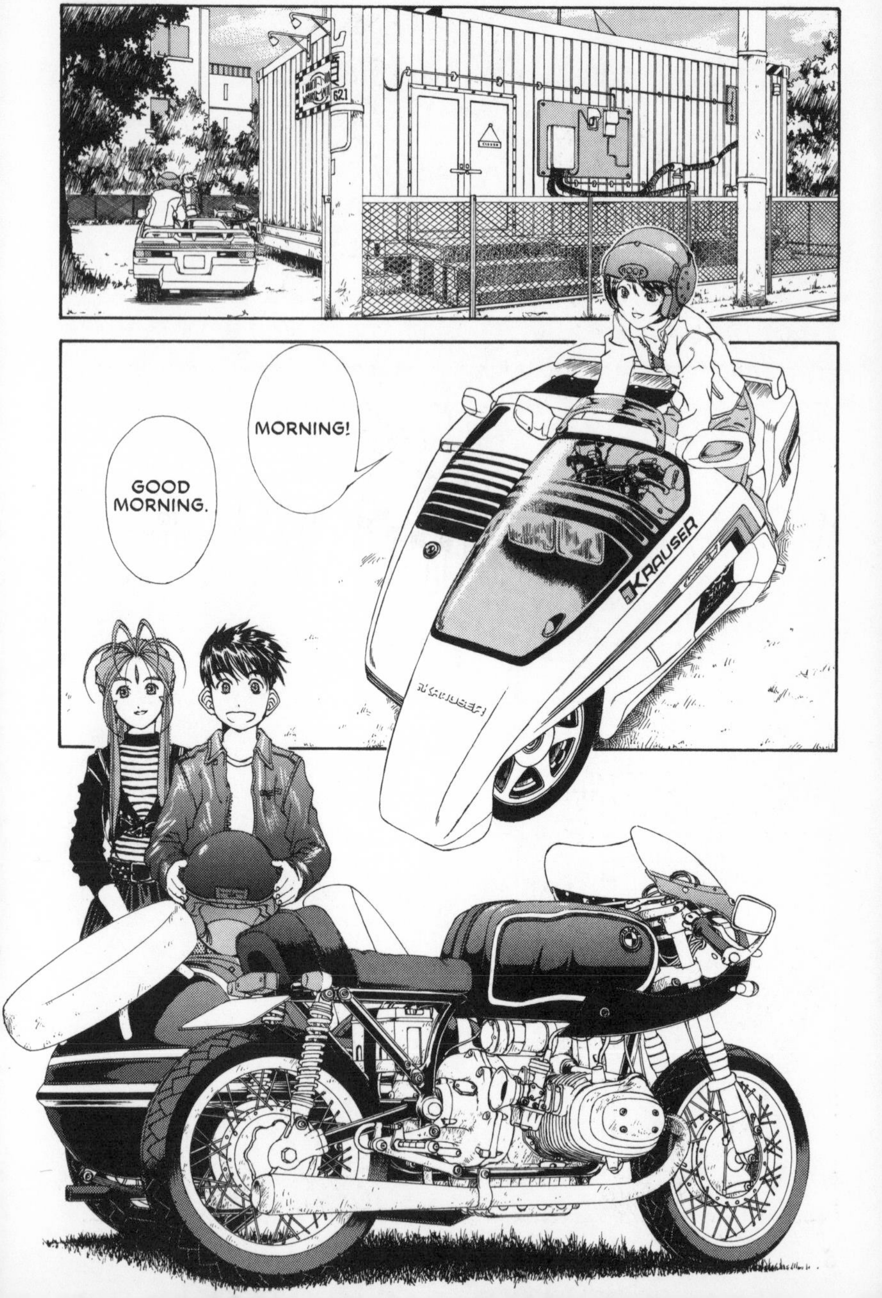
MORNING!
GOOD MORNING.
KRAUSER

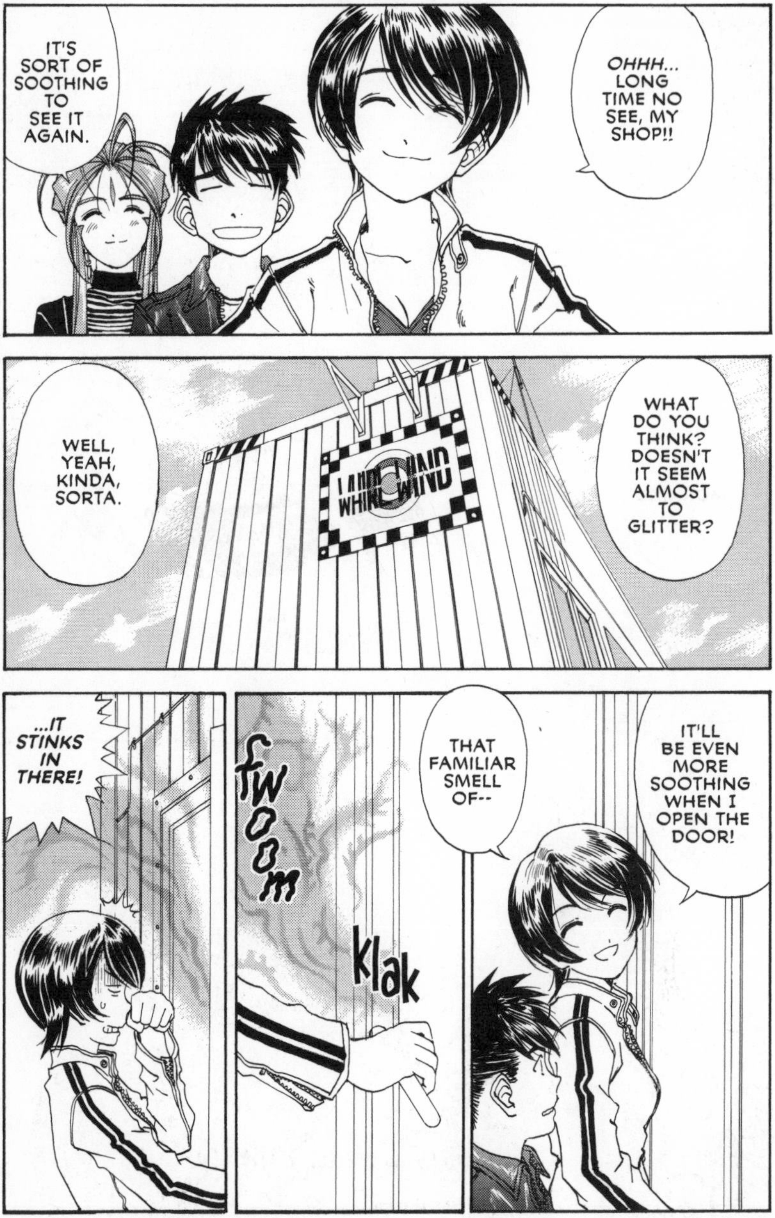
OHHH... LONG TIME NO SEE, MY SHOP!!
IT'S SORT OF SOOTHING TO SEE IT AGAIN.
WHAT DO YOU THINK? DOESN'T IT SEEM ALMOST TO GLITTER?
WELL, YEAH, KINDA, SORTA.
IT'LL BE EVEN MORE SOOTHING WHEN I OPEN THE DOOR!
THAT FAMILIAR SMELL OF--
klak
fwoom
...IT STINKS IN THERE!

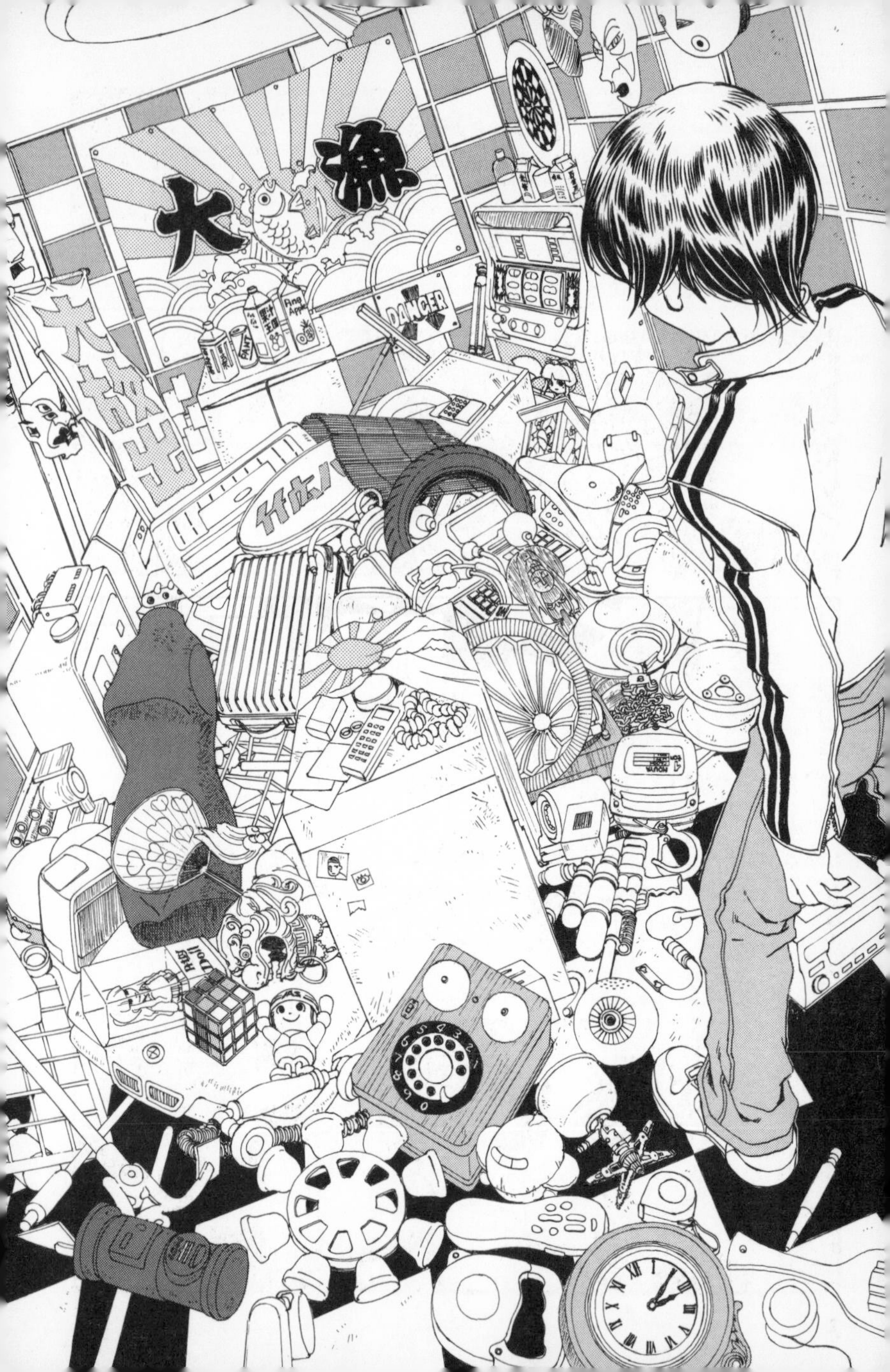
大漁
DANGER

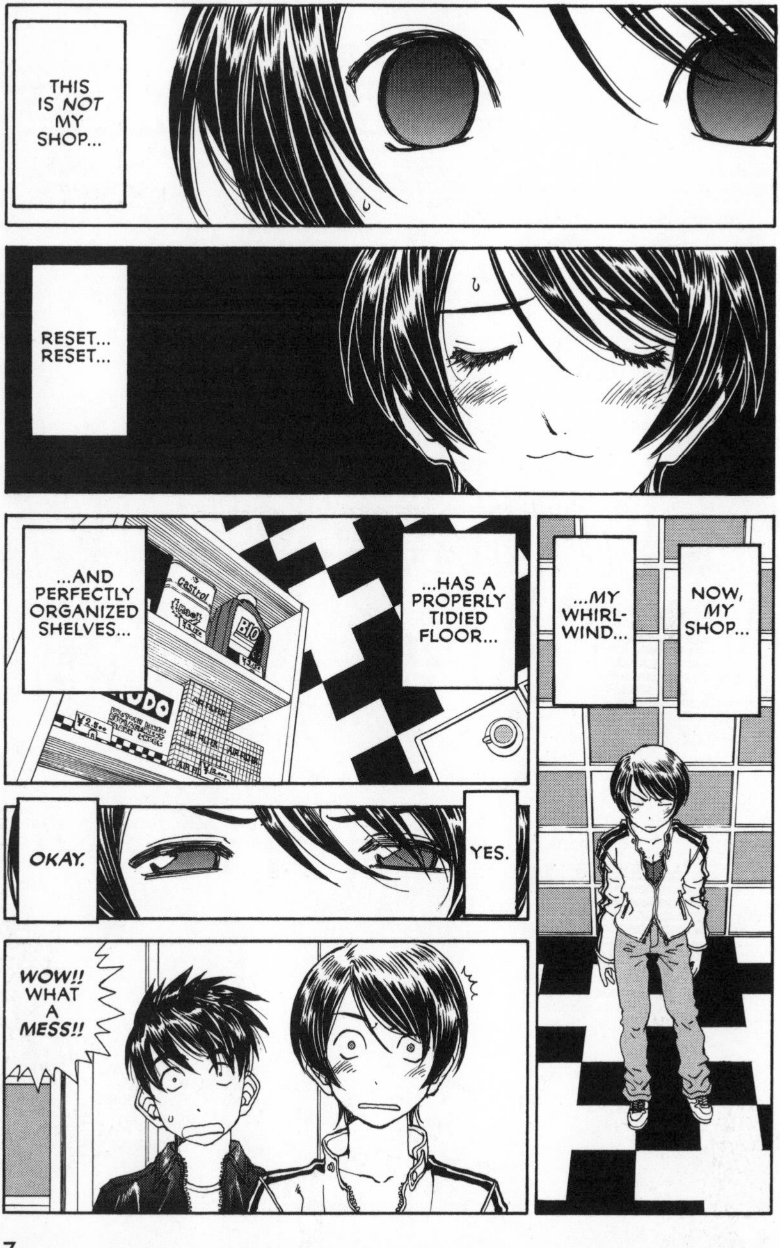
THIS IS *NOT* MY SHOP...
RESET... RESET...
NOW, *MY* SHOP...
...*MY* WHIRL-WIND...
...HAS A PROPERLY TIDIED FLOOR...
...AND PERFECTLY ORGANIZED SHELVES...
Castrol
YES.
OKAY.
WOW!! WHAT A *MESS!!*

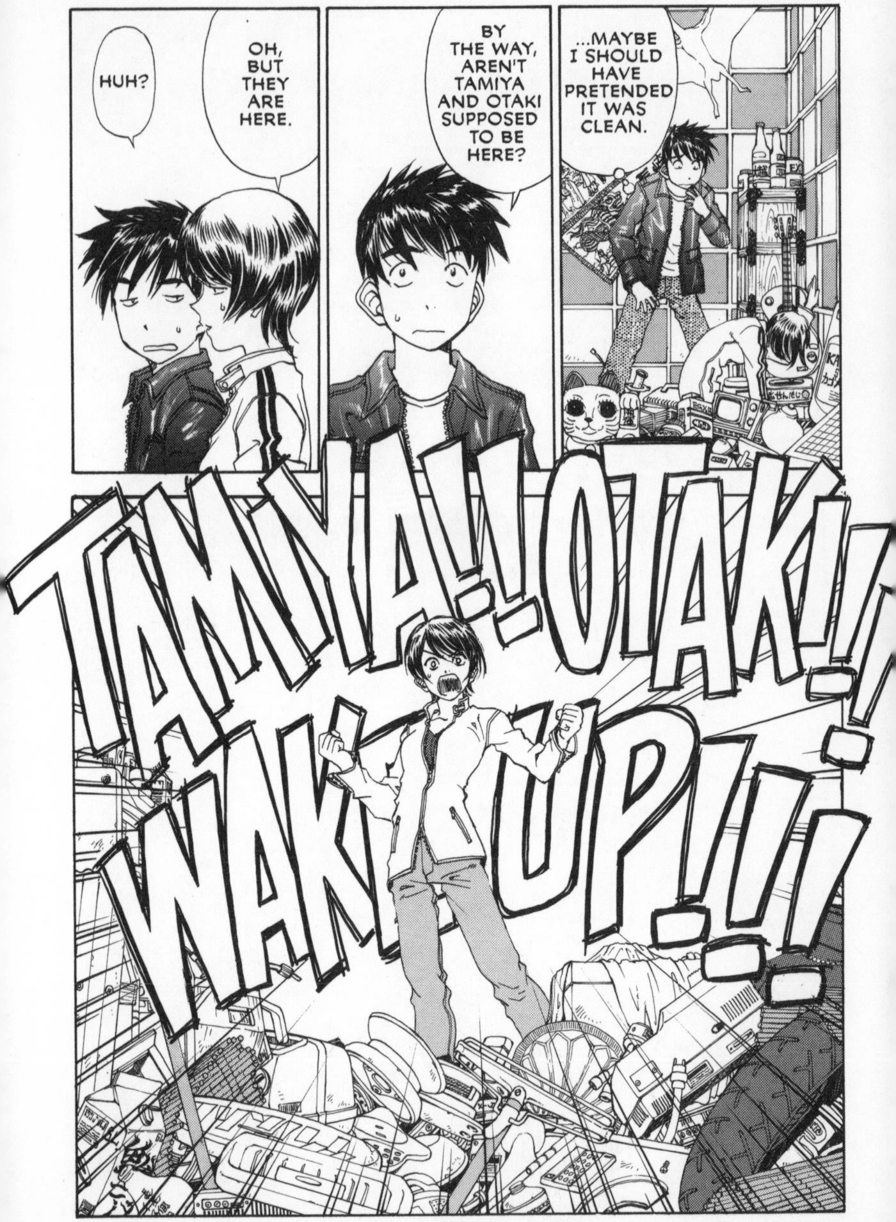
...MAYBE I SHOULD HAVE PRETENDED IT WAS CLEAN.
BY THE WAY, AREN'T TAMIYA AND OTAKI SUPPOSED TO BE HERE?
OH, BUT THEY ARE HERE.
HUH?
TAMIYA!! OTAKI!!
WAKE UP!!!

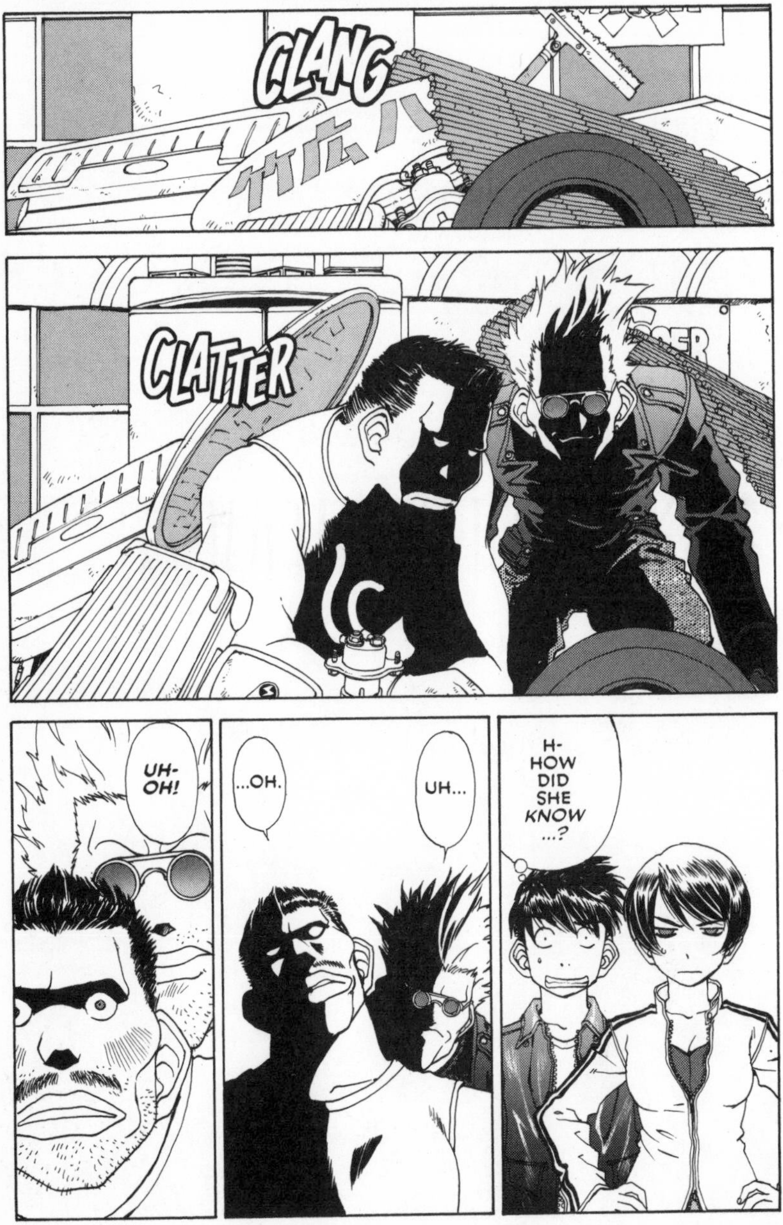
CLANG
CLATTER
H-HOW DID SHE KNOW ...?
UH...
...OH.
UH-OH!

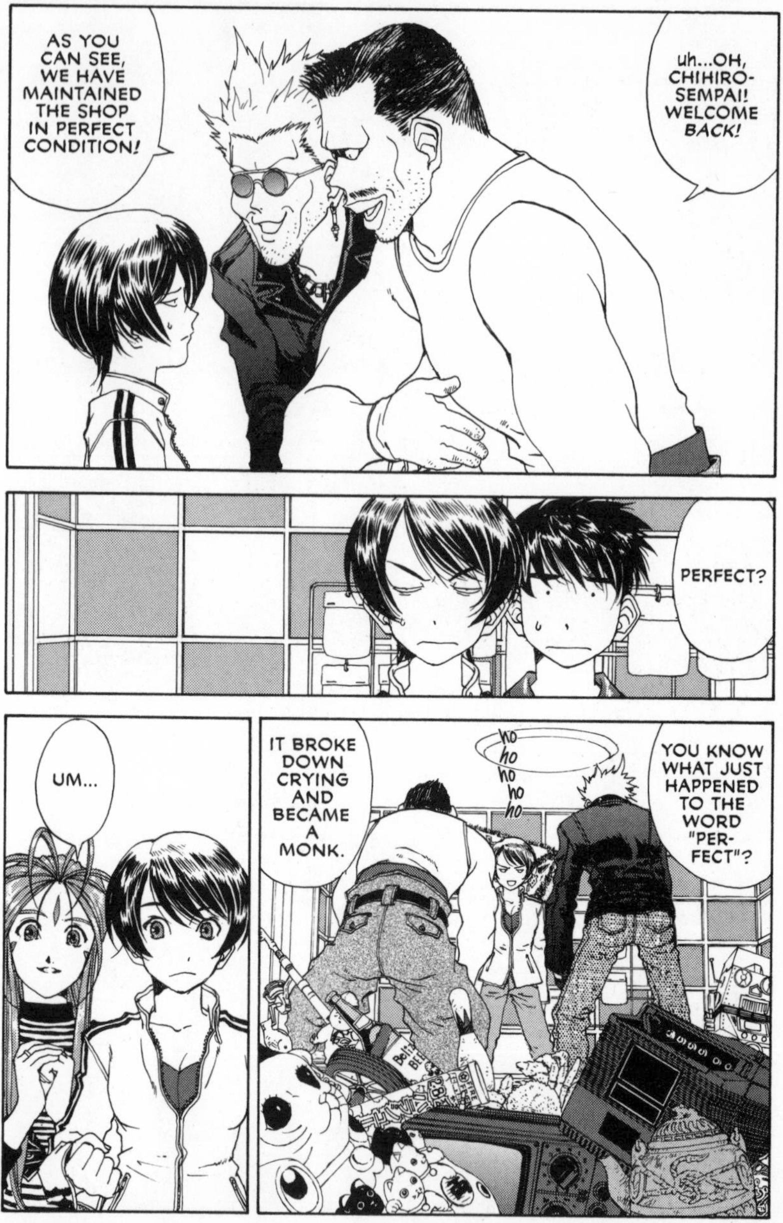
uh...OH, CHIHIRO-SEMPAI! WELCOME BACK!
AS YOU CAN SEE, WE HAVE MAINTAINED THE SHOP IN PERFECT CONDITION!
PERFECT?
YOU KNOW WHAT JUST HAPPENED TO THE WORD "PER-FECT"?
ho ho ho ho ho
IT BROKE DOWN CRYING AND BECAME A MONK.
UM...

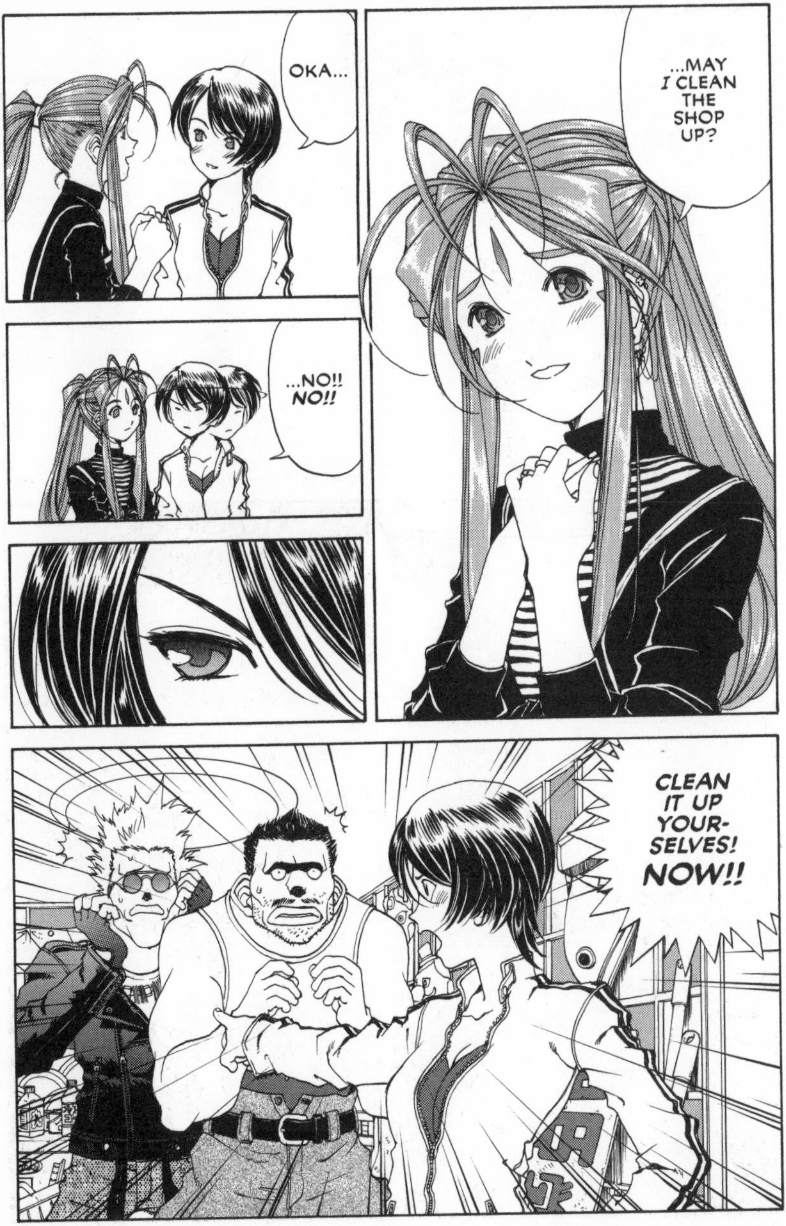
...MAY I CLEAN THE SHOP UP?
OKA...
...NO!! NO!!
CLEAN IT UP YOURSELVES! NOW!!

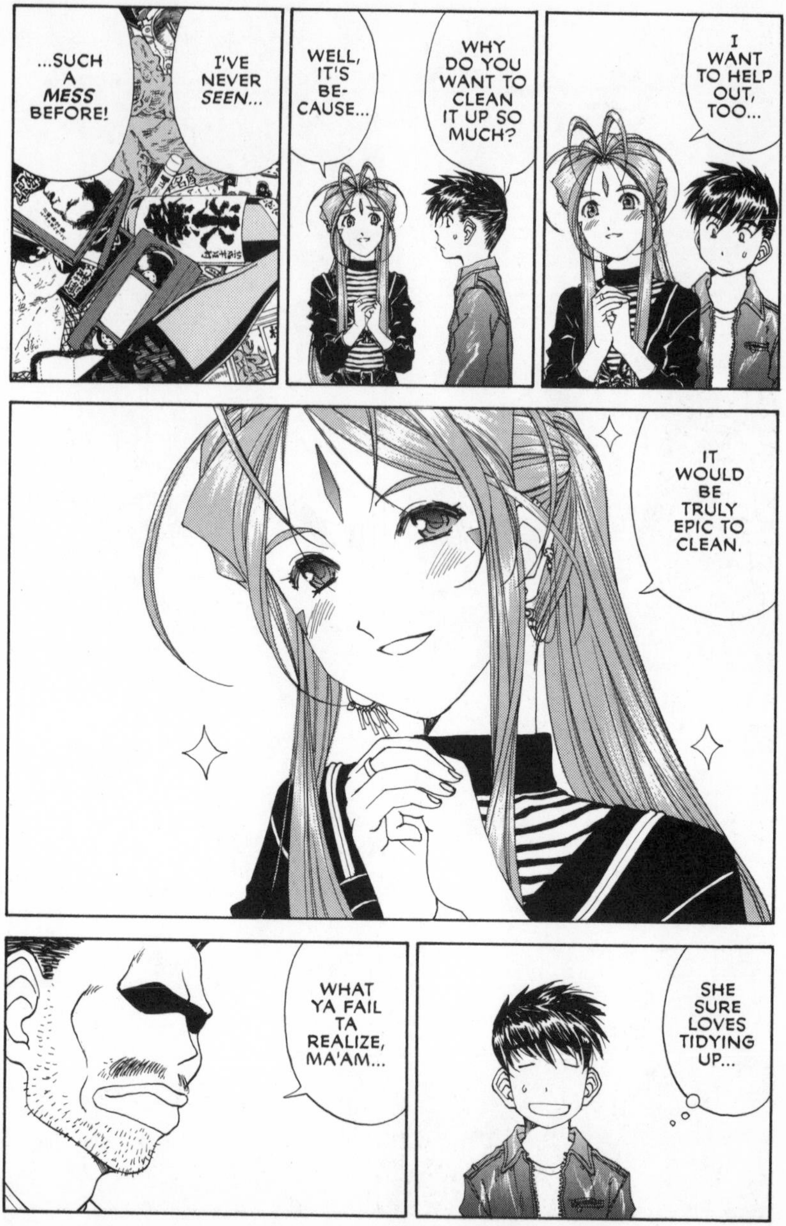
I WANT TO HELP OUT, TOO...
WHY DO YOU WANT TO CLEAN IT UP SO MUCH?
WELL, IT'S BE-CAUSE...
I'VE NEVER *SEEN*...
...SUCH A *MESS* BEFORE!
IT WOULD BE TRULY EPIC TO CLEAN.
SHE SURE LOVES TIDYING UP...
WHAT YA FAIL TA REALIZE, MA'AM...

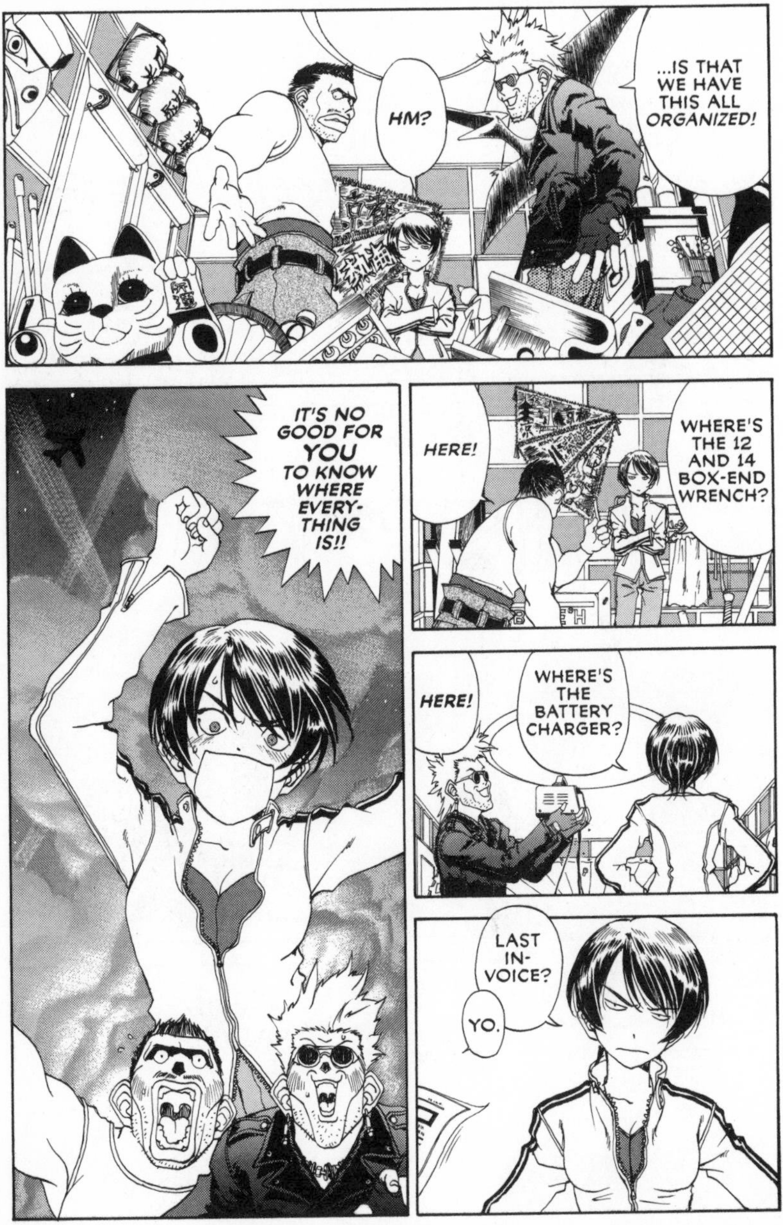

...IS THAT WE HAVE THIS ALL ORGANIZED!
HM?
WHERE'S THE 12 AND 14 BOX-END WRENCH?
HERE!
WHERE'S THE BATTERY CHARGER?
HERE!
LAST IN-VOICE?
YO.
IT'S NO GOOD FOR YOU TO KNOW WHERE EVERY-THING IS!!

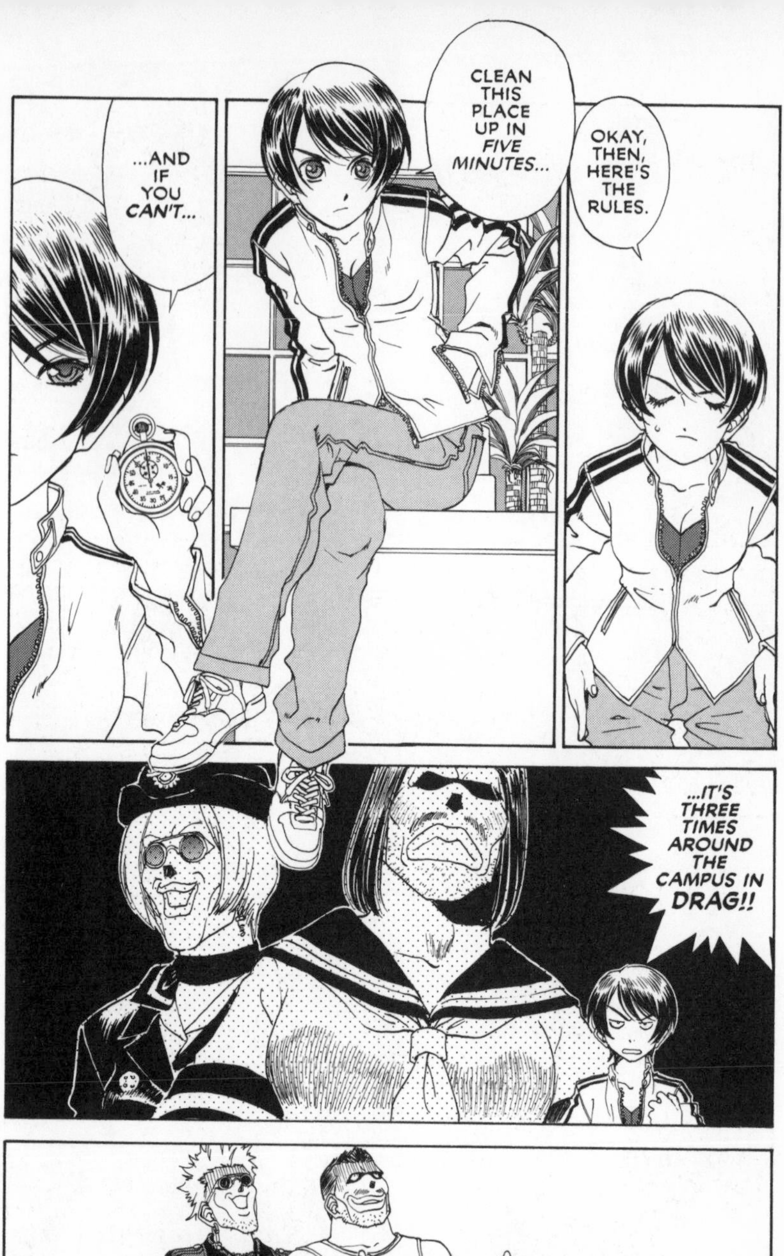
OKAY, THEN, HERE'S THE RULES.
CLEAN THIS PLACE UP IN *FIVE MINUTES*...
...AND IF YOU *CAN'T*...
...IT'S THREE TIMES AROUND THE CAMPUS IN **DRAG!!**

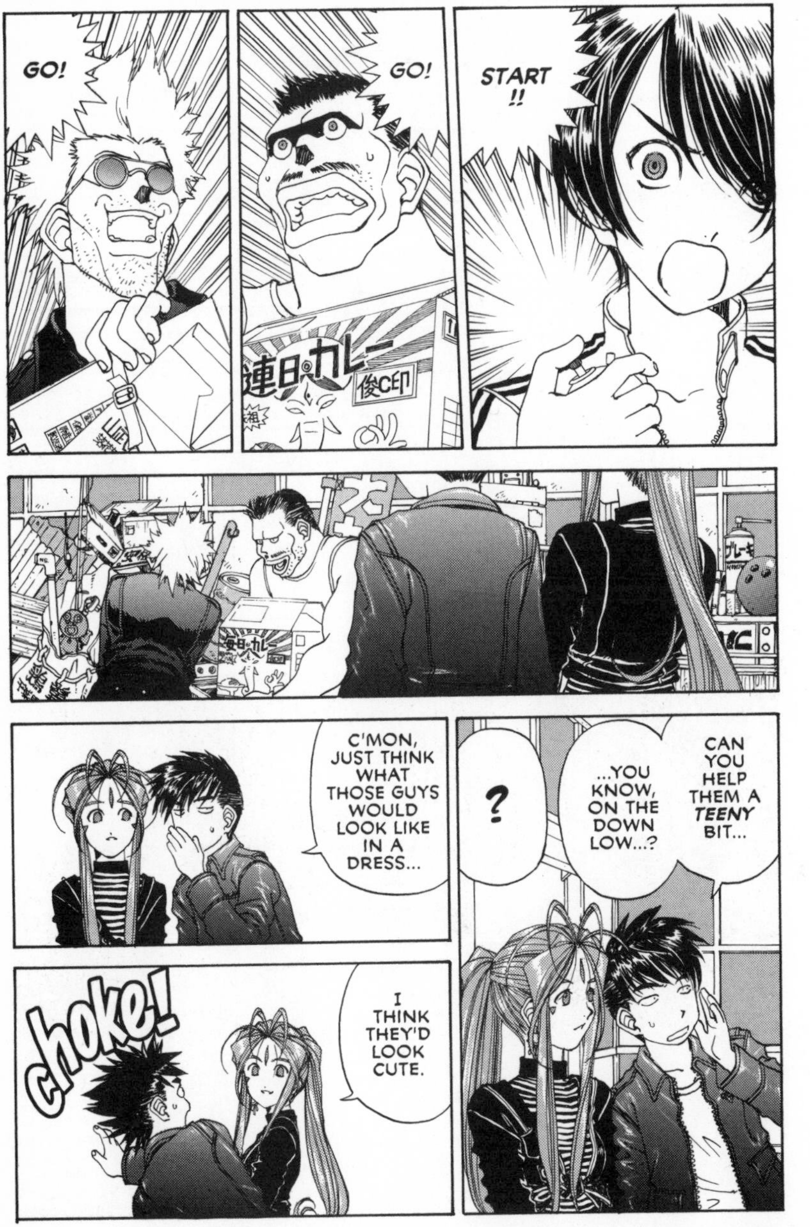
START !!
GO!
連日カレー
GO!
CAN YOU HELP THEM A *TEENY* BIT...
...YOU KNOW, ON THE DOWN LOW...?
?
C'MON, JUST THINK WHAT THOSE GUYS WOULD LOOK LIKE IN A DRESS...
I THINK THEY'D LOOK CUTE.
choke!

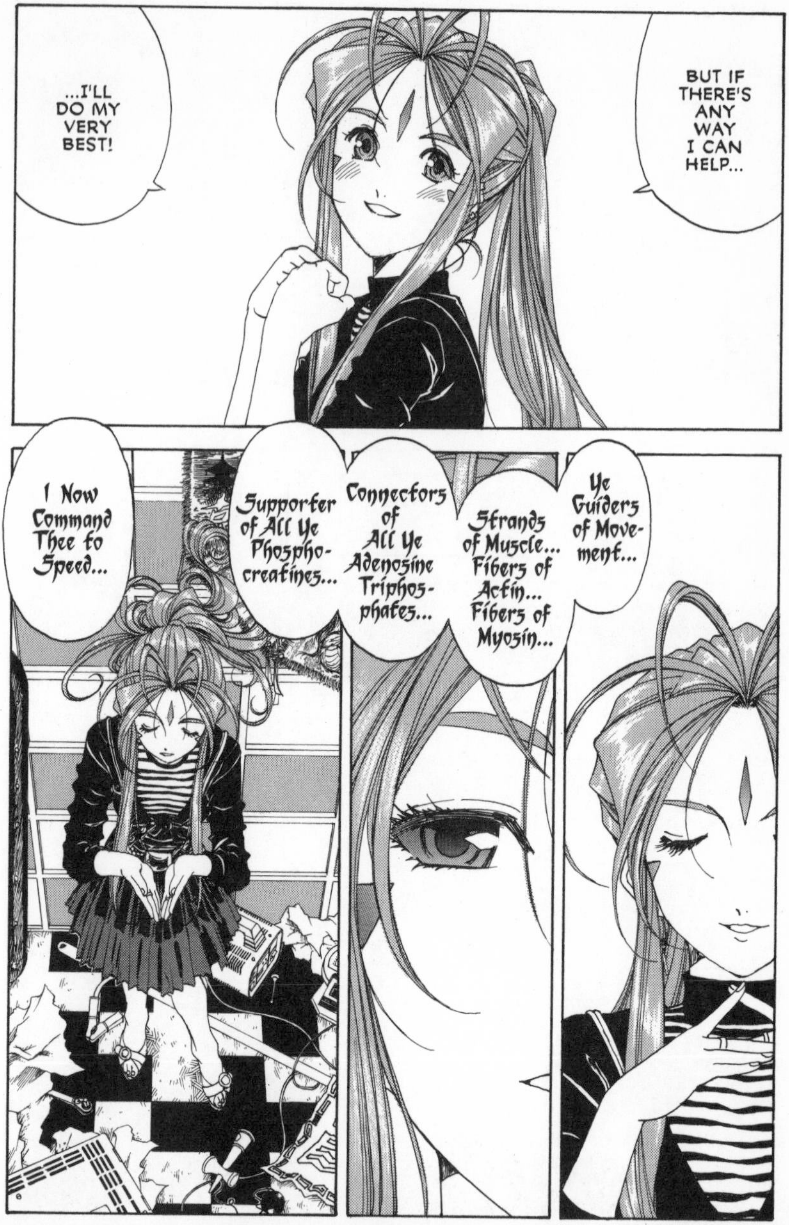
BUT IF THERE'S ANY WAY I CAN HELP...
...I'LL DO MY VERY BEST!
Ye Guiders of Move-ment...
Strands of Muscle... Fibers of Actin... Fibers of Myosin...
Connectors of All Ye Adenosine Triphos-phates...
Supporter of All Ye Phospho-creatines...
I Now Command Thee to Speed...

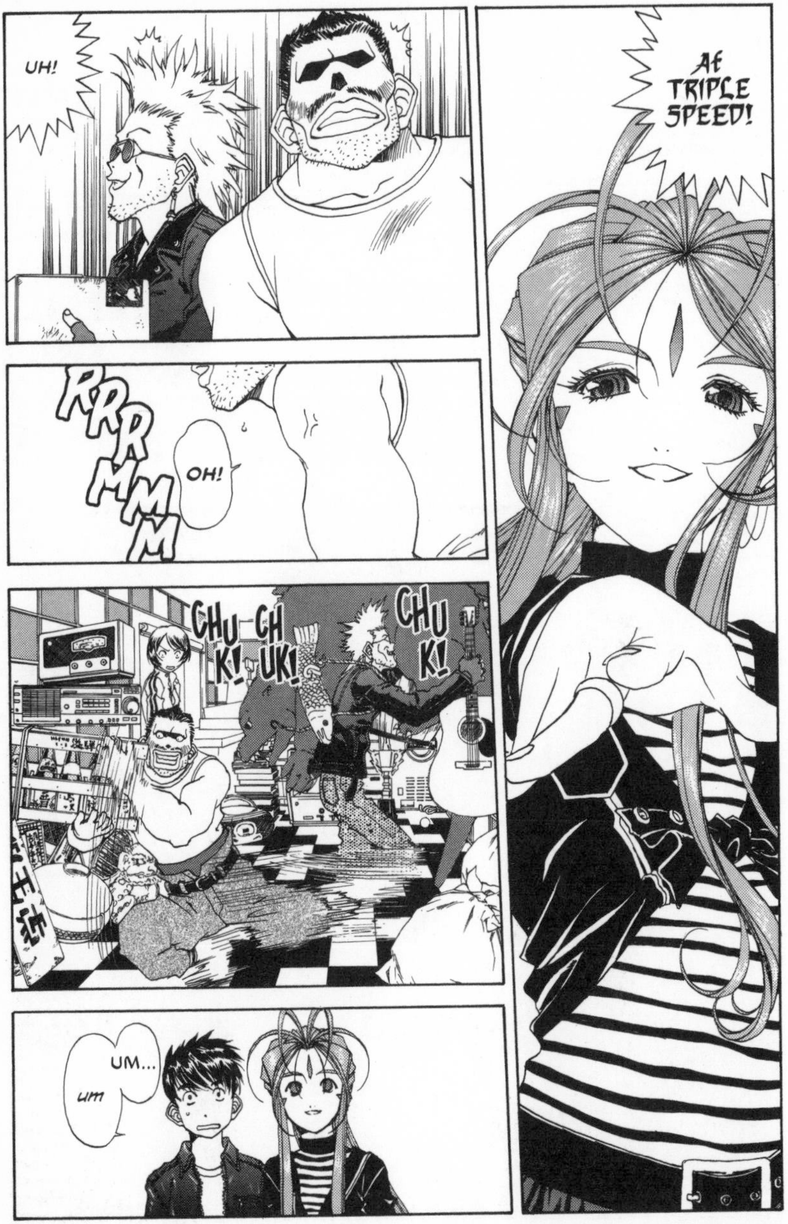

AT TRIPLE SPEED!
UH!
RRRMMMM
OH!
CHUK!
CHUK!
CHUK!
UM...
um

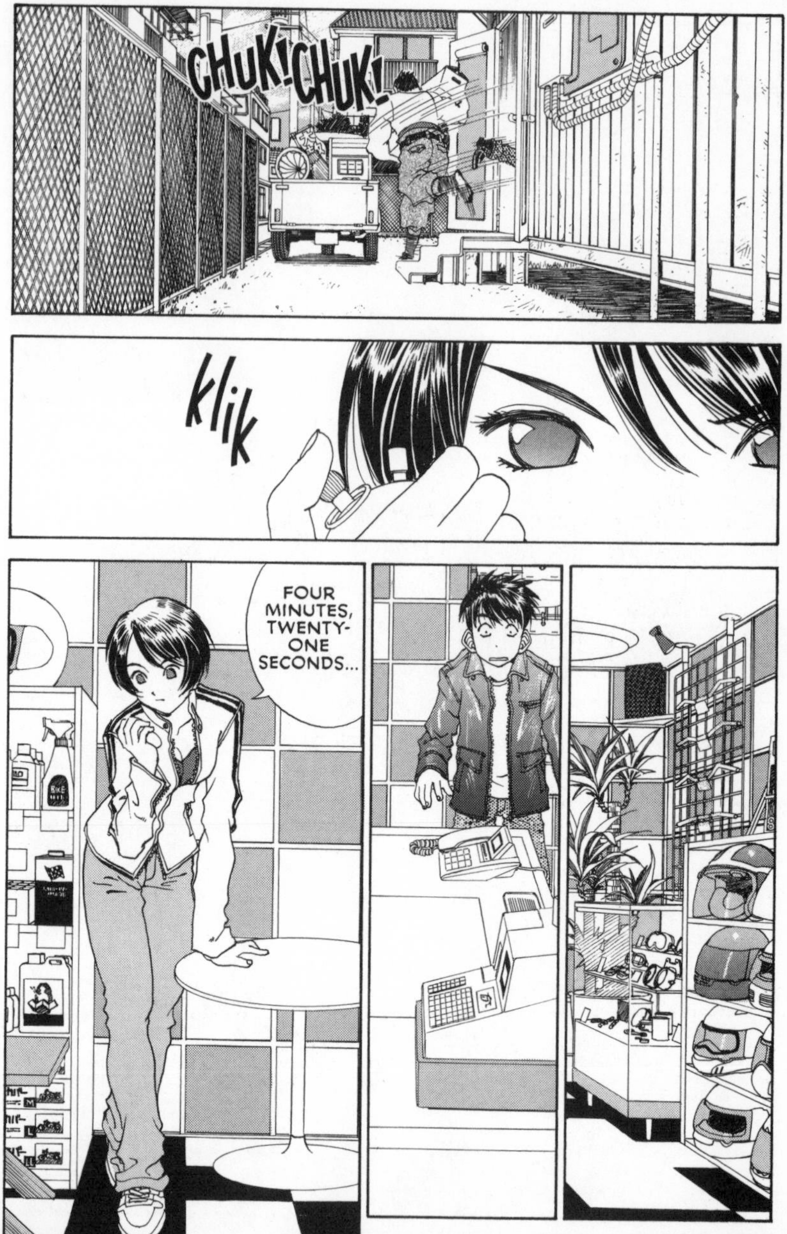
CHUK!CHUK!
klik
FOUR MINUTES, TWENTY-ONE SECONDS...

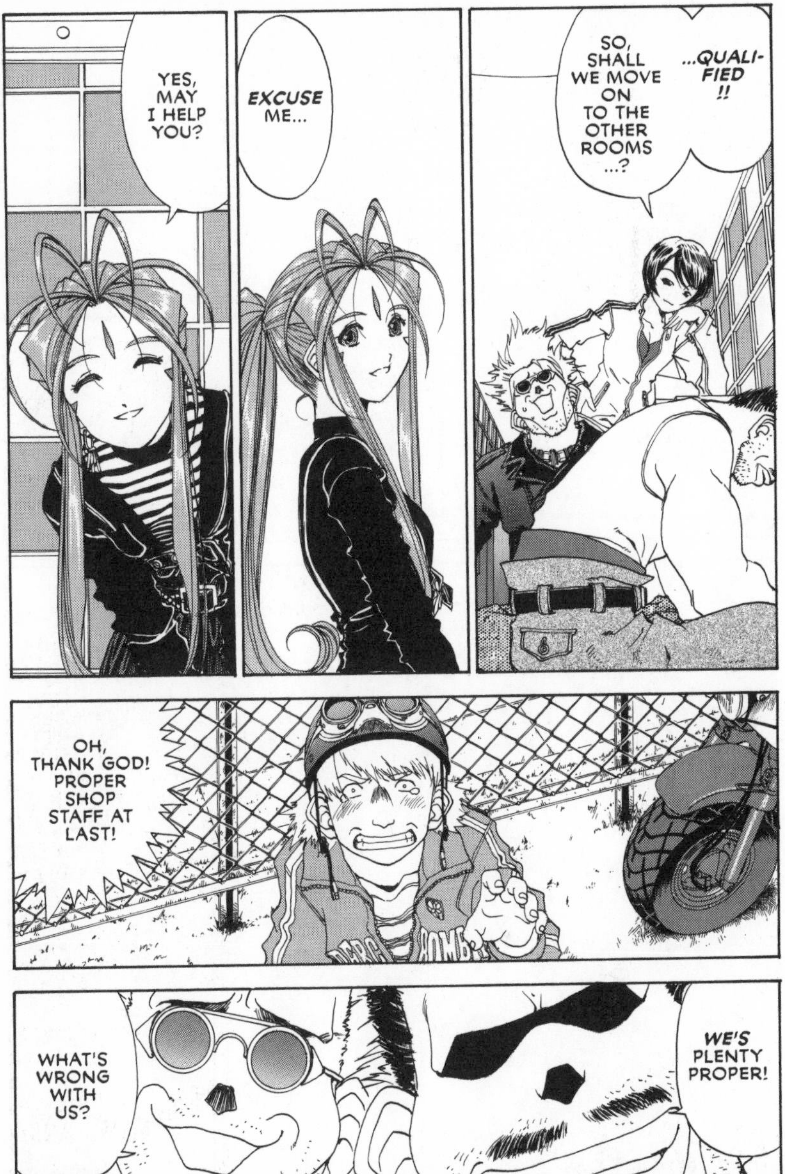

...*QUALIFIED* !!
SO, SHALL WE MOVE ON TO THE OTHER ROOMS ...?
*EXCUSE* ME...
YES, MAY I HELP YOU?
OH, THANK GOD! PROPER SHOP STAFF AT LAST!
*WE'S* PLENTY PROPER!
WHAT'S WRONG WITH US?

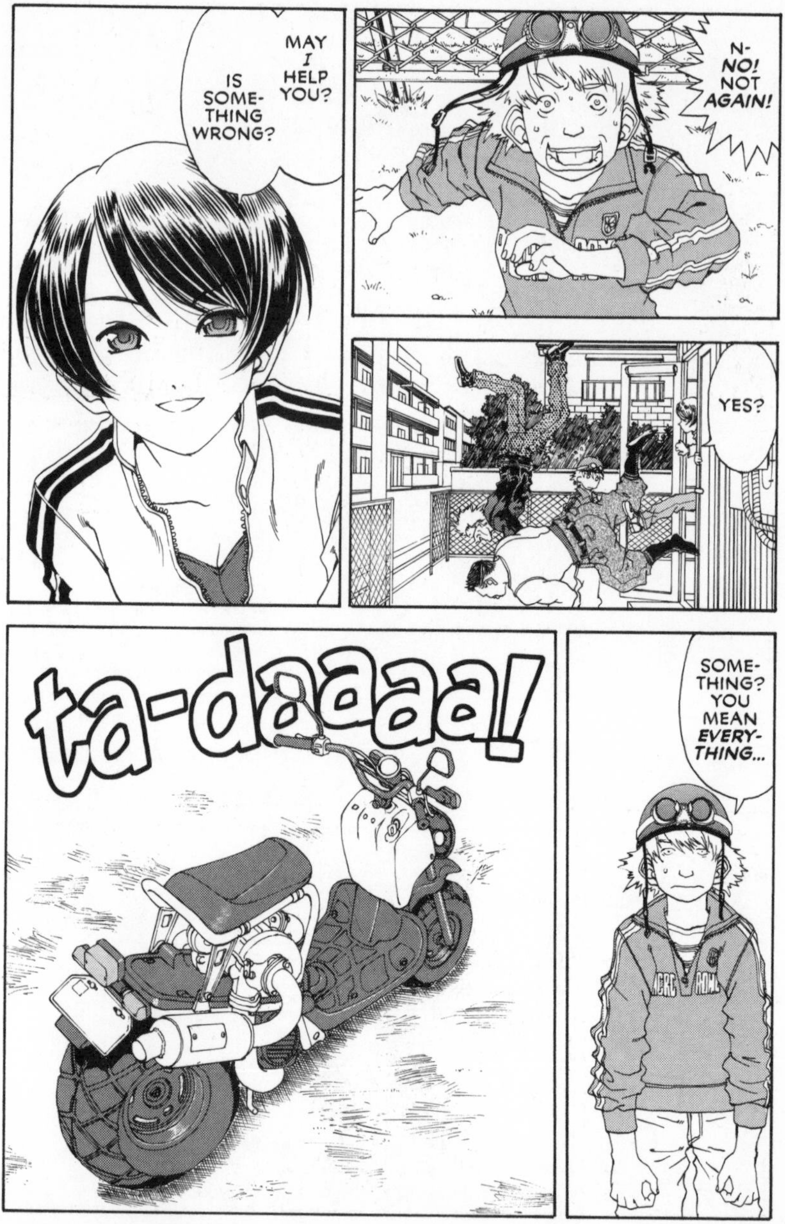
N-NO! NOT AGAIN!
YES?
MAY I HELP YOU?
IS SOMETHING WRONG?
SOMETHING? YOU MEAN EVERYTHING...
ta-daaaaa!

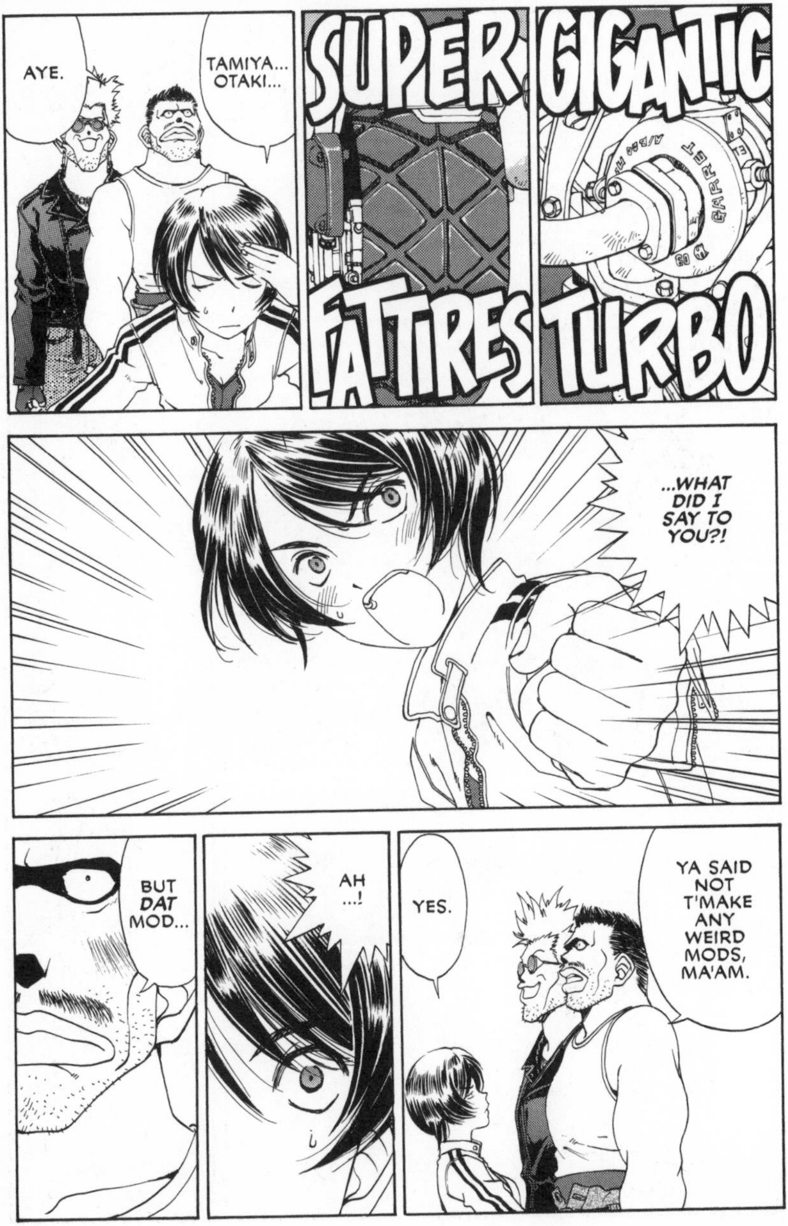
GIGANTIC
TURBO
SUPER
FAT TIRES
TAMIYA... OTAKI...
AYE.
...WHAT DID I SAY TO YOU?!
YA SAID NOT T'MAKE ANY WEIRD MODS, MA'AM.
YES.
AH ...!
BUT *DAT* MOD...

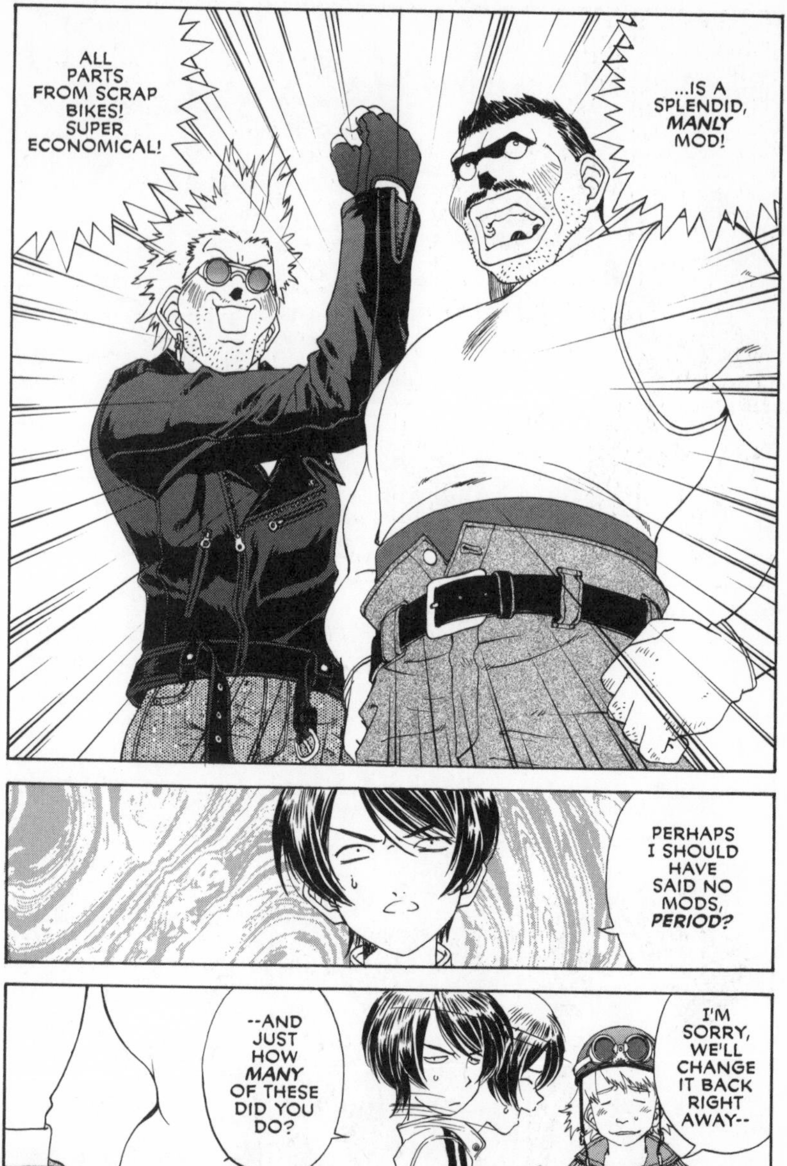
...IS A SPLENDID, *MANLY* MOD!
ALL PARTS FROM SCRAP BIKES! SUPER ECONOMICAL!
PERHAPS I SHOULD HAVE SAID NO MODS, *PERIOD?*
I'M SORRY, WE'LL CHANGE IT BACK RIGHT AWAY--
--AND JUST HOW *MANY* OF THESE DID YOU DO?

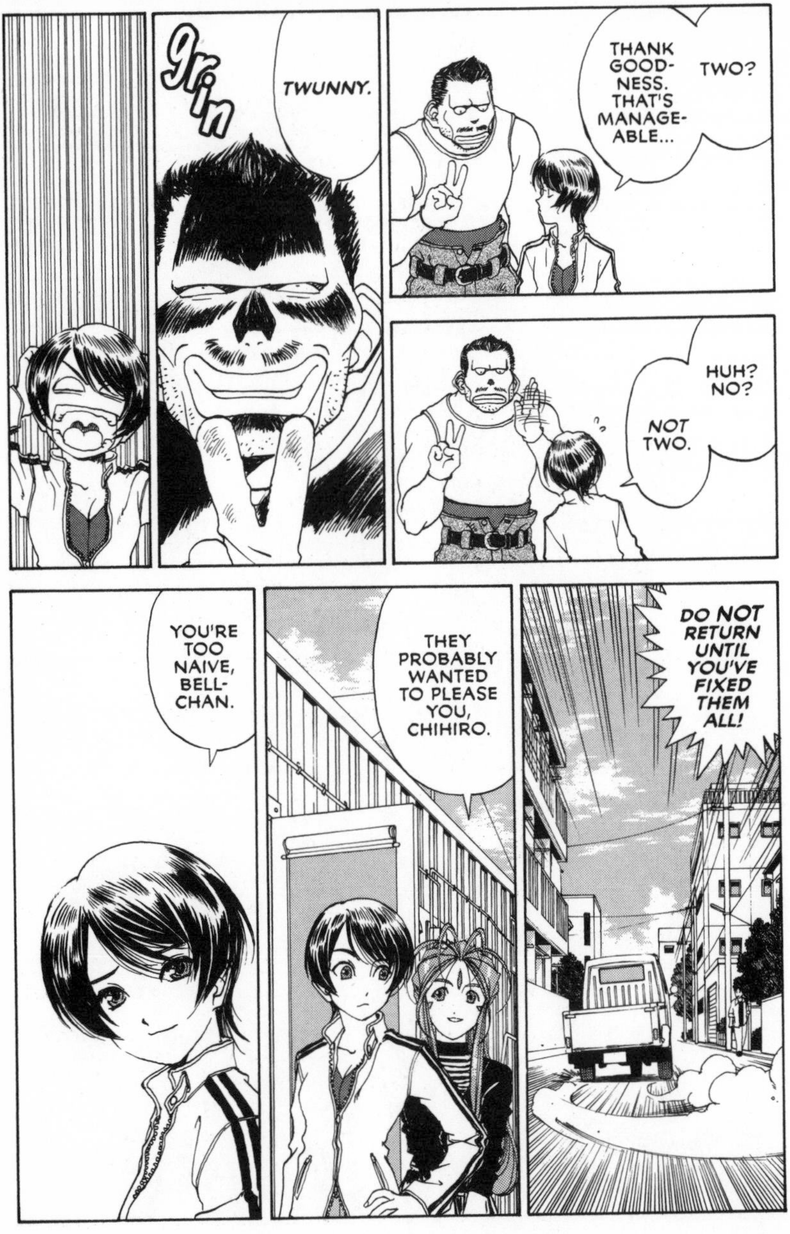
TWO?
THANK GOODNESS. THAT'S MANAGEABLE...
HUH? NO?
NOT TWO.
grin
TWUNNY.
DO NOT RETURN UNTIL YOU'VE FIXED THEM ALL!
THEY PROBABLY WANTED TO PLEASE YOU, CHIHIRO.
YOU'RE TOO NAIVE, BELL-CHAN.

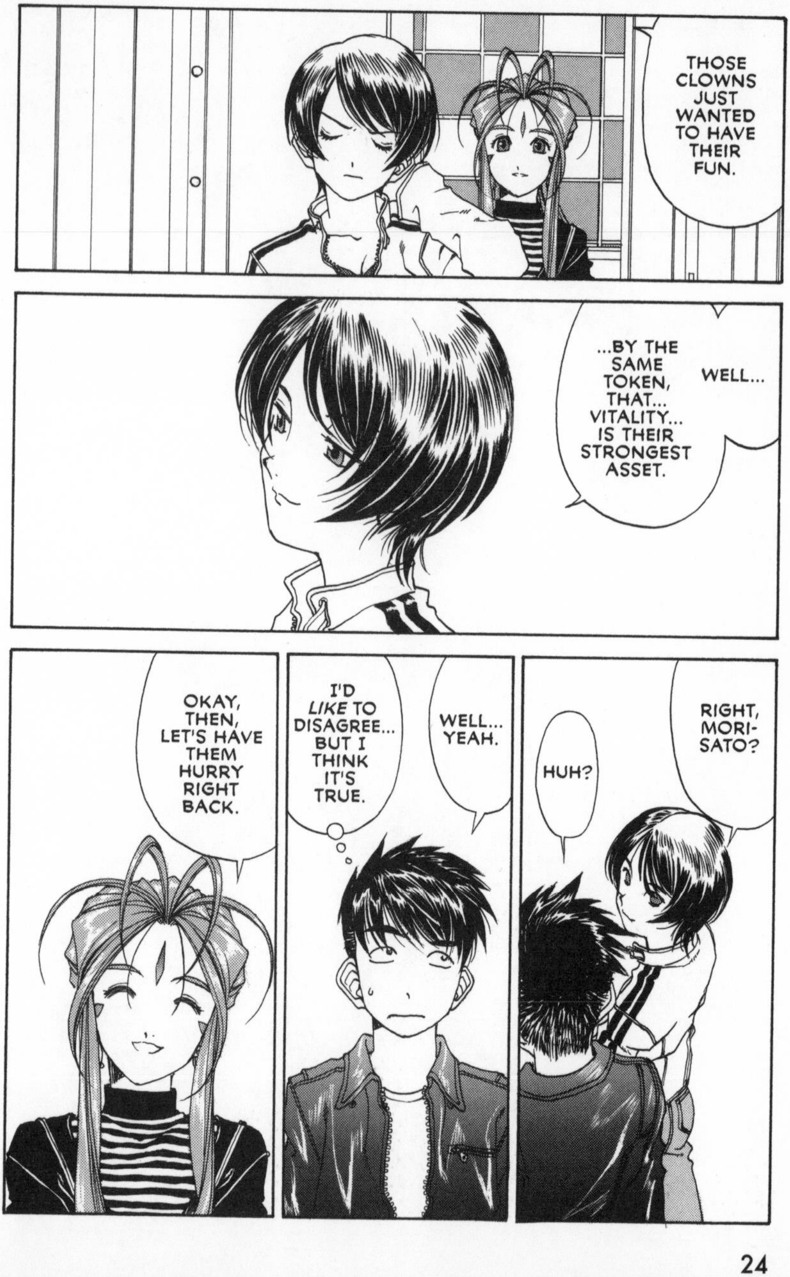
THOSE CLOWNS JUST WANTED TO HAVE THEIR FUN.
WELL...
...BY THE SAME TOKEN, THAT... VITALITY... IS THEIR STRONGEST ASSET.
RIGHT, MORI-SATO?
HUH?
WELL... YEAH.
I'D *LIKE* TO DISAGREE... BUT I THINK IT'S TRUE.
OKAY, THEN, LET'S HAVE THEM HURRY RIGHT BACK.

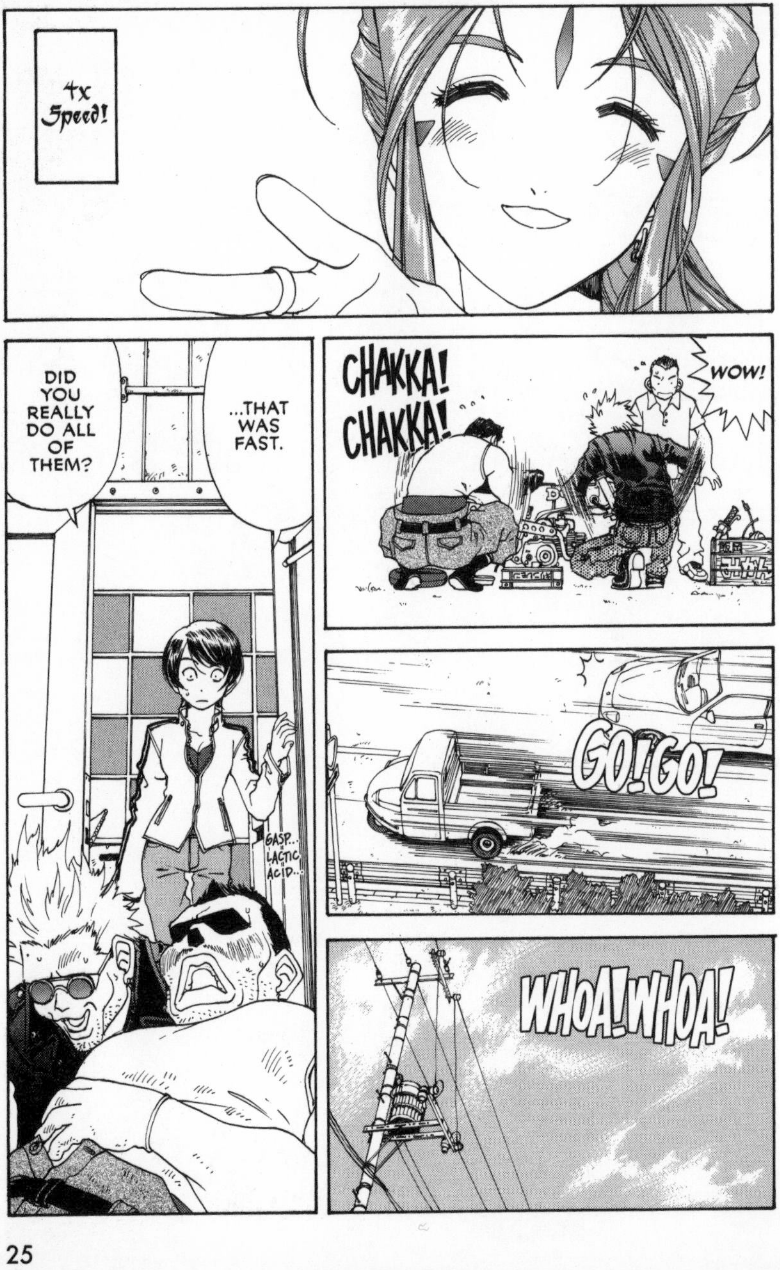
4x Speed!
WOW!
CHAKKA! CHAKKA!
GO!GO!
WHOA!WHOA!
...THAT WAS FAST.
DID YOU REALLY DO ALL OF THEM?
GASP... LACTIC ACID...

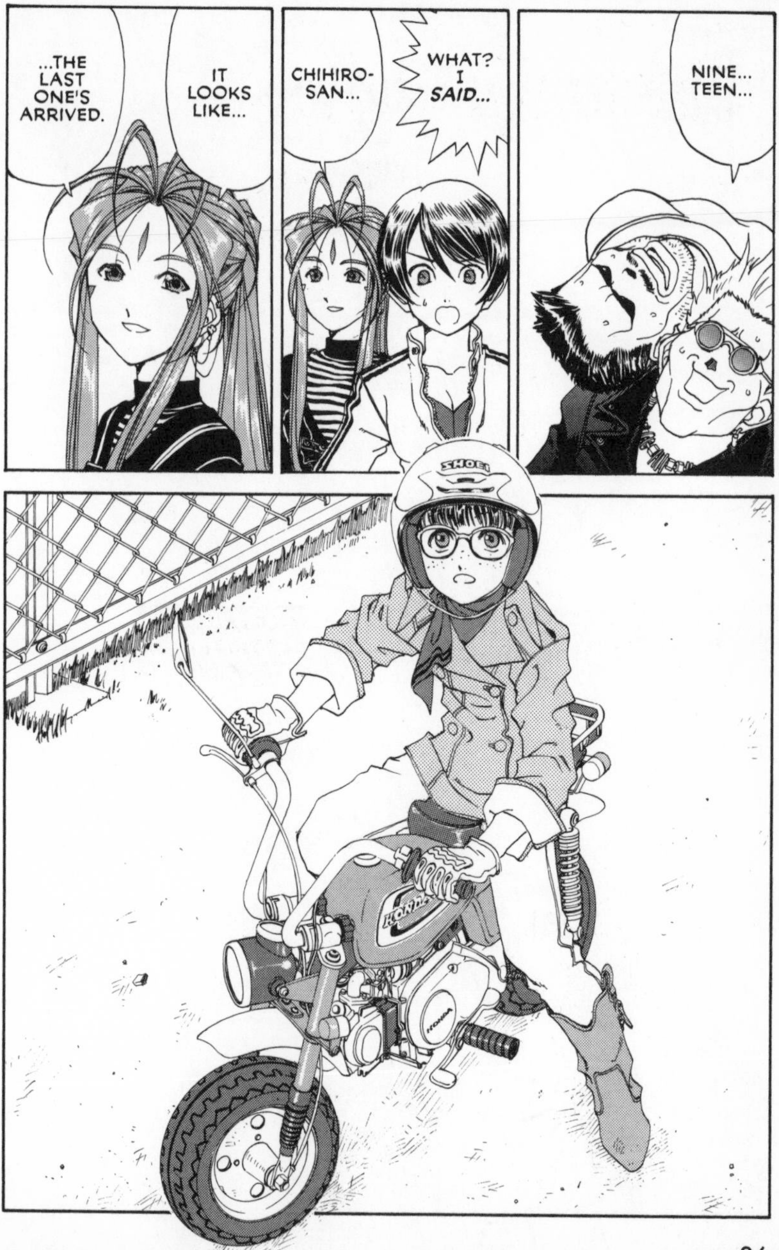
NINE... TEEN...
WHAT? I *SAID*...
CHIHIRO-SAN...
IT LOOKS LIKE...
...THE LAST ONE'S ARRIVED.

CHAPTER 214

# Jubilation Engine

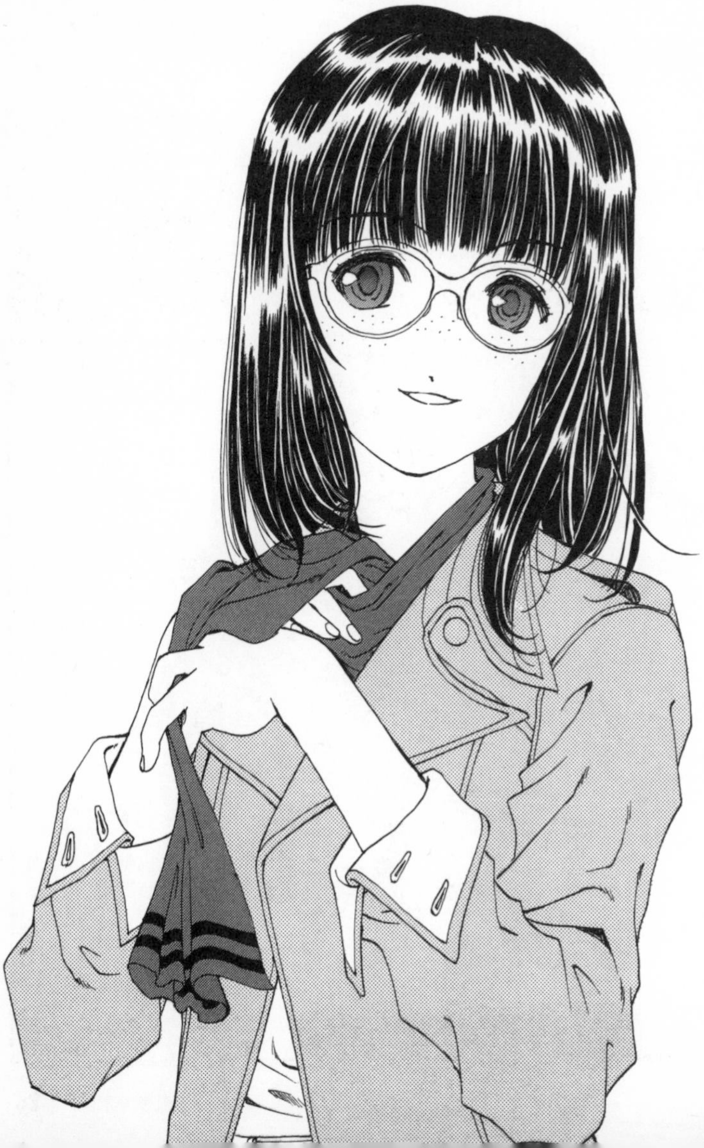

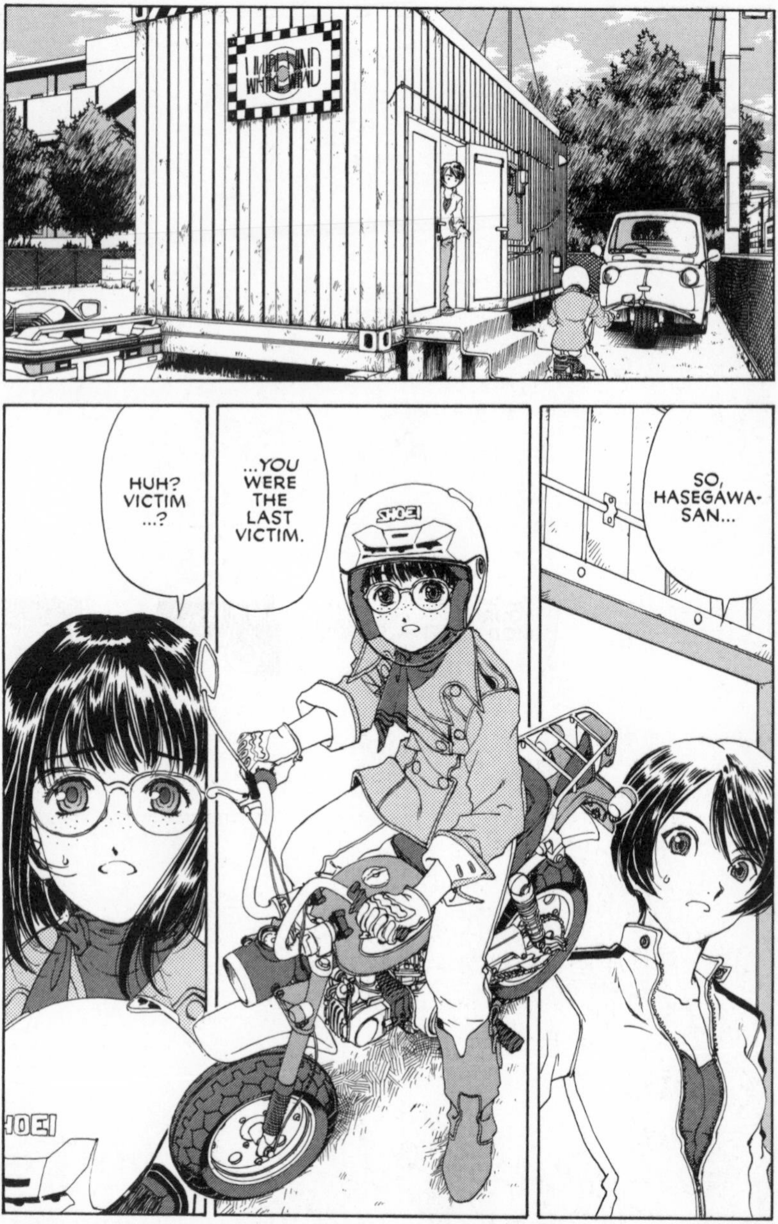
SO, HASEGAWA-SAN...
...*YOU* WERE THE LAST VICTIM.
SHOEI
HUH? VICTIM ...?

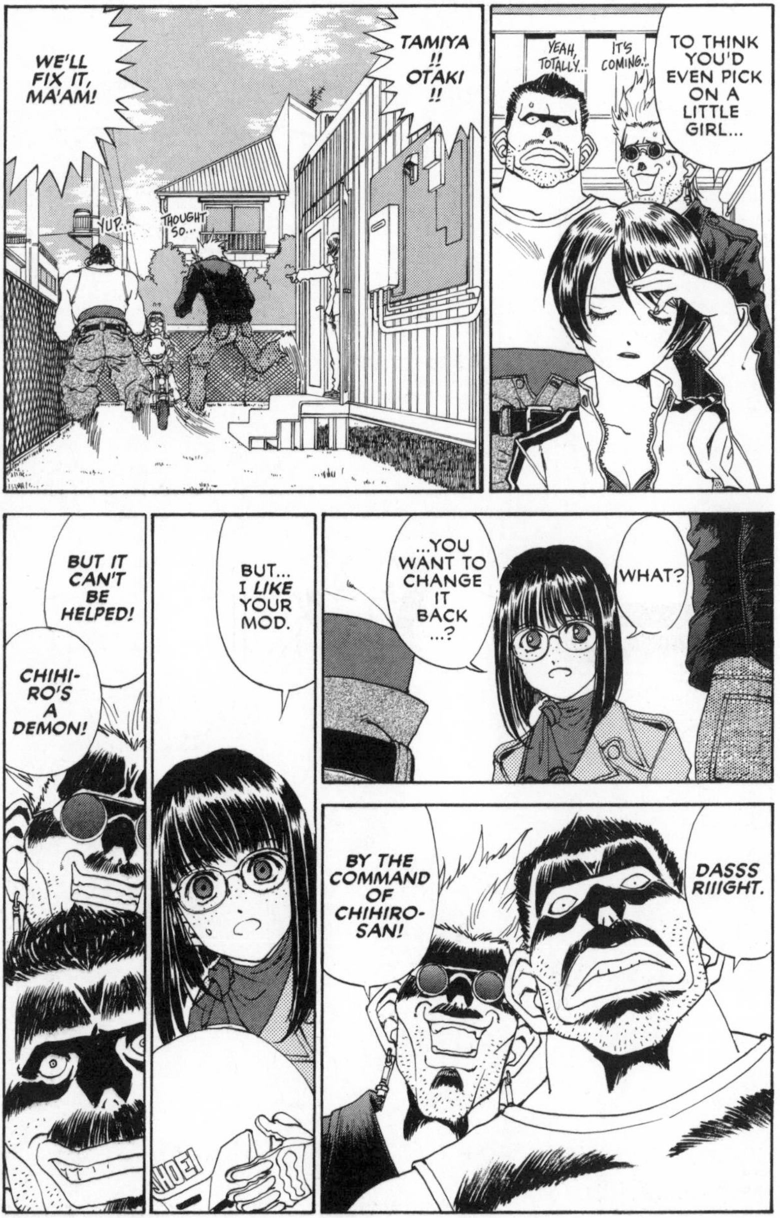
TO THINK YOU'D EVEN PICK ON A LITTLE GIRL...
IT'S COMING..
YEAH, TOTALLY...
TAMIYA!! OTAKI!!
WE'LL FIX IT, MA'AM!
THOUGHT SO...
YUP...
WHAT?
...YOU WANT TO CHANGE IT BACK ...?
DASSS RIIIGHT.
BY THE COMMAND OF CHIHIRO-SAN!
BUT... I *LIKE* YOUR MOD.
BUT IT CAN'T BE HELPED!
CHIHI-RO'S A DEMON!

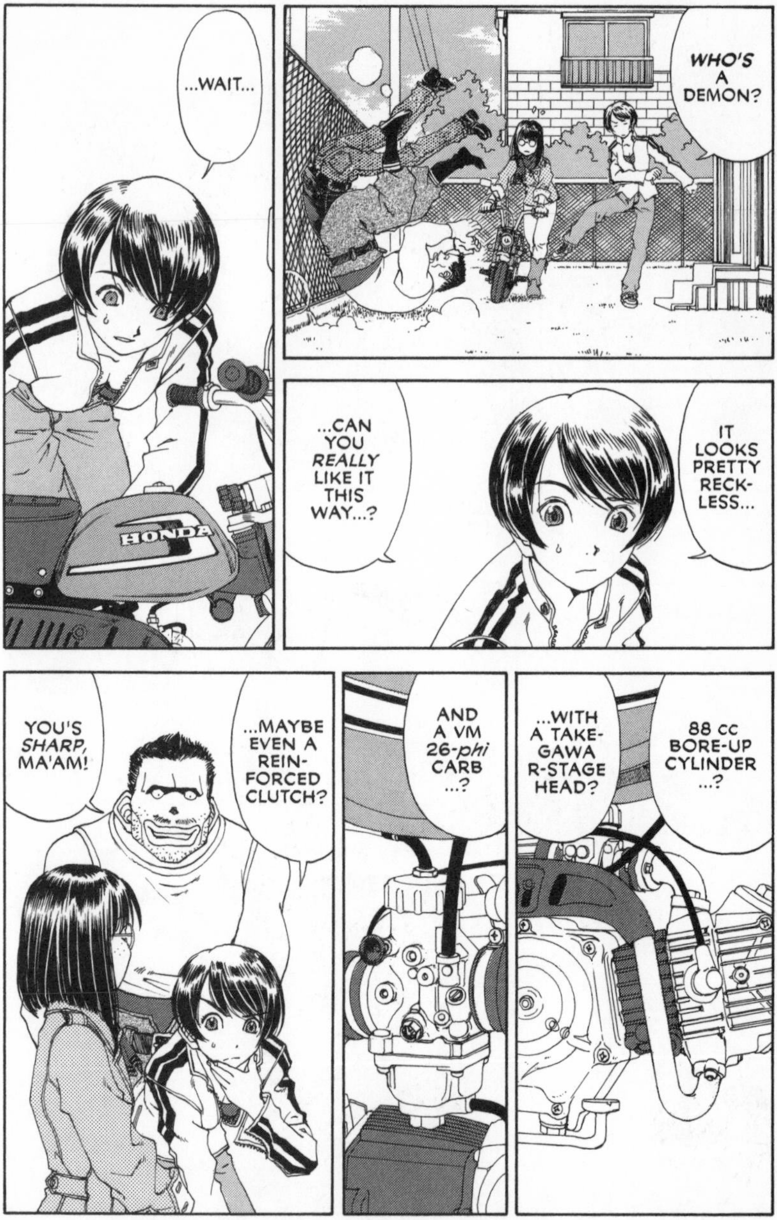
WHO'S A DEMON?
IT LOOKS PRETTY RECK-LESS...
...CAN YOU REALLY LIKE IT THIS WAY...?
...WAIT...
HONDA
88 cc BORE-UP CYLINDER ...?
...WITH A TAKE-GAWA R-STAGE HEAD?
AND A VM 26-phi CARB ...?
...MAYBE EVEN A REIN-FORCED CLUTCH?
YOU'S SHARP, MA'AM!

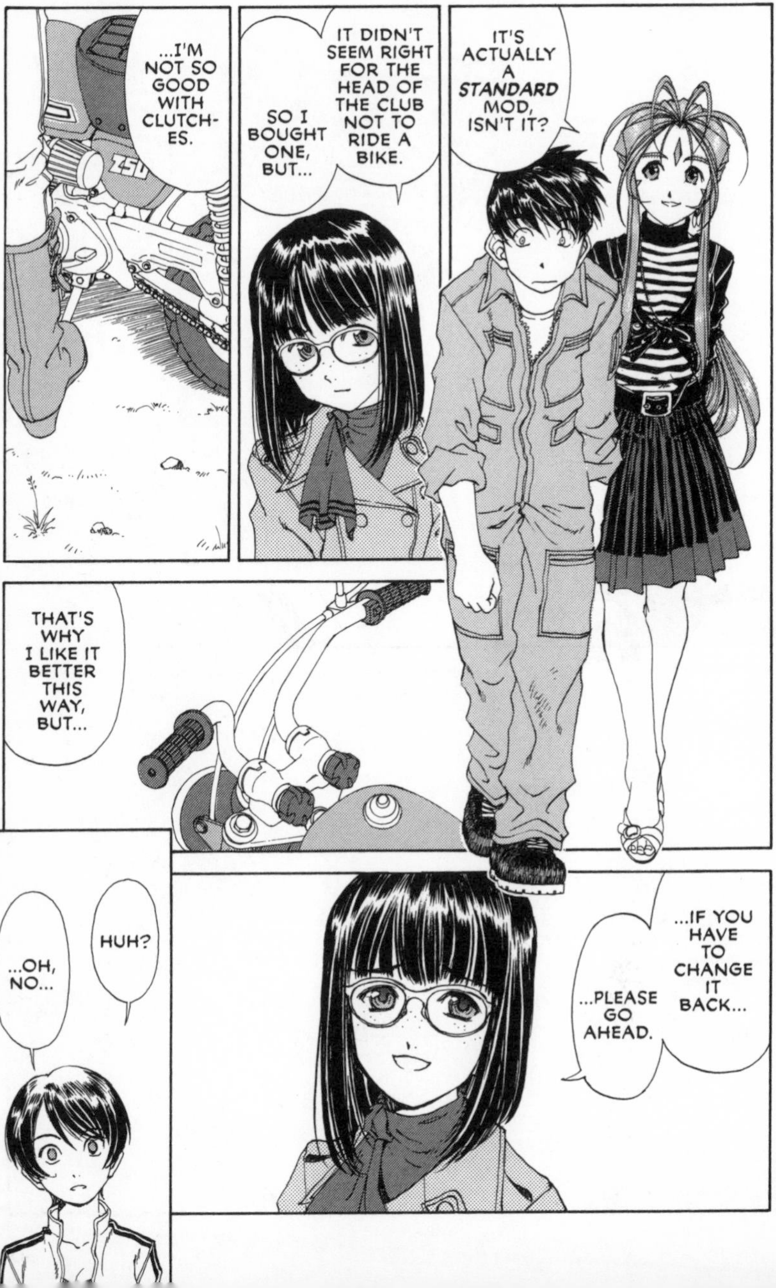
IT'S ACTUALLY A STANDARD MOD, ISN'T IT?
IT DIDN'T SEEM RIGHT FOR THE HEAD OF THE CLUB NOT TO RIDE A BIKE.
SO I BOUGHT ONE, BUT...
...I'M NOT SO GOOD WITH CLUTCH-ES.
THAT'S WHY I LIKE IT BETTER THIS WAY, BUT...
...IF YOU HAVE TO CHANGE IT BACK...
...PLEASE GO AHEAD.
HUH?
...OH, NO...

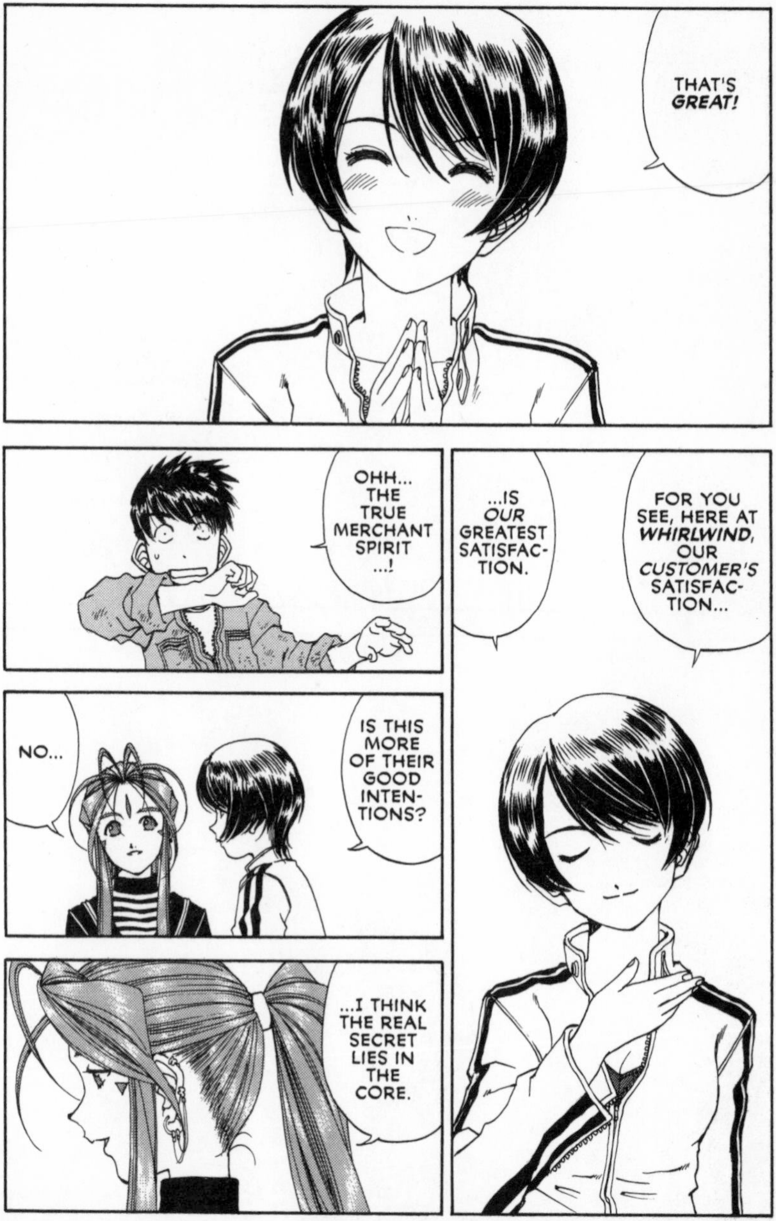
THAT'S GREAT!
FOR YOU SEE, HERE AT WHIRLWIND, OUR CUSTOMER'S SATISFACTION...
...IS OUR GREATEST SATISFACTION.
OHH... THE TRUE MERCHANT SPIRIT ...!
IS THIS MORE OF THEIR GOOD INTENTIONS?
NO...
...I THINK THE REAL SECRET LIES IN THE CORE.

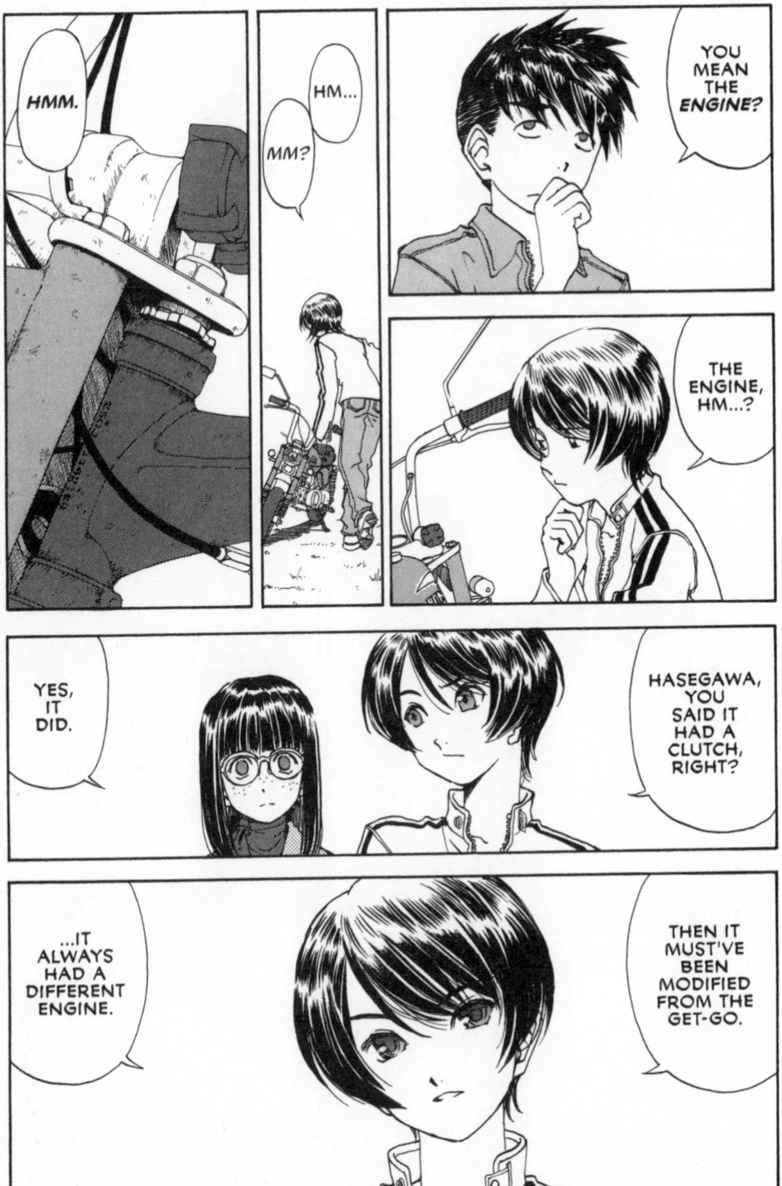
YOU MEAN THE *ENGINE?*
THE ENGINE, HM...?
HM...
MM?
*HMM.*
HASEGAWA, YOU SAID IT HAD A CLUTCH, RIGHT?
YES, IT DID.
THEN IT MUST'VE BEEN MODIFIED FROM THE GET-GO.
...IT ALWAYS HAD A DIFFERENT ENGINE.

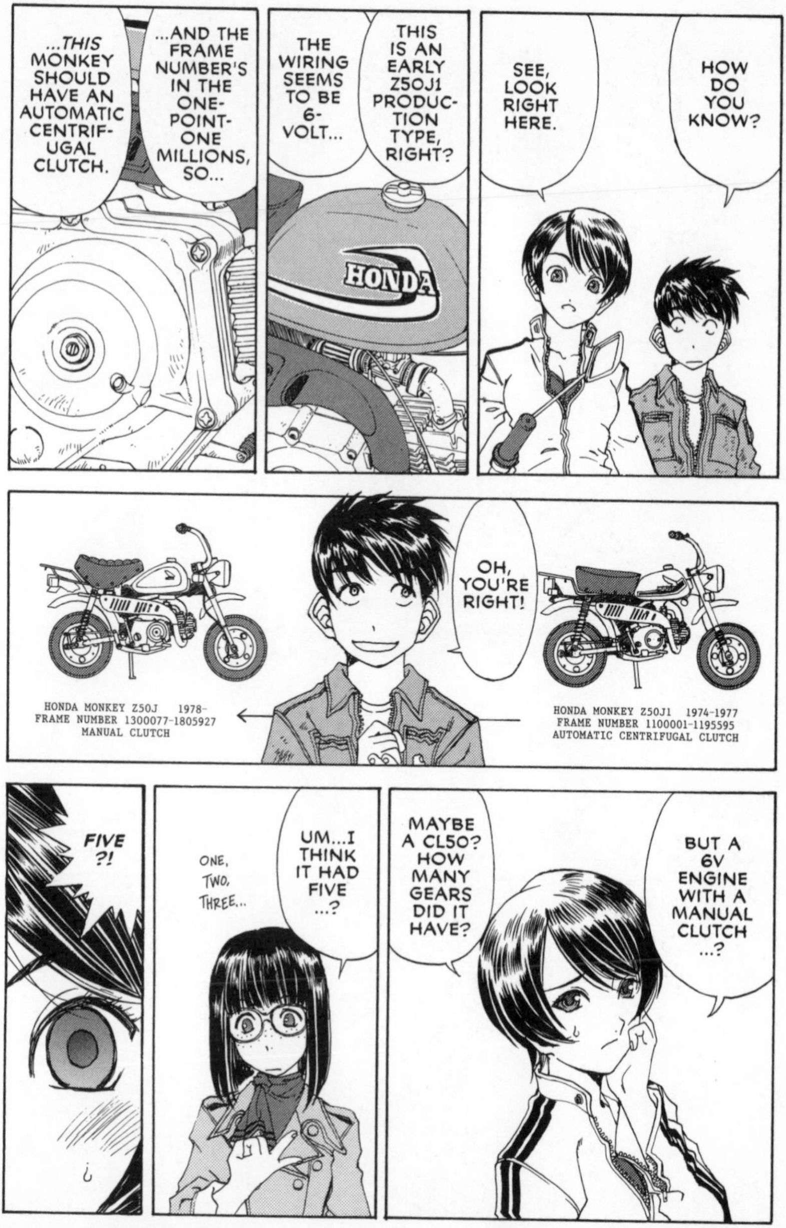
HOW DO YOU KNOW?
SEE, LOOK RIGHT HERE.
THIS IS AN EARLY Z50J1 PRODUCTION TYPE, RIGHT?
THE WIRING SEEMS TO BE 6-VOLT...
...AND THE FRAME NUMBER'S IN THE ONE-POINT-ONE MILLIONS, SO...
...*THIS* MONKEY SHOULD HAVE AN AUTOMATIC CENTRIFUGAL CLUTCH.
HONDA
OH, YOU'RE RIGHT!
HONDA MONKEY Z50J1 1974-1977
FRAME NUMBER 1100001-1195595
AUTOMATIC CENTRIFUGAL CLUTCH
HONDA MONKEY Z50J 1978-
FRAME NUMBER 1300077-1805927
MANUAL CLUTCH
BUT A 6V ENGINE WITH A MANUAL CLUTCH ...?
MAYBE A CL50? HOW MANY GEARS DID IT HAVE?
UM...I THINK IT HAD FIVE ...?
ONE, TWO, THREE...
*FIVE ?!*

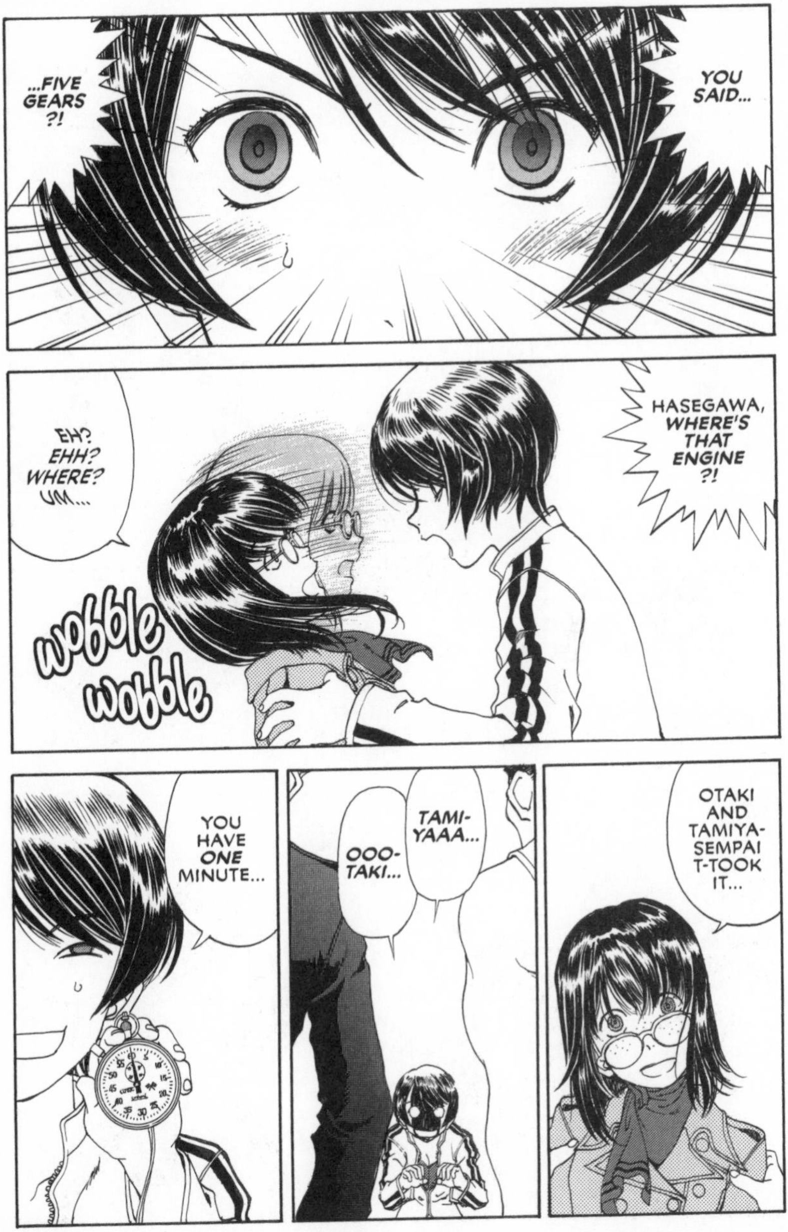
YOU SAID...
...FIVE GEARS ?!
HASEGAWA, WHERE'S THAT ENGINE ?!
EH? EHH? WHERE? UM...
wobble wobble
OTAKI AND TAMIYA-SEMPAI T-TOOK IT...
TAMI-YAAA...
OOO-TAKI...
YOU HAVE ONE MINUTE...

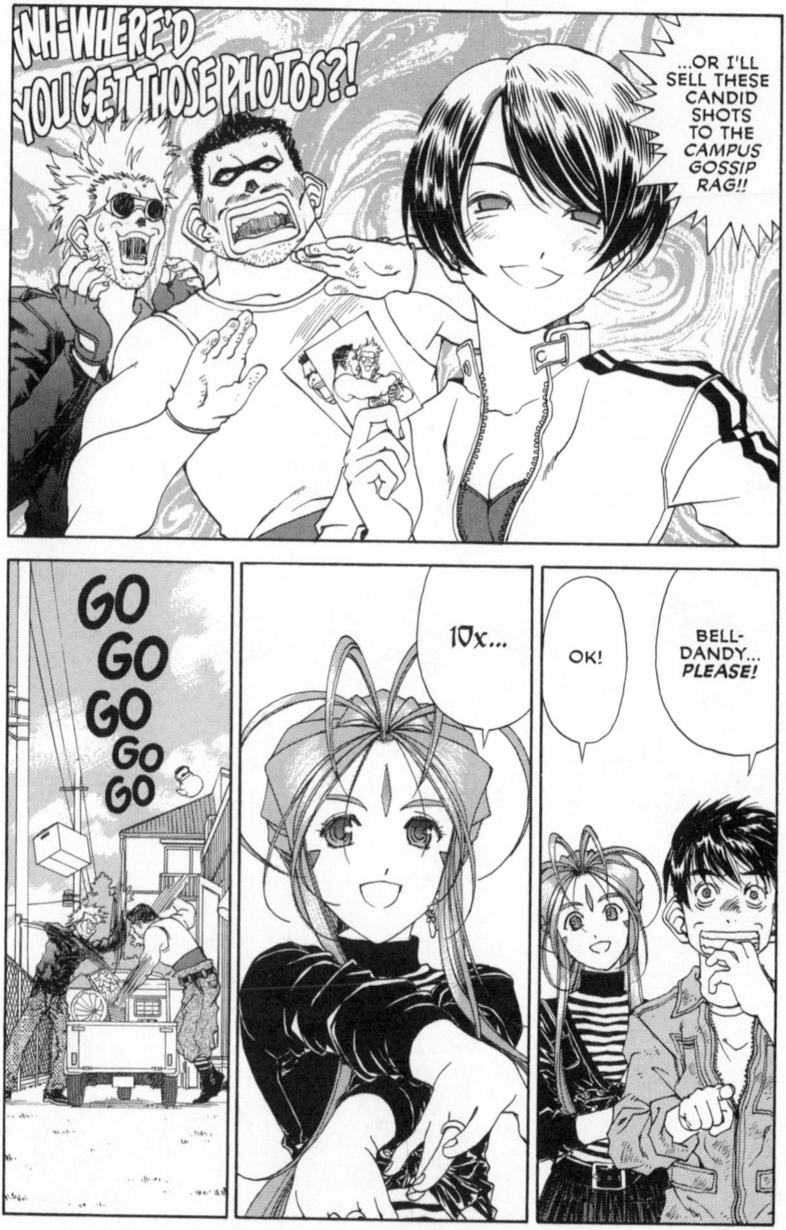
...OR I'LL SELL THESE CANDID SHOTS TO THE CAMPUS GOSSIP RAG!!
WH-WHERE'D YOU GET THOSE PHOTOS?!
BELL-DANDY... PLEASE!
OK!
10x...
GO GO GO GO GO

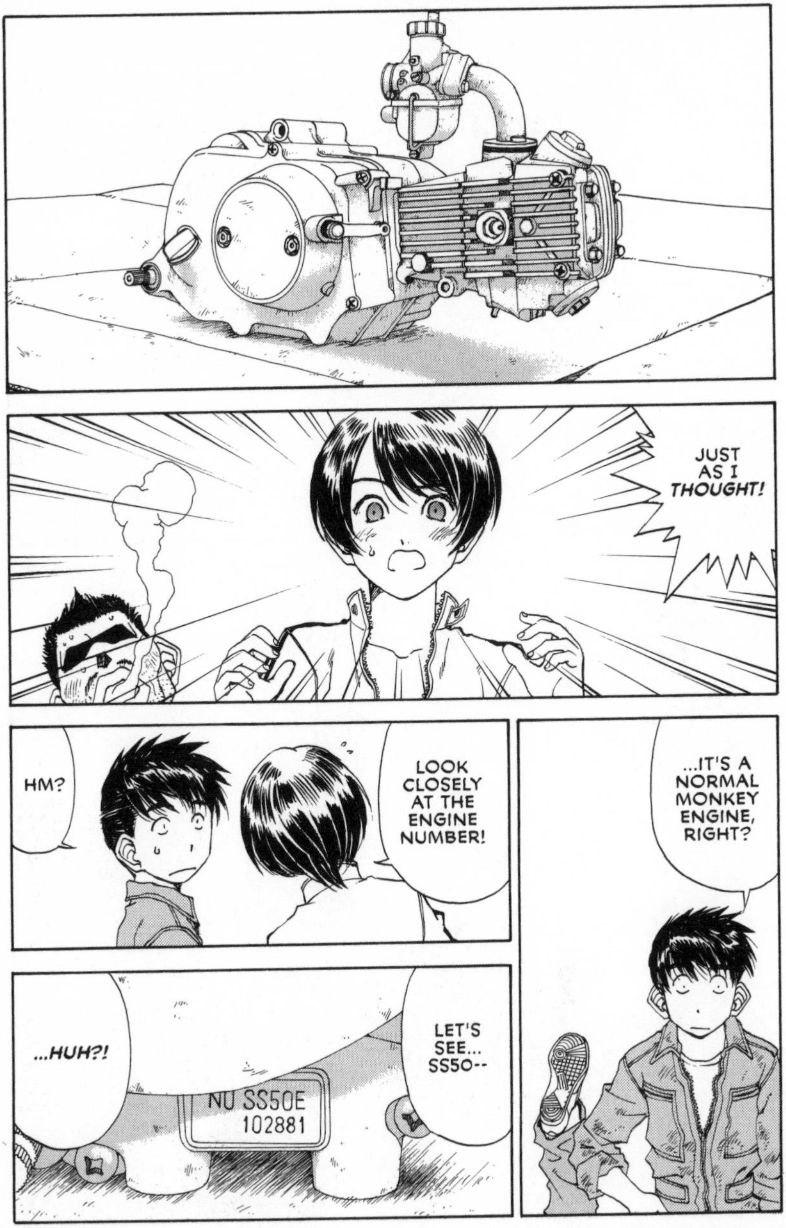
JUST AS I *THOUGHT!*
...IT'S A NORMAL MONKEY ENGINE, RIGHT?
LOOK CLOSELY AT THE ENGINE NUMBER!
HM?
LET'S SEE... SS50--
NU SS50E 102881
*...HUH?!*

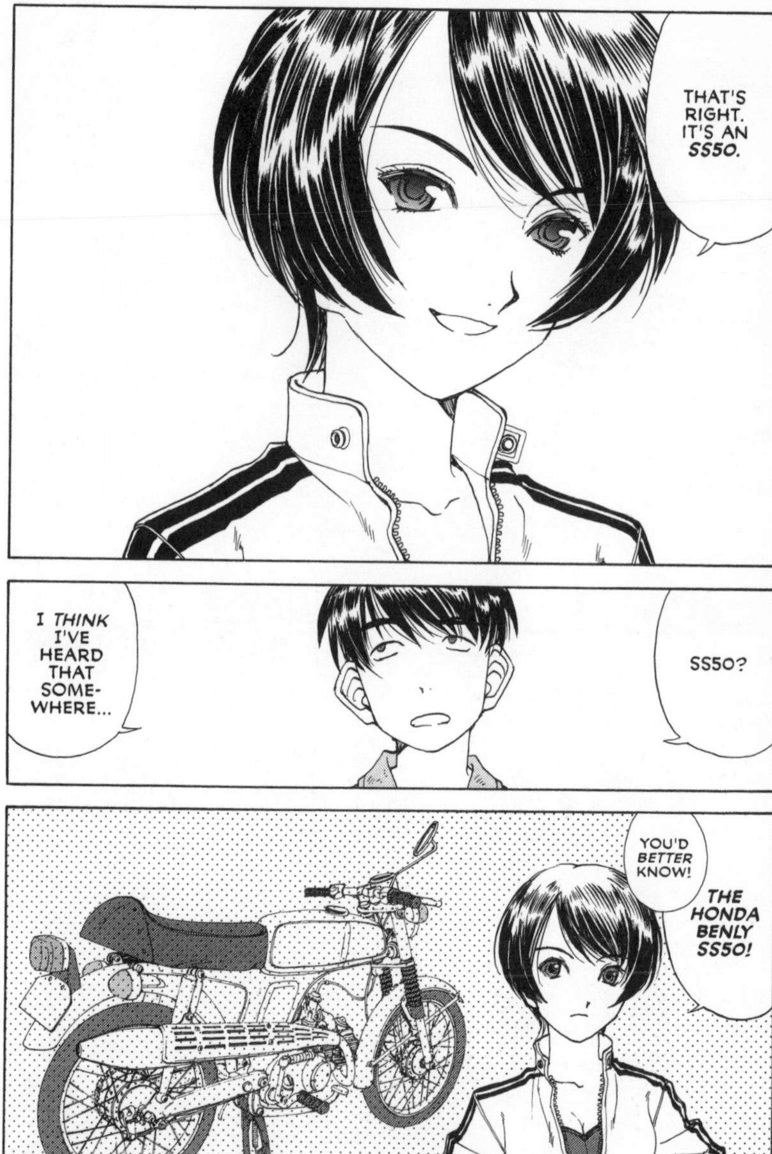
THAT'S RIGHT. IT'S AN *SS50.*
SS50?
I *THINK* I'VE HEARD THAT SOME-WHERE...
YOU'D *BETTER* KNOW!
***THE HONDA BENLY SS50!***

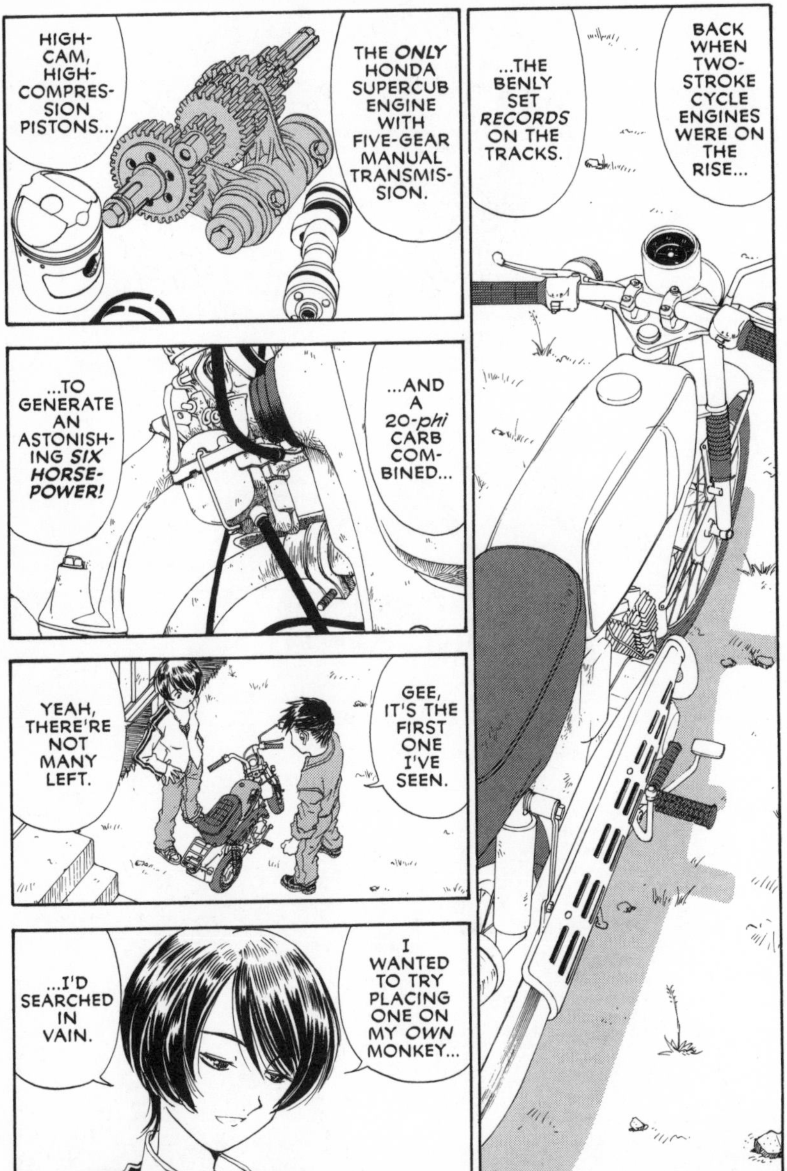
BACK WHEN TWO-STROKE CYCLE ENGINES WERE ON THE RISE...
...THE BENLY SET *RECORDS* ON THE TRACKS.
THE *ONLY* HONDA SUPERCUB ENGINE WITH FIVE-GEAR MANUAL TRANSMISSION.
HIGH-CAM, HIGH-COMPRESSION PISTONS...
...AND A 20-*phi* CARB COMBINED...
...TO GENERATE AN ASTONISHING *SIX HORSE-POWER!*
GEE, IT'S THE FIRST ONE I'VE SEEN.
YEAH, THERE'RE NOT MANY LEFT.
I WANTED TO TRY PLACING ONE ON MY *OWN* MONKEY...
...I'D SEARCHED IN VAIN.

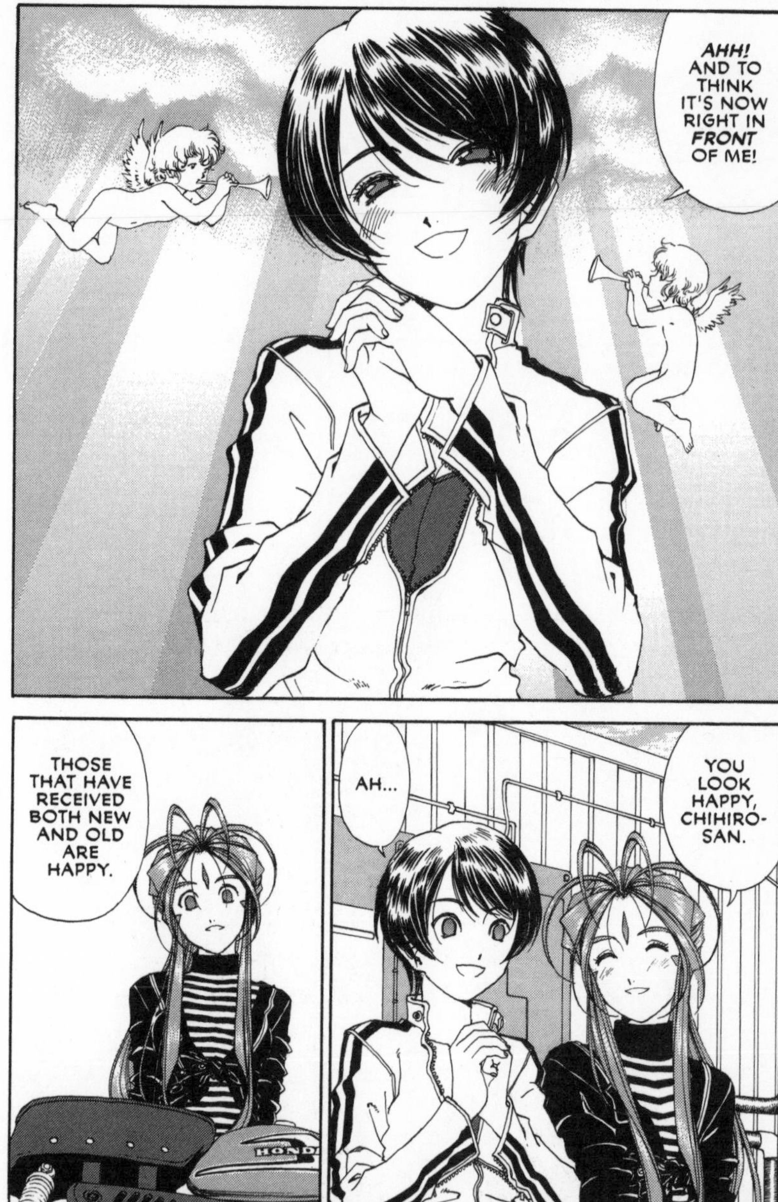

AHH! AND TO THINK IT'S NOW RIGHT IN FRONT OF ME!
YOU LOOK HAPPY, CHIHIRO-SAN.
AH...
THOSE THAT HAVE RECEIVED BOTH NEW AND OLD ARE HAPPY.
HONDA

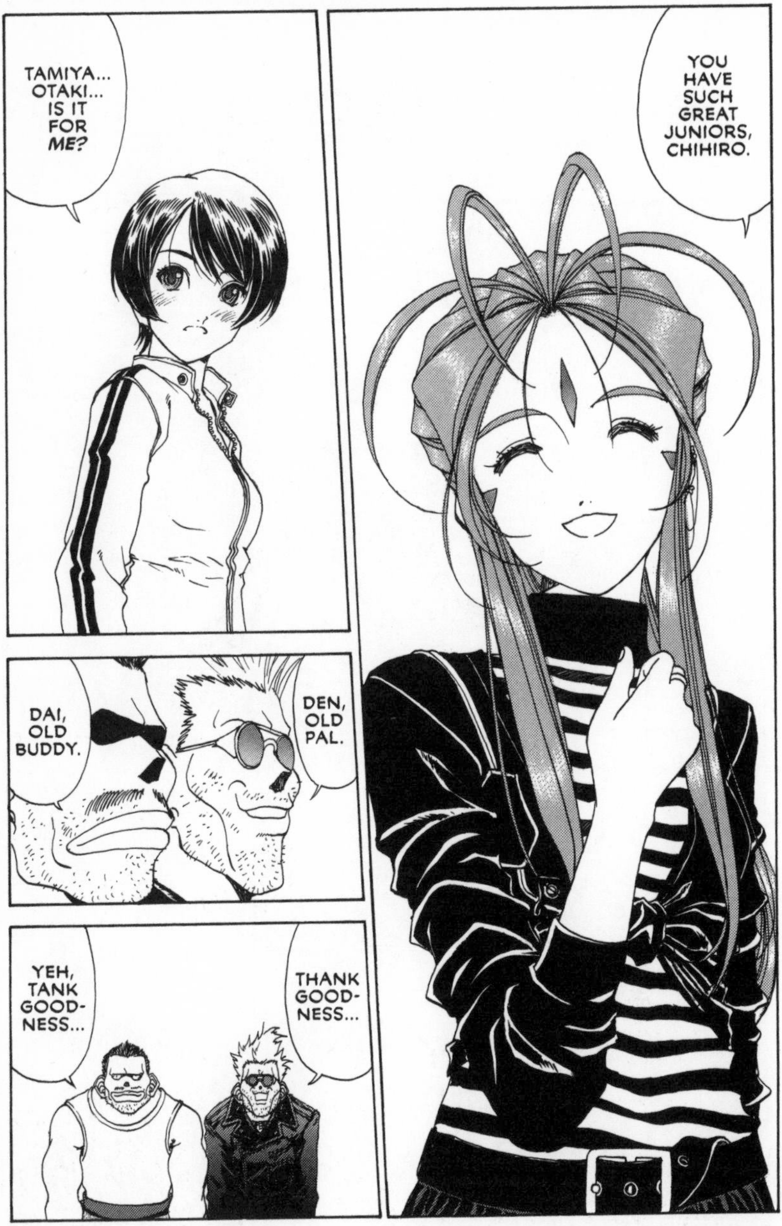
YOU HAVE SUCH GREAT JUNIORS, CHIHIRO.
TAMIYA... OTAKI... IS IT FOR *ME?*
DEN, OLD PAL.
DAI, OLD BUDDY.
THANK GOODNESS...
YEH, TANK GOODNESS...

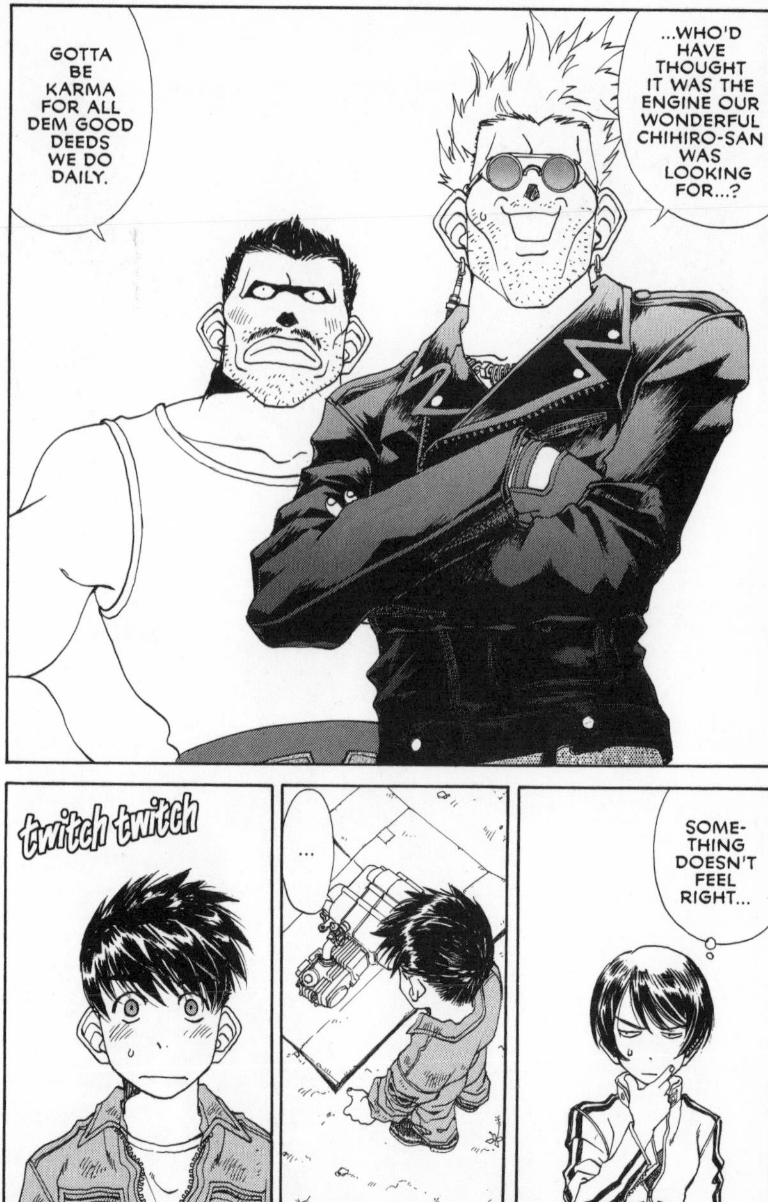
...WHO'D HAVE THOUGHT IT WAS THE ENGINE OUR WONDERFUL CHIHIRO-SAN WAS LOOKING FOR...?
GOTTA BE KARMA FOR ALL DEM GOOD DEEDS WE DO DAILY.
SOME-THING DOESN'T FEEL RIGHT...
...
twitch twitch

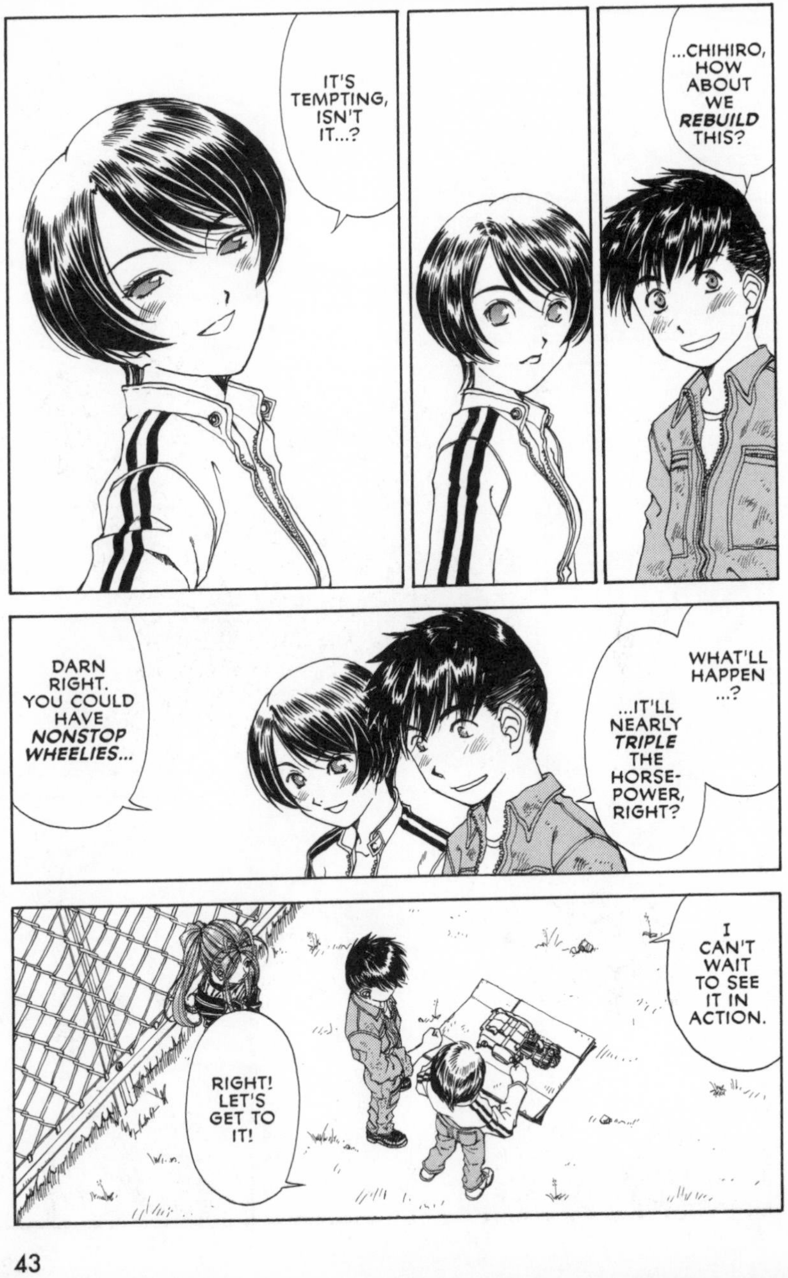
...CHIHIRO, HOW ABOUT WE *REBUILD* THIS?
IT'S TEMPTING, ISN'T IT...?
WHAT'LL HAPPEN ...?
...IT'LL NEARLY *TRIPLE* THE HORSE-POWER, RIGHT?
DARN RIGHT. YOU COULD HAVE *NONSTOP WHEELIES...*
I CAN'T WAIT TO SEE IT IN ACTION.
RIGHT! LET'S GET TO IT!

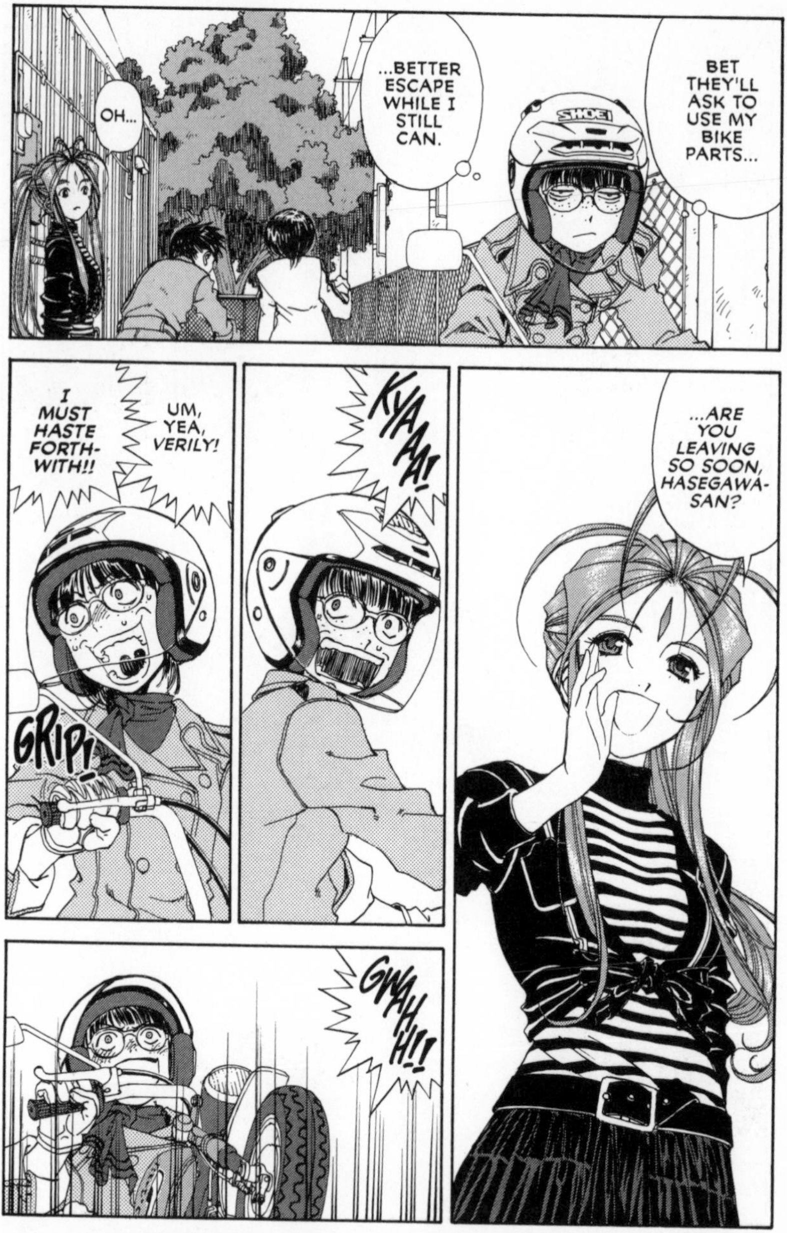
BET THEY'LL ASK TO USE MY BIKE PARTS...
...BETTER ESCAPE WHILE I STILL CAN.
OH...
...ARE YOU LEAVING SO SOON, HASEGAWA-SAN?
KYAAAA!
UM, YEA, VERILY!
I MUST HASTE FORTH-WITH!!
GRIP!
GWAHH!!

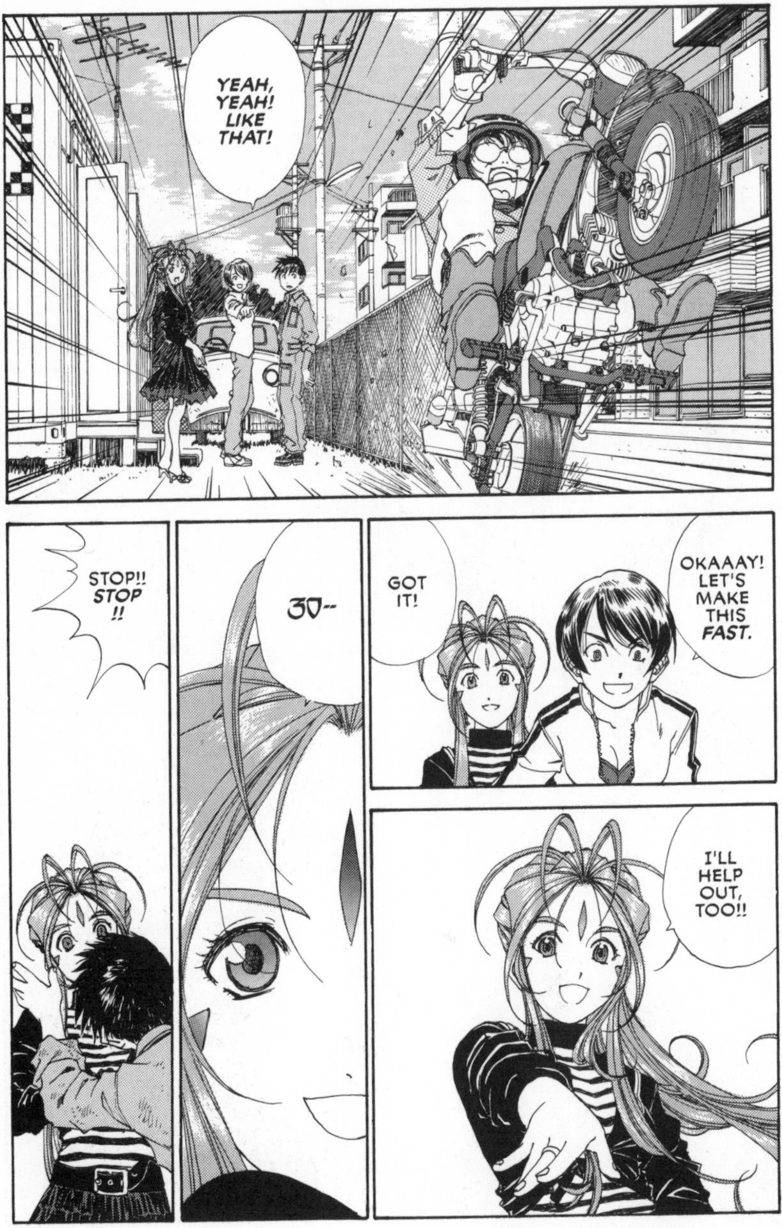
YEAH, YEAH! LIKE THAT!
OKAAAY! LET'S MAKE THIS FAST.
GOT IT!
I'LL HELP OUT, TOO!!
30--
STOP!! STOP !!

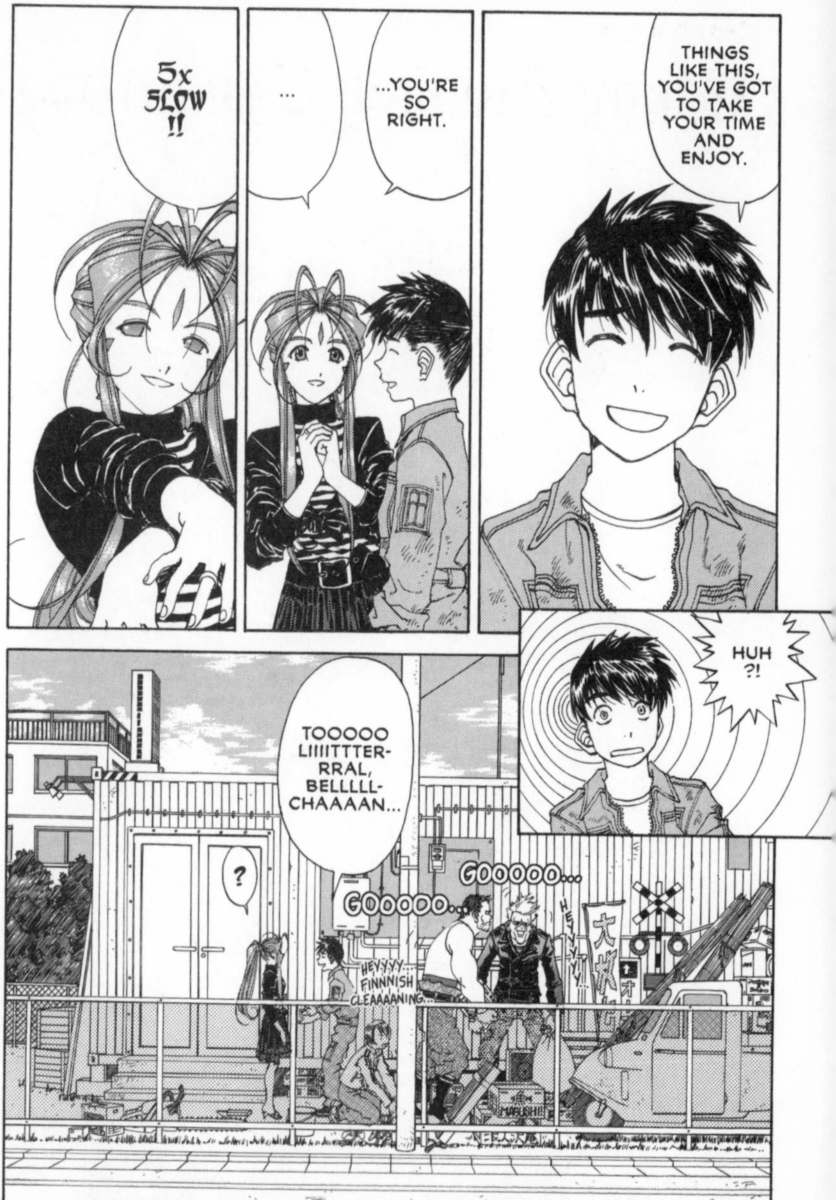
THINGS LIKE THIS, YOU'VE GOT TO TAKE YOUR TIME AND ENJOY.
...YOU'RE SO RIGHT.
...
5x SLOW !!
HUH ?!
TOOOOO LIIIITTTER-RRAL, BELLLLL-CHAAAAN...
?
GOOOOO...
GOOOOO...
HEYYYYY... FINNNISH CLEAAAANING...

CHAPTER 215

# Happy Monkey Generations

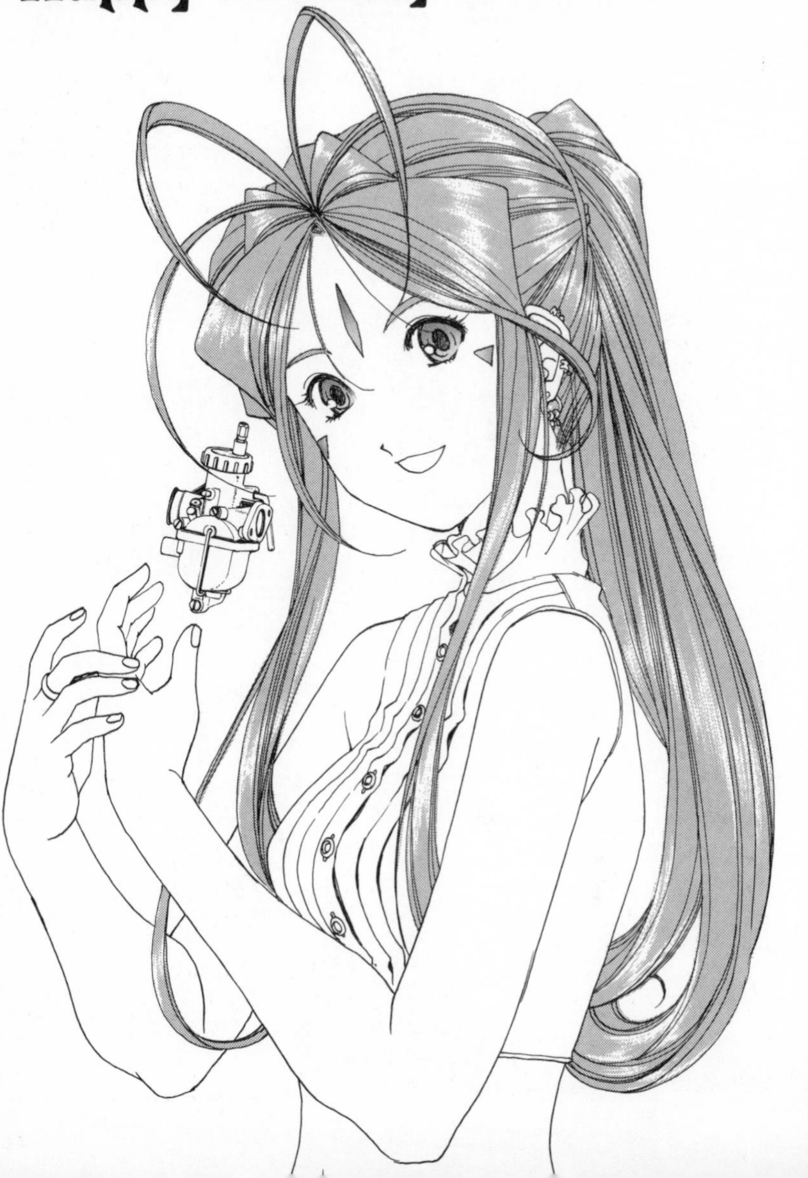

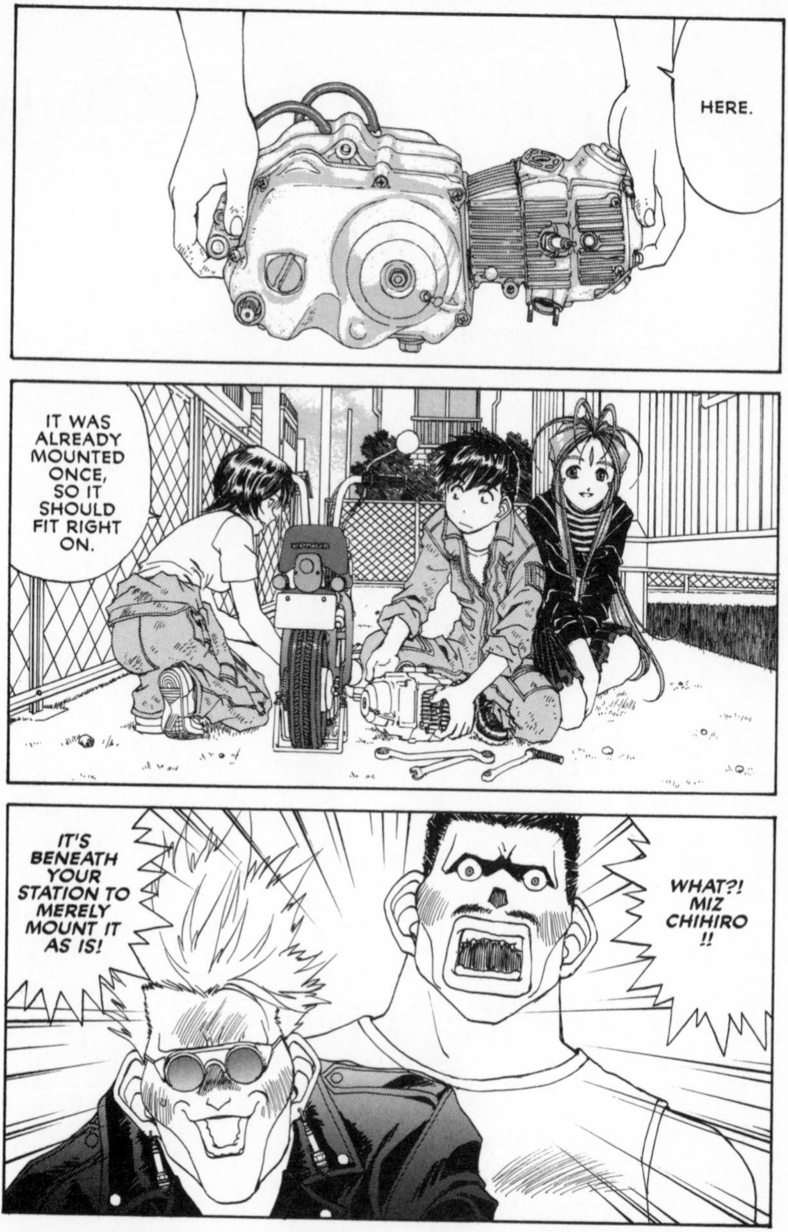
HERE.
IT WAS ALREADY MOUNTED ONCE, SO IT SHOULD FIT RIGHT ON.
WHAT?! MIZ CHIHIRO !!
IT'S BENEATH YOUR STATION TO MERELY MOUNT IT AS IS!

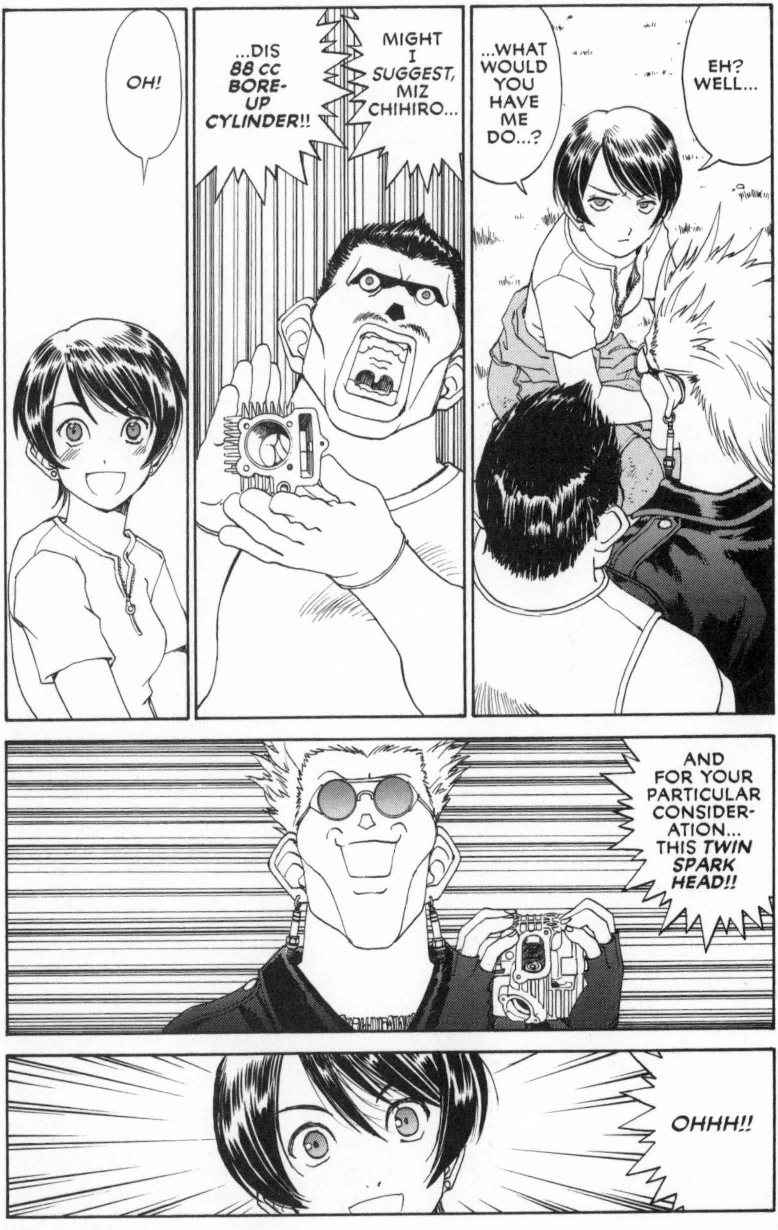
EH? WELL...
...WHAT WOULD YOU HAVE ME DO...?
MIGHT I SUGGEST, MIZ CHIHIRO...
...DIS 88 CC BORE-UP CYLINDER!!
OH!
AND FOR YOUR PARTICULAR CONSIDERATION... THIS TWIN SPARK HEAD!!
OHHH!!

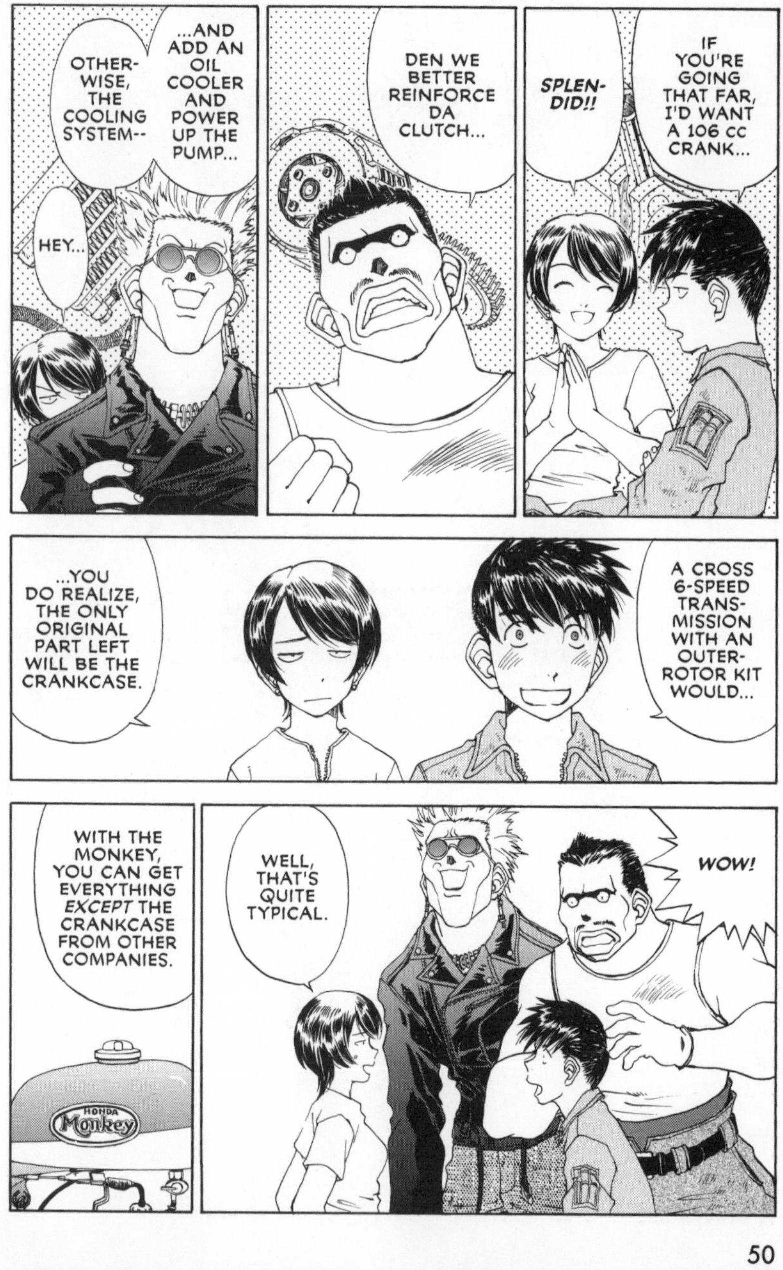
IF YOU'RE GOING THAT FAR, I'D WANT A 106 cc CRANK...
*SPLEN-DID!!*
DEN WE BETTER REINFORCE DA CLUTCH...
...AND ADD AN OIL COOLER AND POWER UP THE PUMP...
OTHER-WISE, THE COOLING SYSTEM--
HEY...
A CROSS 6-SPEED TRANS-MISSION WITH AN OUTER-ROTOR KIT WOULD...
...YOU DO REALIZE, THE ONLY ORIGINAL PART LEFT WILL BE THE CRANKCASE.
*WOW!*
WELL, THAT'S QUITE TYPICAL.
WITH THE MONKEY, YOU CAN GET EVERYTHING *EXCEPT* THE CRANKCASE FROM OTHER COMPANIES.
HONDA
Monkey

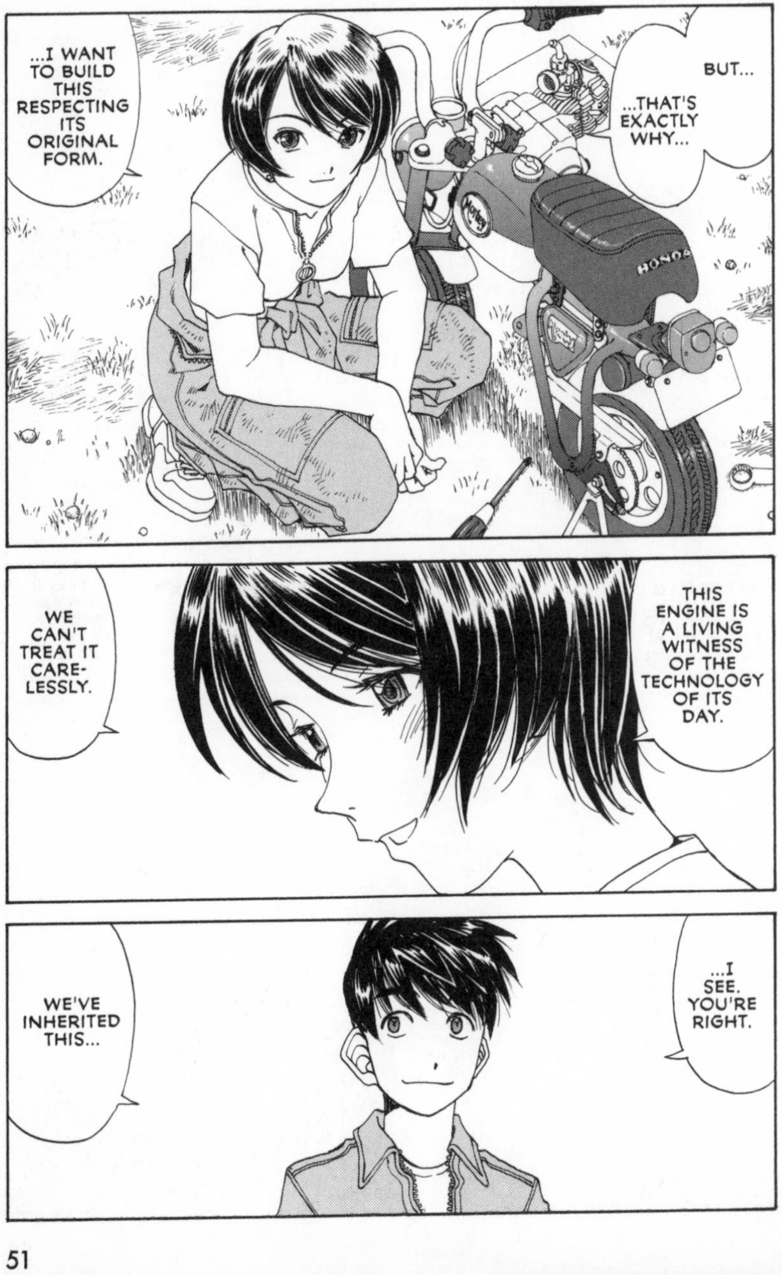
BUT...
...THAT'S EXACTLY WHY...
...I WANT TO BUILD THIS RESPECTING ITS ORIGINAL FORM.
HONDA
THIS ENGINE IS A LIVING WITNESS OF THE TECHNOLOGY OF ITS DAY.
WE CAN'T TREAT IT CARE-LESSLY.
...I SEE. YOU'RE RIGHT.
WE'VE INHERITED THIS...

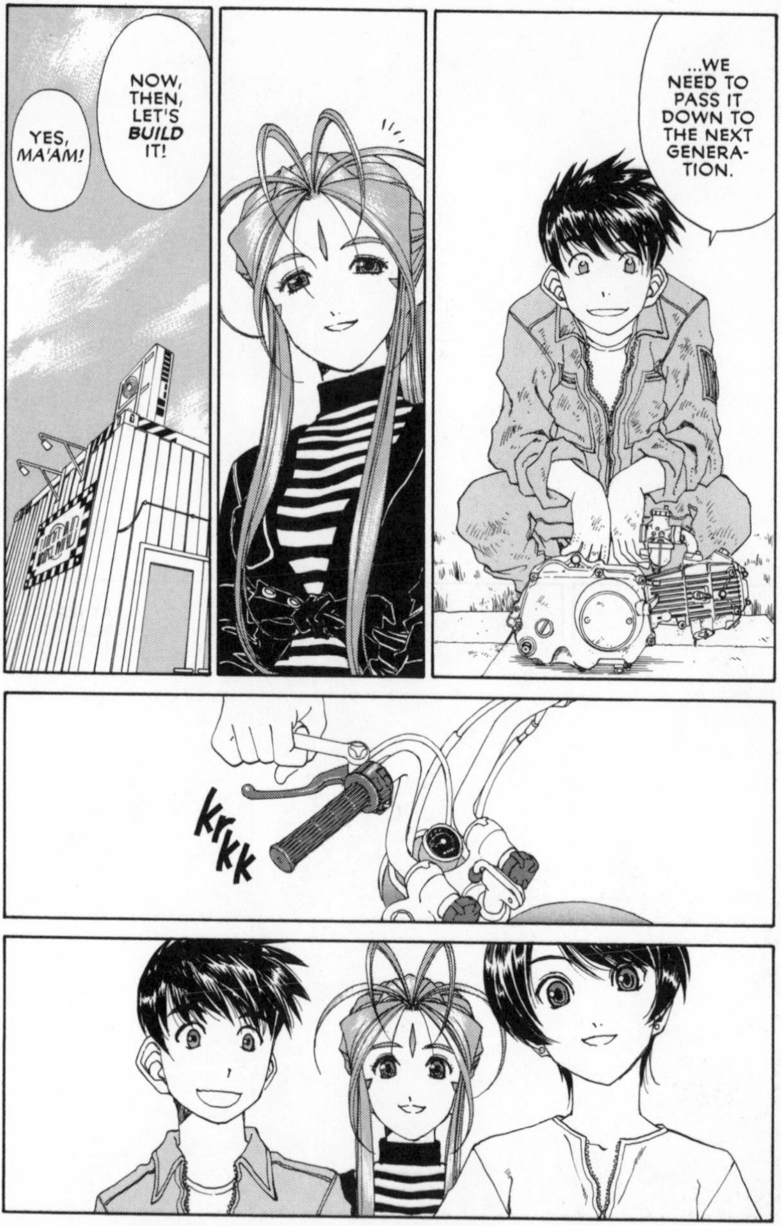
...WE NEED TO PASS IT DOWN TO THE NEXT GENERATION.
NOW, THEN, LET'S BUILD IT!
YES, MA'AM!
KRKK

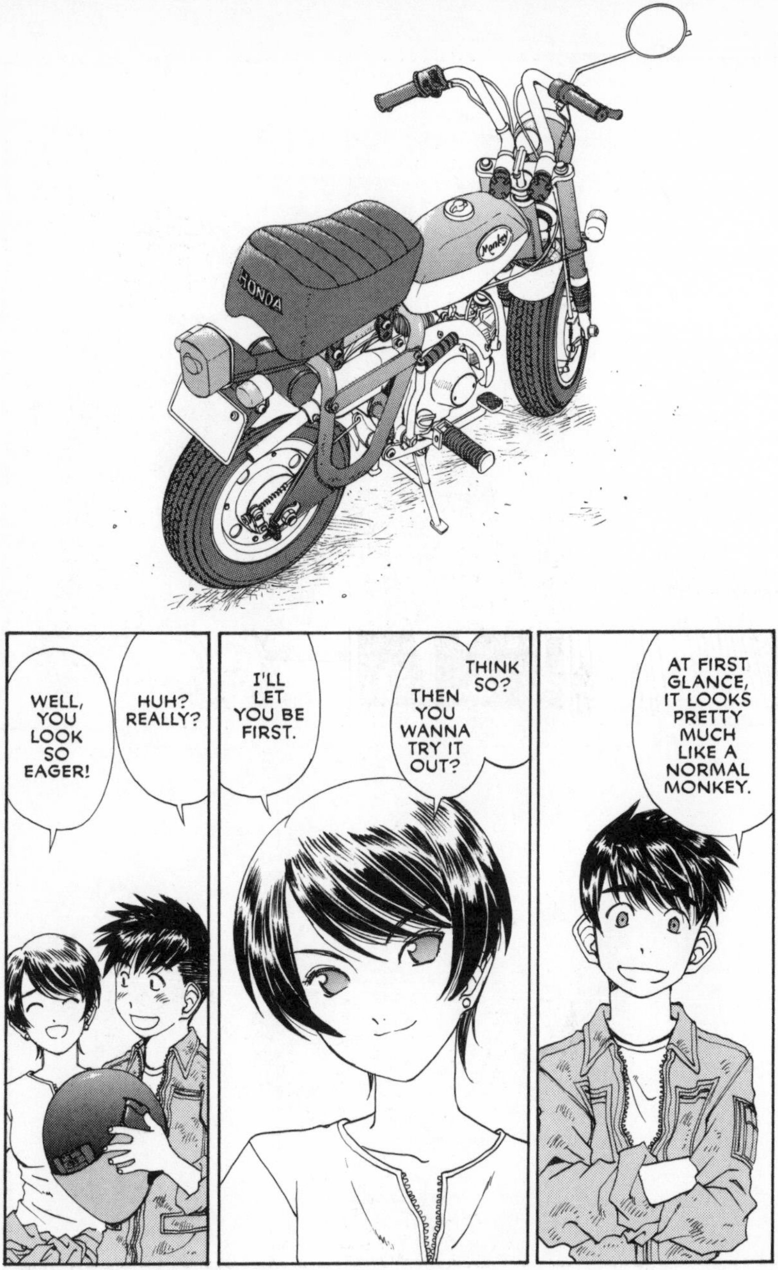
HONDA
Monkey
AT FIRST GLANCE, IT LOOKS PRETTY MUCH LIKE A NORMAL MONKEY.
THINK SO?
THEN YOU WANNA TRY IT OUT?
I'LL LET YOU BE FIRST.
HUH? REALLY?
WELL, YOU LOOK SO EAGER!

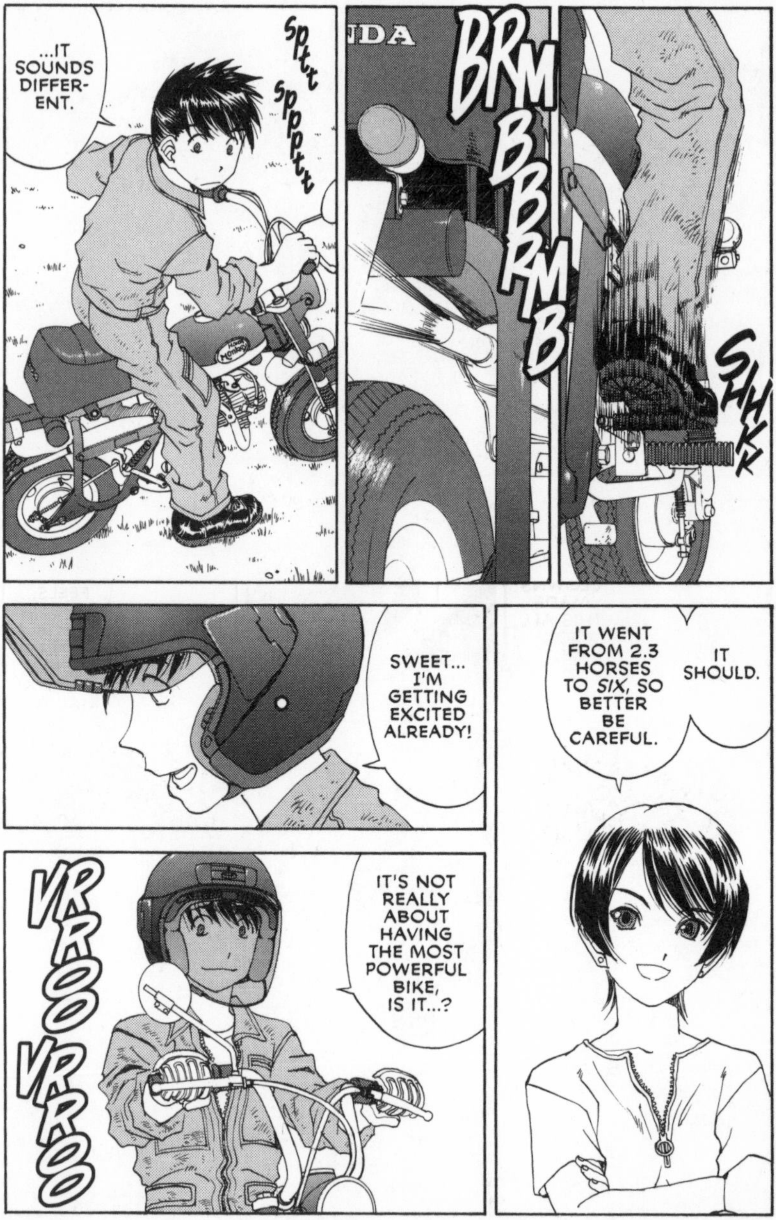
SHHKK
BRM BBRMB
NDA
SPTTT SPPPTTT
...IT SOUNDS DIFFERENT.
IT SHOULD.
IT WENT FROM 2.3 HORSES TO *SIX*, SO BETTER BE CAREFUL.
SWEET... I'M GETTING EXCITED ALREADY!
IT'S NOT REALLY ABOUT HAVING THE MOST POWERFUL BIKE, IS IT...?
VRROO VRROO

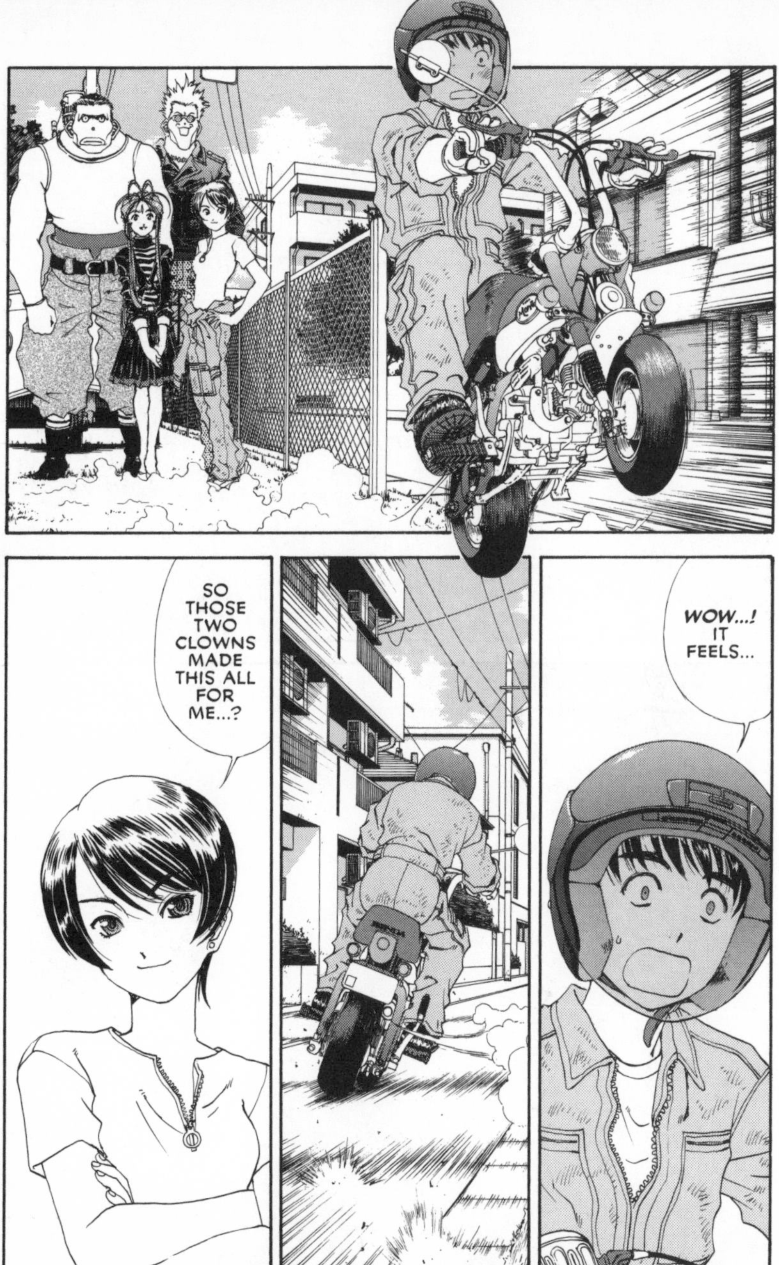
*WOW...!* IT FEELS...
SO THOSE TWO CLOWNS MADE THIS ALL FOR ME...?

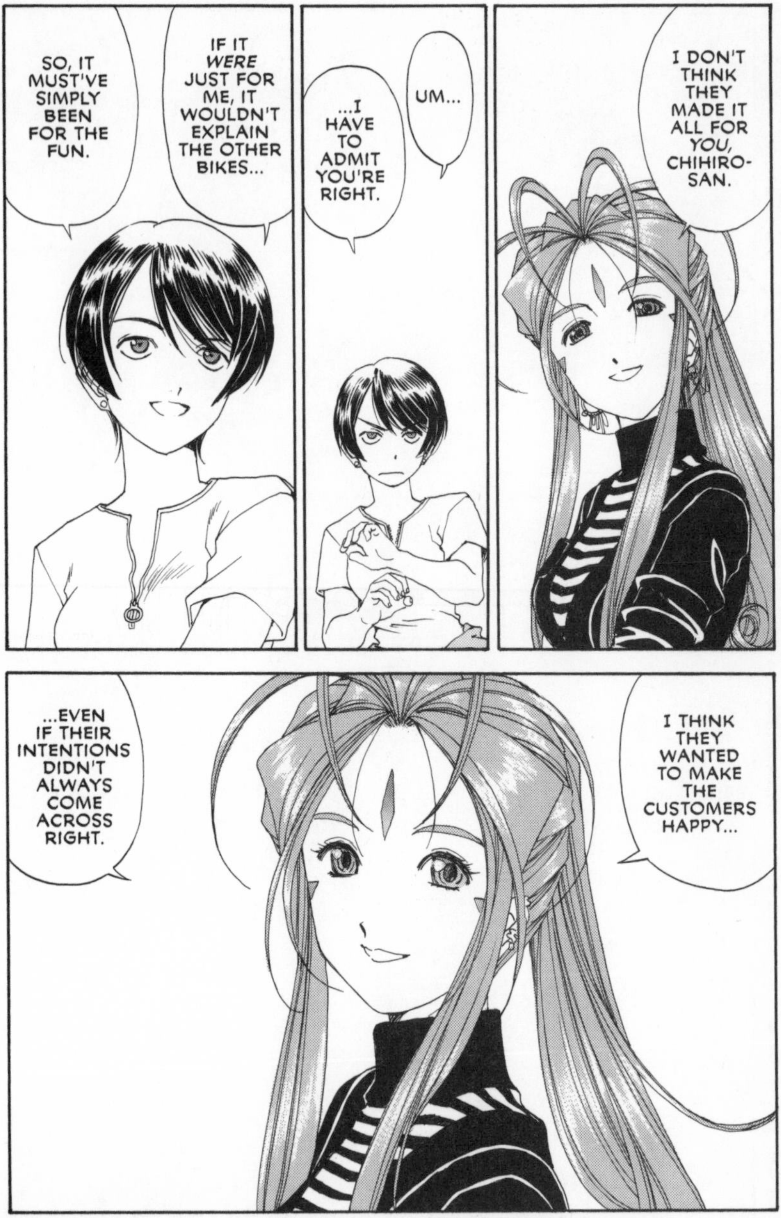
I DON'T THINK THEY MADE IT ALL FOR *YOU*, CHIHIRO-SAN.
UM...
...I HAVE TO ADMIT YOU'RE RIGHT.
IF IT *WERE* JUST FOR ME, IT WOULDN'T EXPLAIN THE OTHER BIKES...
SO, IT MUST'VE SIMPLY BEEN FOR THE FUN.
I THINK THEY WANTED TO MAKE THE CUSTOMERS HAPPY...
...EVEN IF THEIR INTENTIONS DIDN'T ALWAYS COME ACROSS RIGHT.

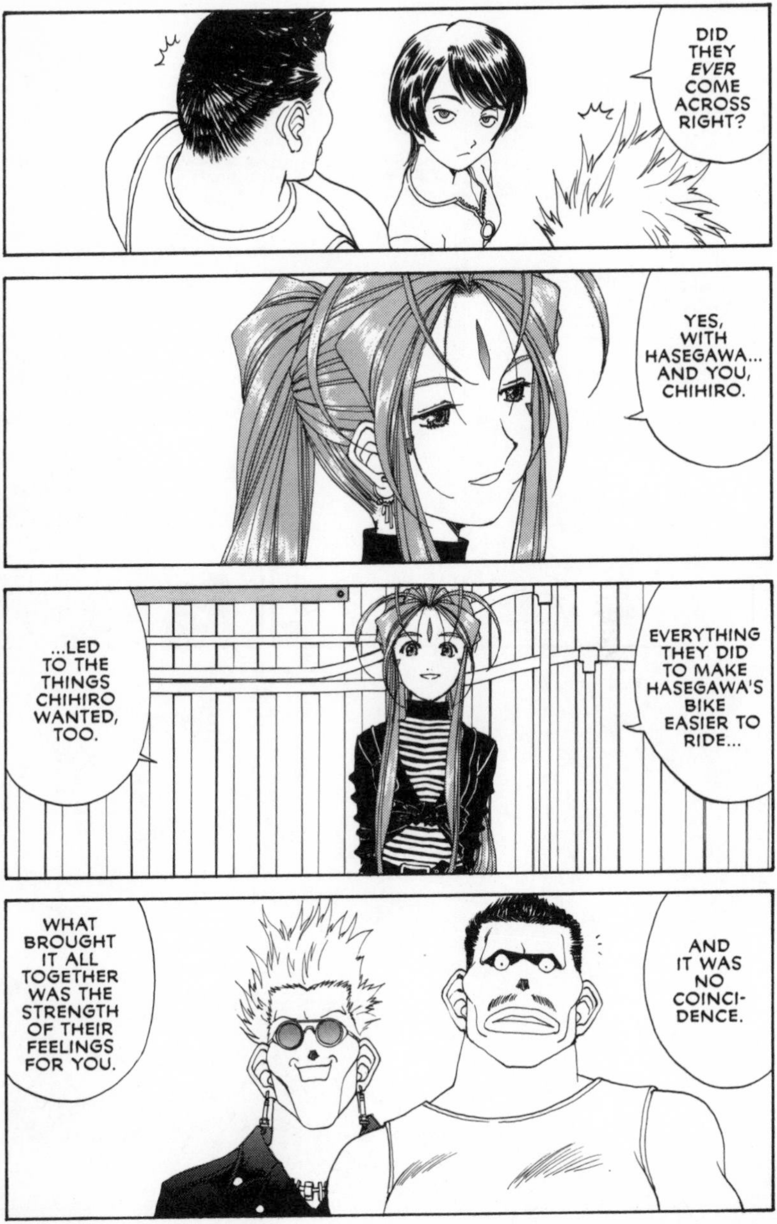
DID THEY *EVER* COME ACROSS RIGHT?
YES, WITH HASEGAWA... AND YOU, CHIHIRO.
EVERYTHING THEY DID TO MAKE HASEGAWA'S BIKE EASIER TO RIDE...
...LED TO THE THINGS CHIHIRO WANTED, TOO.
AND IT WAS NO COINCI-DENCE.
WHAT BROUGHT IT ALL TOGETHER WAS THE STRENGTH OF THEIR FEELINGS FOR YOU.

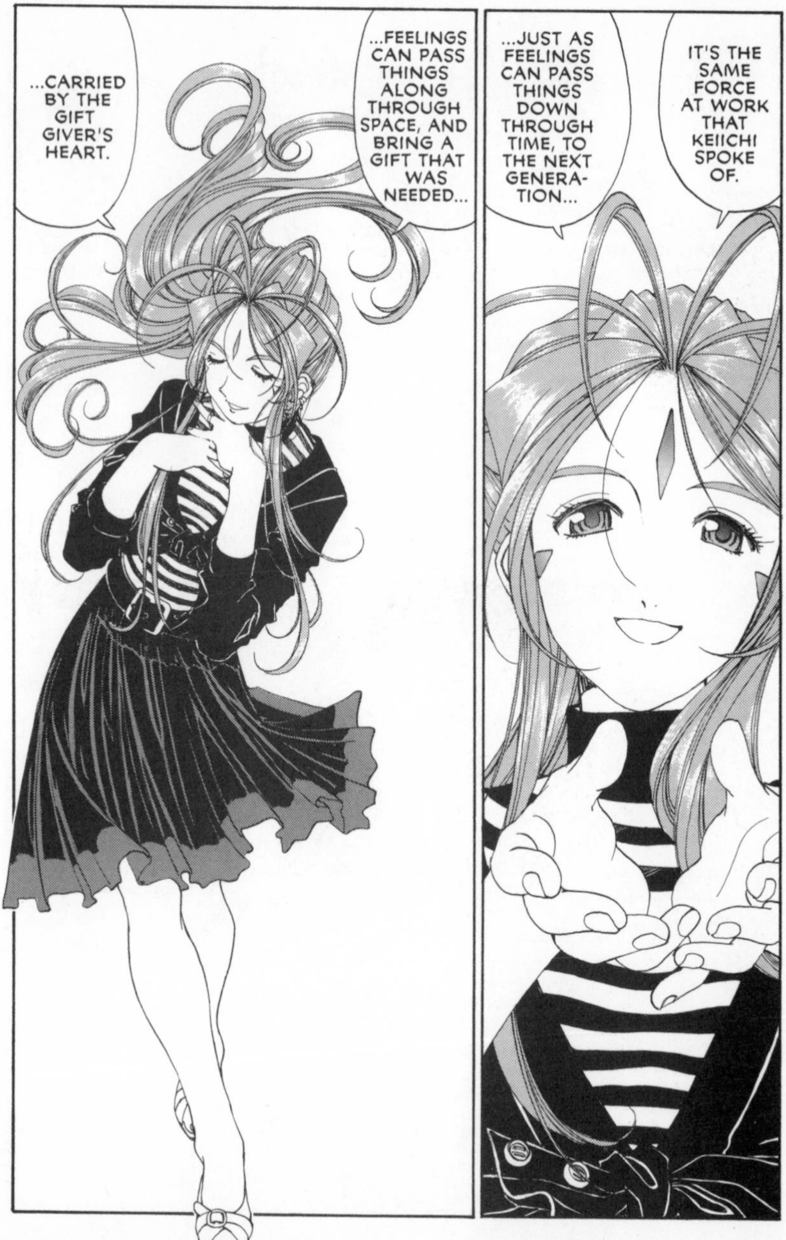
IT'S THE SAME FORCE AT WORK THAT KEIICHI SPOKE OF.
...JUST AS FEELINGS CAN PASS THINGS DOWN THROUGH TIME, TO THE NEXT GENERATION...
...FEELINGS CAN PASS THINGS ALONG THROUGH SPACE, AND BRING A GIFT THAT WAS NEEDED...
...CARRIED BY THE GIFT GIVER'S HEART.

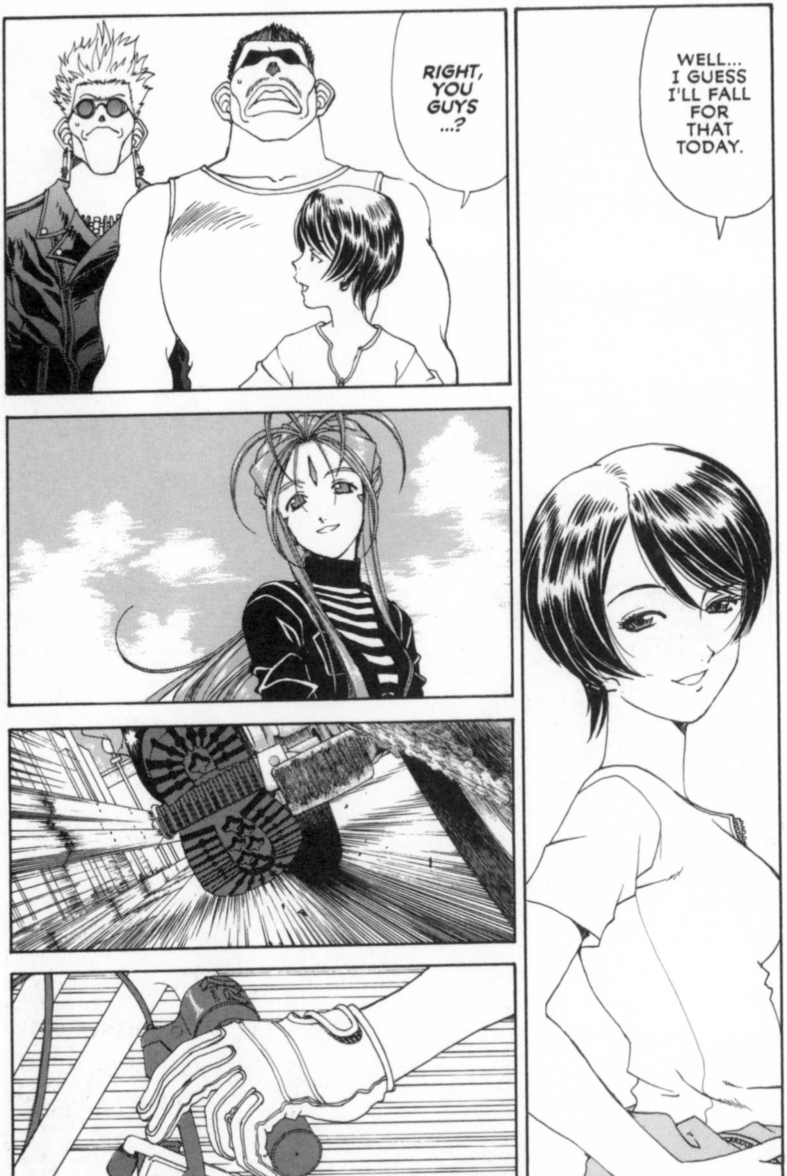
WELL... I GUESS I'LL FALL FOR THAT TODAY.
RIGHT, YOU GUYS ...?

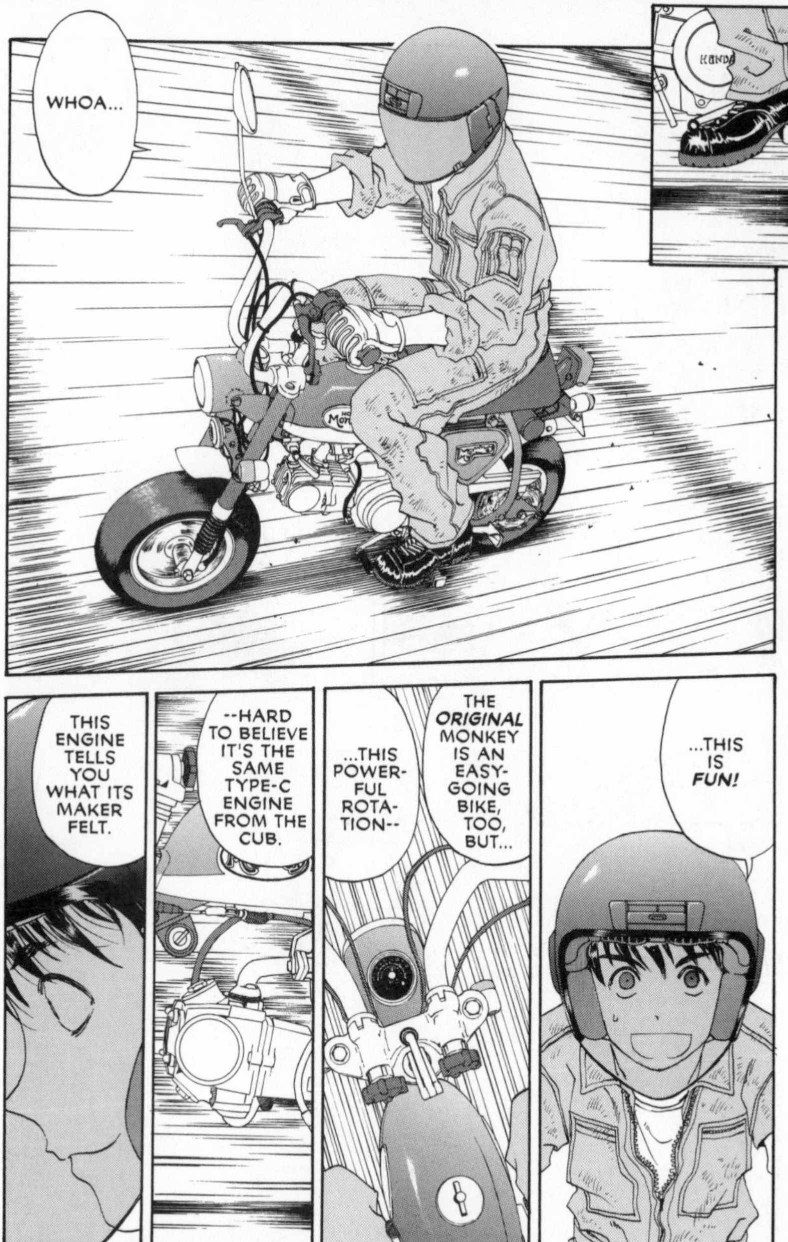
HONDA
WHOA...
...THIS IS *FUN!*
THE *ORIGINAL* MONKEY IS AN EASY-GOING BIKE, TOO, BUT...
...THIS POWERFUL ROTATION--
--HARD TO BELIEVE IT'S THE SAME TYPE-C ENGINE FROM THE CUB.
THIS ENGINE TELLS YOU WHAT ITS MAKER FELT.

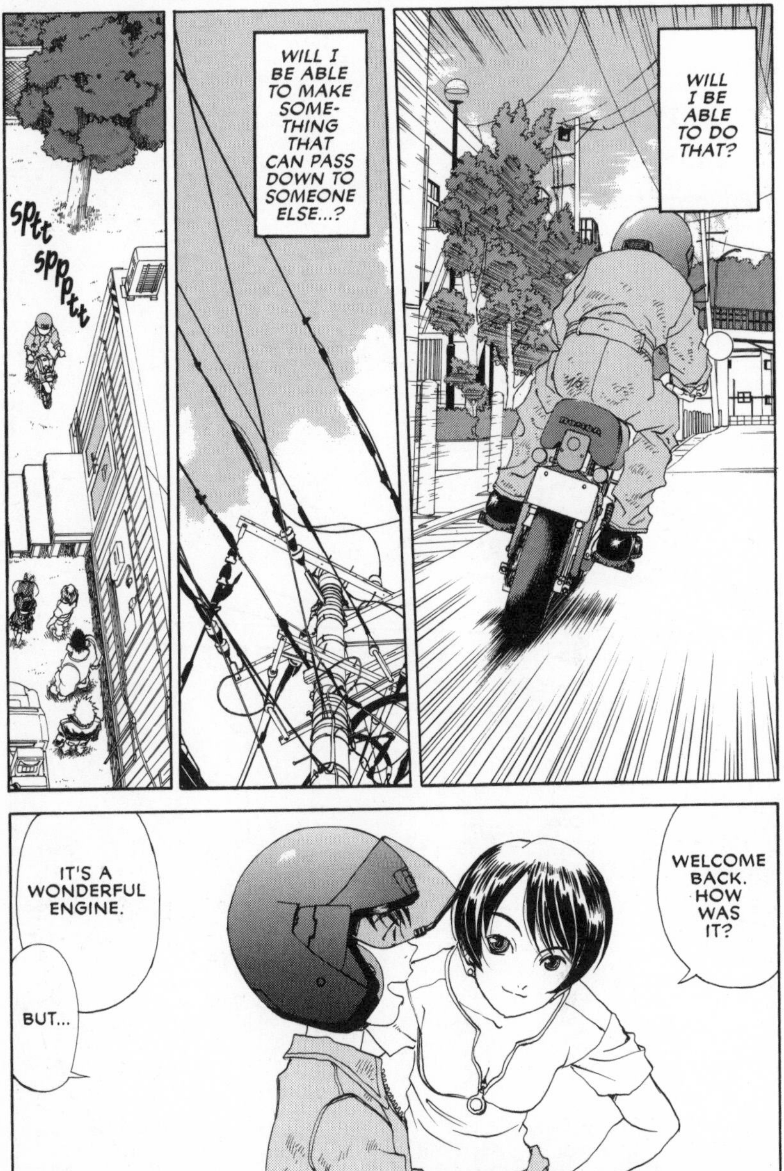
WILL I BE ABLE TO DO THAT?
WILL I BE ABLE TO MAKE SOMETHING THAT CAN PASS DOWN TO SOMEONE ELSE...?
sptt
sppptt
WELCOME BACK. HOW WAS IT?
IT'S A WONDERFUL ENGINE.
BUT...

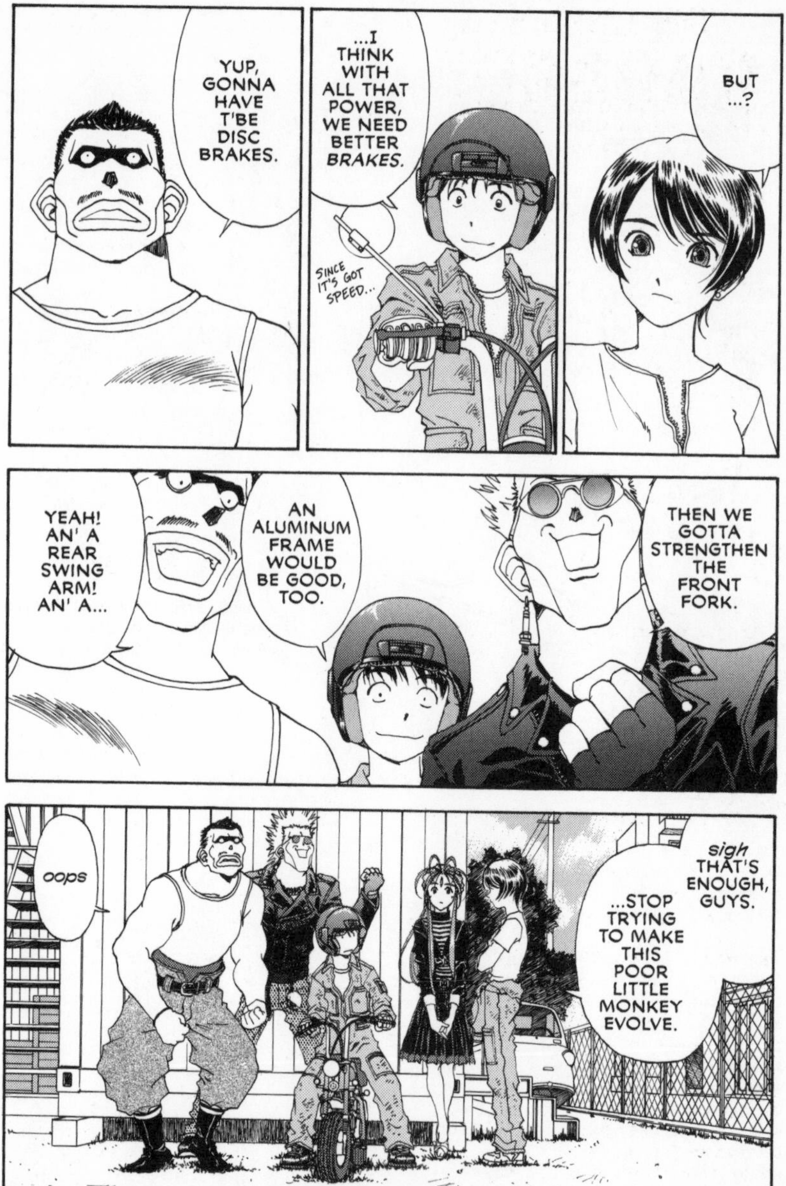
BUT ...?
...I THINK WITH ALL THAT POWER, WE NEED BETTER *BRAKES.*
SINCE IT'S GOT SPEED...
YUP, GONNA HAVE T'BE DISC BRAKES.
THEN WE GOTTA STRENGTHEN THE FRONT FORK.
AN ALUMINUM FRAME WOULD BE GOOD, TOO.
YEAH! AN' A REAR SWING ARM! AN' A...
*sigh* THAT'S ENOUGH, GUYS.
...STOP TRYING TO MAKE THIS POOR LITTLE MONKEY EVOLVE.
*oops*

# THE *GODDESS!* GARAGE

女神用語の基礎知識 ガレージ拝見

**A look at the vehicles owned by each character**

By guest writer and artist Kouji Akimoto

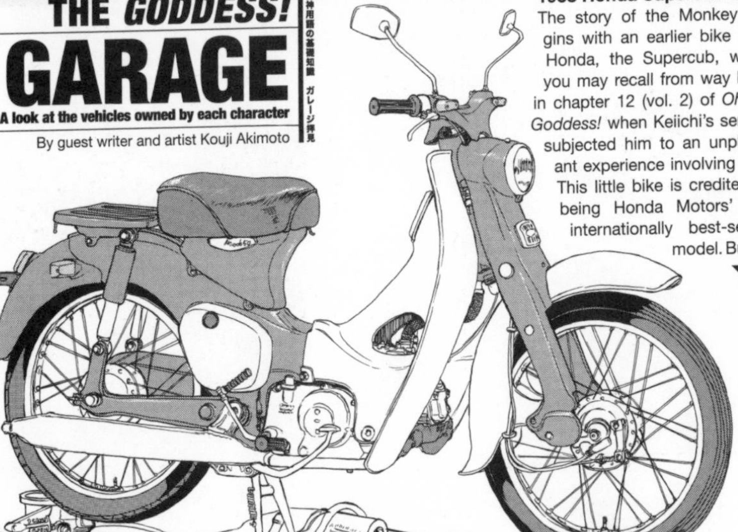

**1958 Honda Supercub C100**

The story of the Monkey begins with an earlier bike from Honda, the Supercub, which you may recall from way back in chapter 12 (vol. 2) of *Oh My Goddess!* when Keiichi's seniors subjected him to an unpleasant experience involving one. This little bike is credited as being Honda Motors' first internationally best-selling model. But it's hardly a relic of the past! It's still being manufactured, and with over 60 million sold, it's the most successful powered vehicle in human history! Particularly in developing countries, the Supercub has provided motorized transport to individuals that had never been able to afford it before. Adjusted for inflation and exchange rates (which since World War Two have varied between a maximum of 360 and a minimum of 79 yen to the dollar) its initial price of 55,000 yen is the equivalent of US$1,100 today.

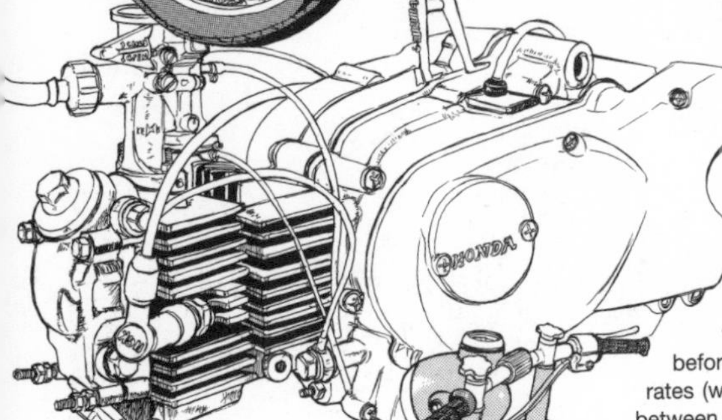

**C100 Engine**

The Supercub C100 is powered by an air-cooled, three-speed, four-stroke 49 cc, maximum speed, 70 km/h!

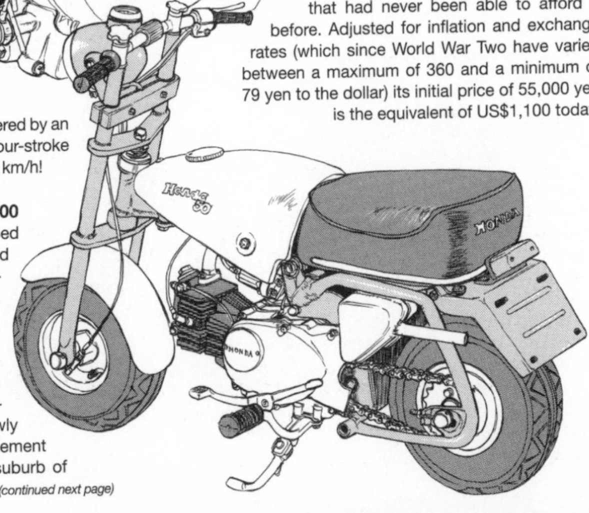

**1961 Honda Monkey Z100**

The C100 engine developed for the Supercub, was used to power the smaller Honda Monkey, making it a little giant! The Monkey wasn't originally meant to be a consumer bike; instead, the first ones were built as something for visitors to ride at Honda's newly opened Tama Tech amusement park; located in Hino, a suburb of Tokyo, Tama Tech closed *(continued next page)*

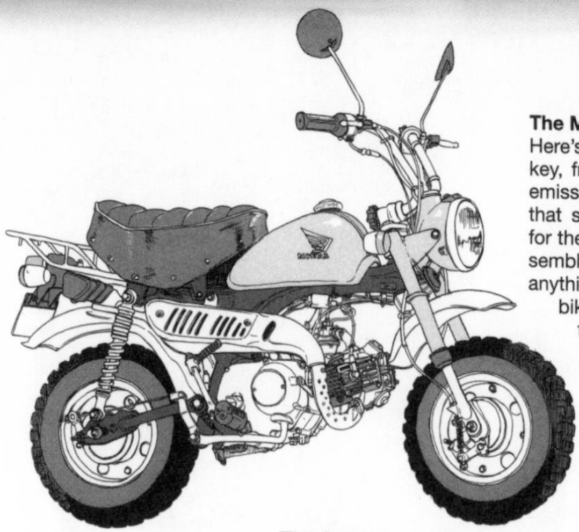

**The Modern Monkey!**
Here's a much more recent Honda Monkey, from 1996. This version has strict emissions controls. The truth is, though, that so many mod parts are available for the bike now that it's possible to assemble a Monkey without actually using anything made in a Honda factory! The bike seen here has an air-cooled, four speed, four-stroke 49 cc kick-start engine, delivering a maximum output of 3.1 PS at 6,000 rpm. It weighs 58 kilos and sold for 239,000 yen (adjusted price about US$3,000 today).

**The Gorilla**
The bulkier brother of the Monkey, the Honda Gorilla has largely the same specs, with two important differences: the Monkey's traditional foldable handle is omitted, and the 9 L fuel tank is twice as big as the Monkey's.

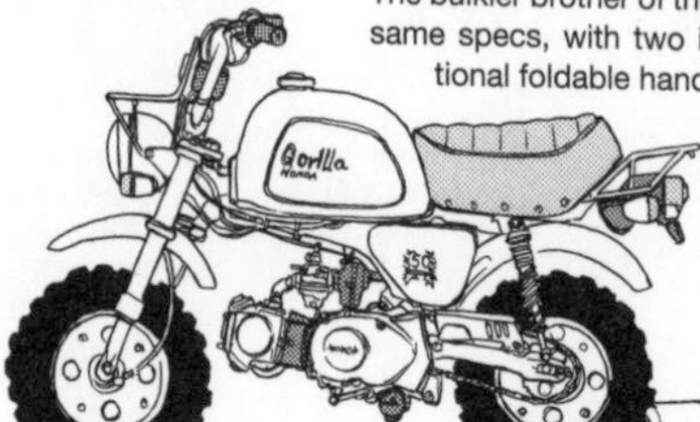
Gorilla

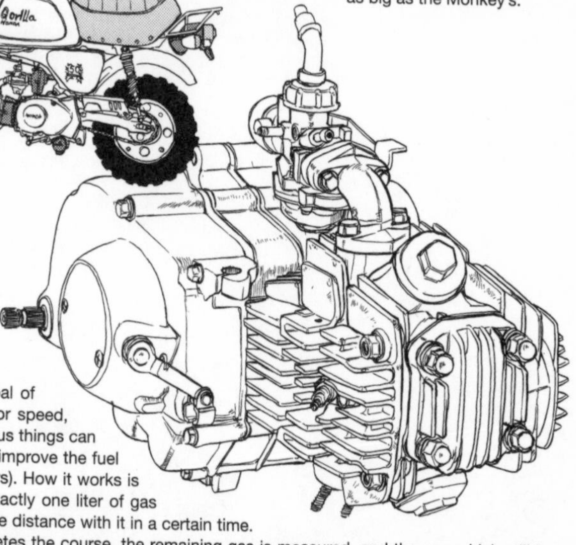

**The Miracle Monkey!**
In *Oh My Goddess!* vol. 4, chapter 30, the NIT Motor Club took part in an "economy run" race. Also called eco-run for short, the goal of such a race is not time or speed, but fuel efficiency (and thus things can be learned that can help improve the fuel efficiency of everyday cars). How it works is that each vehicle gets exactly one liter of gas and has to travel the same distance with it in a certain time. After each vehicle completes the course, the remaining gas is measured, and the one which still has the most is the winner. Now, some models of the Supercub were said to get as much as 180 km/L (423 mpg!) just in normal use, but at the 2001 Honda eco-run, the winning team set a new world record for fuel efficiency by getting an incredible 3,435.33 km/L out of this Monkey engine! That's the equivalent of being able to drive around the world on three and a fifth gallons of gas . . .

**1961 Honda Monkey Z100** *(continued from previous page)*
this September after forty-eight years of operation. Based on its popularity, Honda developed the Monkey CZ100, a street-legal version for both the domestic and export market. There are different stories about where the name "Monkey" comes from; although one often hears it refers to the simian posture you assume when riding one, it is actually said to come from the Yaen ("Wild Monkey") Highway that runs near Tama Tech park.

**Eco-Run Design**
Naturally, a vehicle designed to maximize fuel efficiency above all other factors is not going to look like a regular motorcycle. In an eco-run, the engine will be surrounded by a chassis that is low and a body that is light and aerodynamic. By the way, the Honda eco-run course is seven laps, totaling 16.8 km, and drivers must maintain a speed of at least 25 km/h.

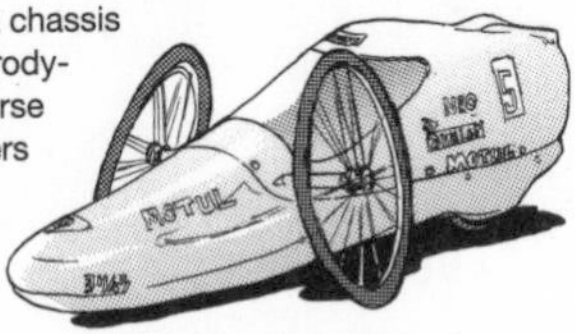

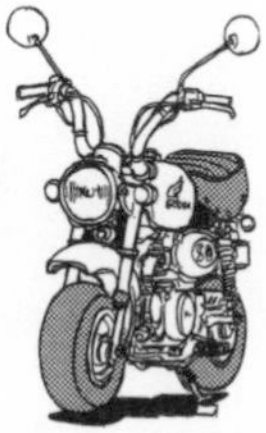

**The Monkey-Benly Connection!**
Ah, you were wondering what the link was between the Monkey and the Benly mentioned on page 38? Well, look closely at Chihiro's 1969 Z50A/Z Monkey . . . and notice it's had a Benly engine installed! That engine, as noted above, could do 95 km/h on its original frame . . . but since the Z50A/Z weighs 13 kg less than the Benly, who knows how fast Chihiro can go now? Note that the front section of the Z50A/Z was detachable, making the bike easy to stow inside an automobile. A standard 1969 Z50A/Z, however, had a performance of 2.6 PS at 7,000 rpm and a maximum speed of 50 km/h, and went for 63,000 yen (adjusted price about US$1,075).

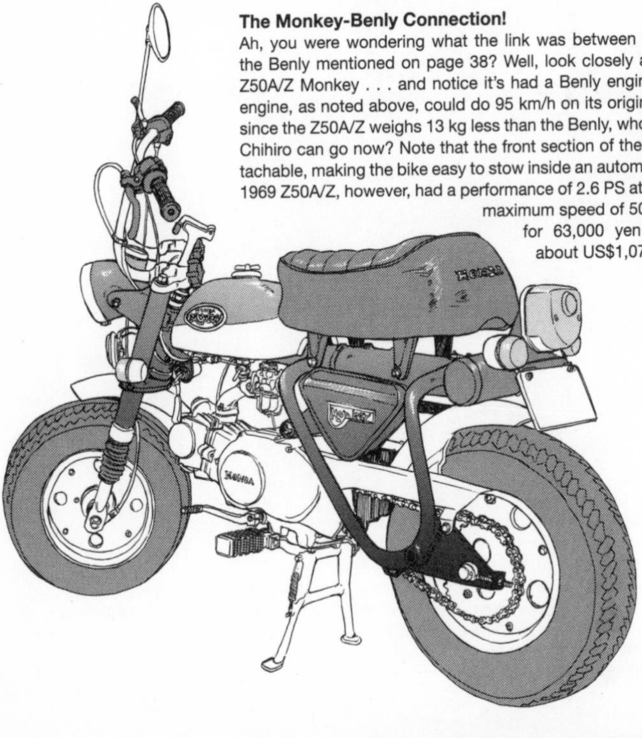

**Honda Benly SS50**

This bike featured a five-speed engine (unusual for a 49 cc unit) and was surprisingly powerful and fast—6 PS at 11,000 rpm. With a top speed of 95 km/h, it's not surprising that it was sometimes known as the "super moped." When released, it cost 62,000 yen (adjusted price about US$1,120 today).

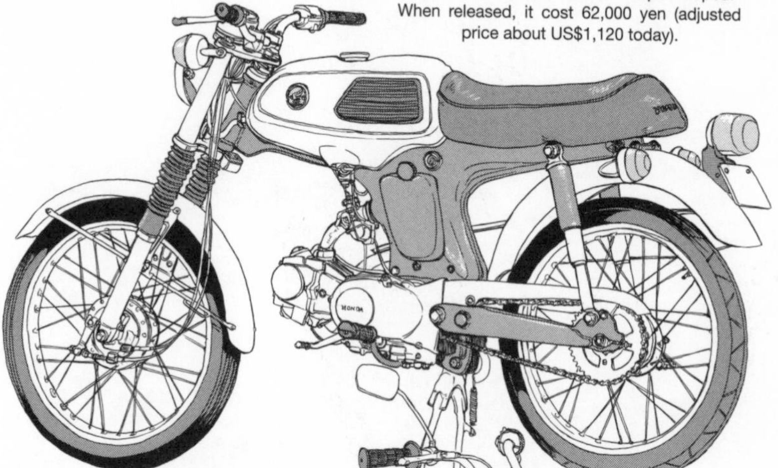

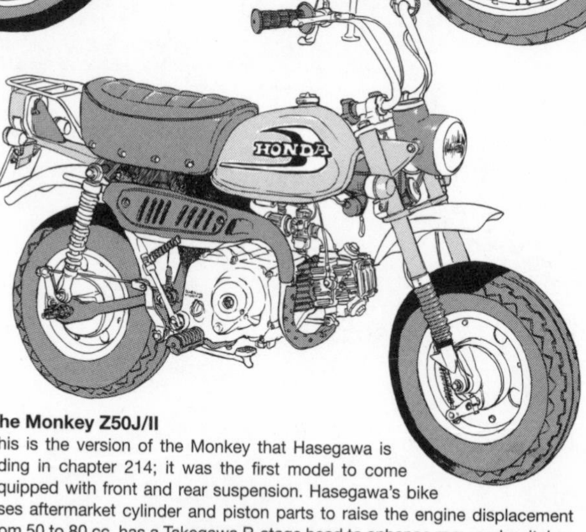
HONDA

**The Monkey Z50J/II**

This is the version of the Monkey that Hasegawa is riding in chapter 214; it was the first model to come equipped with front and rear suspension. Hasegawa's bike uses aftermarket cylinder and piston parts to raise the engine displacement from 50 to 80 cc, has a Takegawa R-stage head to enhance rpm, and switches out the stock carburetor, air cleaner, and muffler to further increase power. Tiny but mighty is the theme here! The stock 1974 Monkey Z50J/II went for 89,000 yen (adjusted price about US$1,500 today).

CHAPTER 216

# I'll Fly for You!

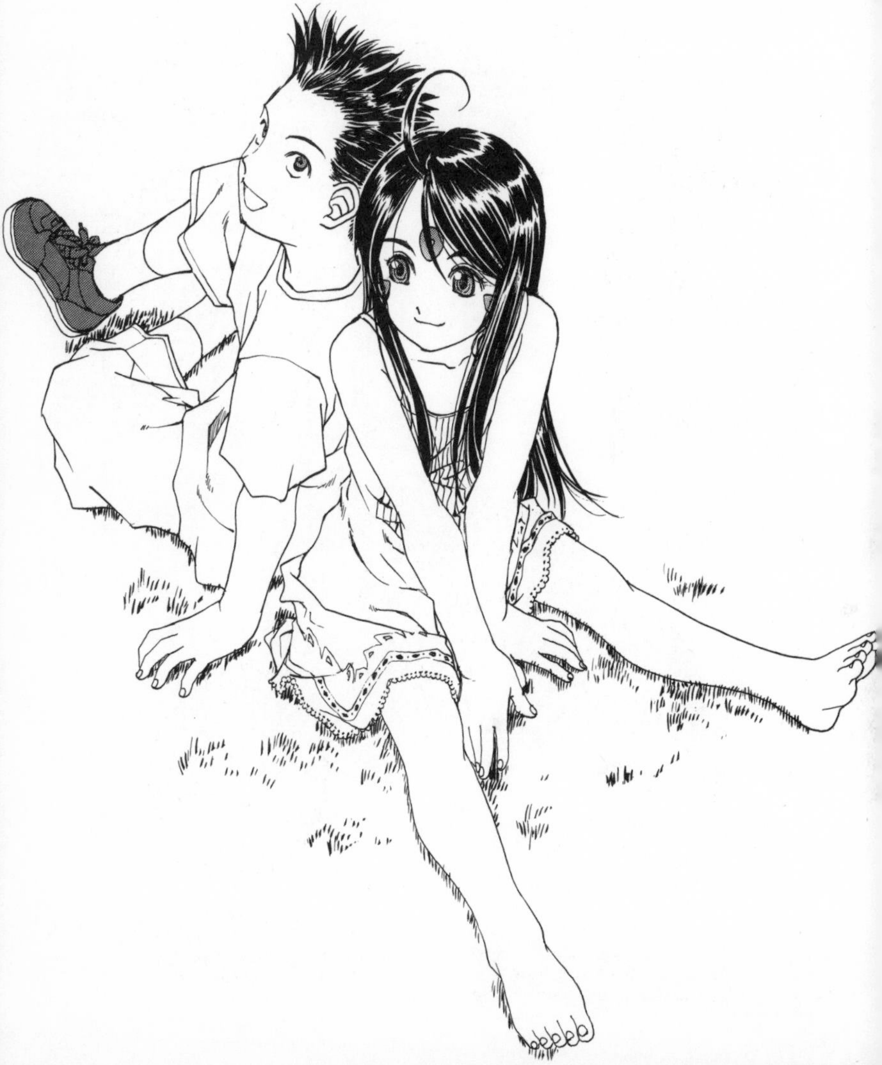

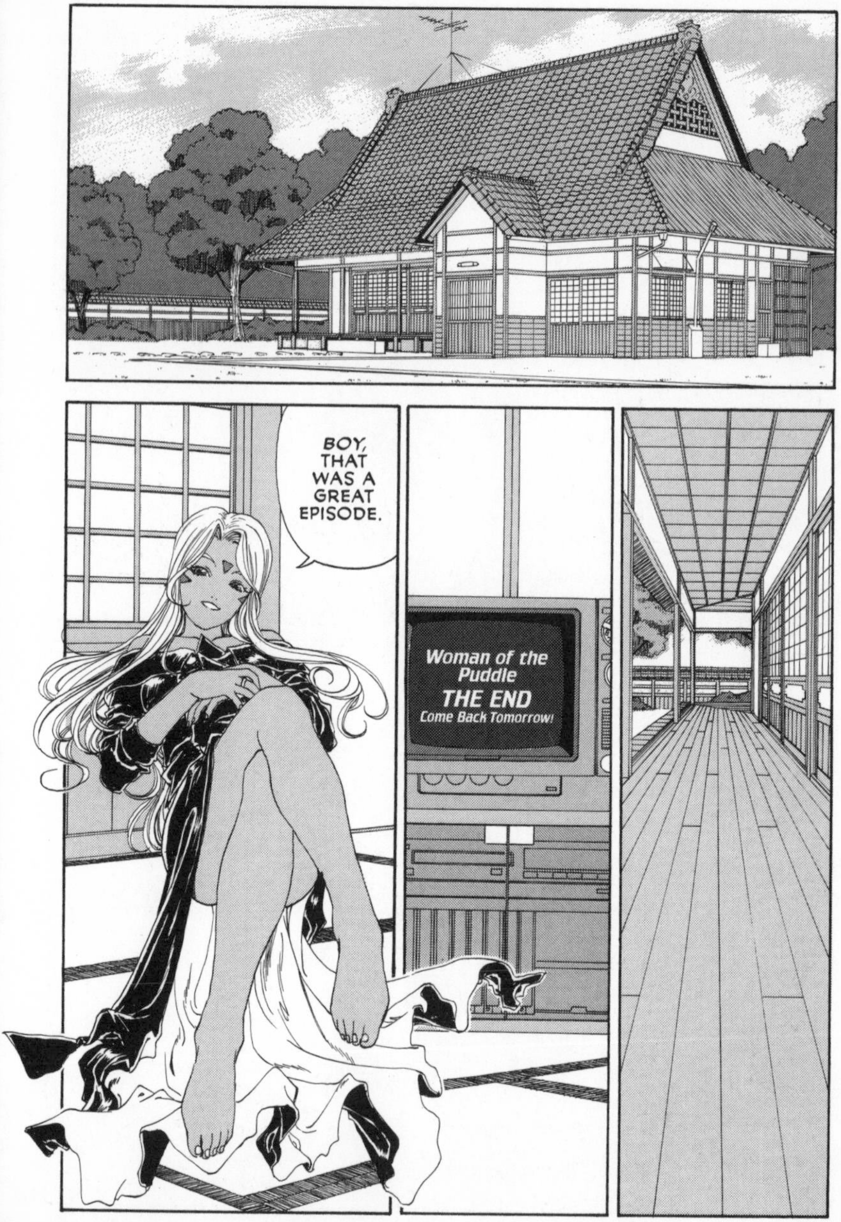
Woman of the Puddle
THE END
Come Back Tomorrow!
BOY, THAT WAS A GREAT EPISODE.

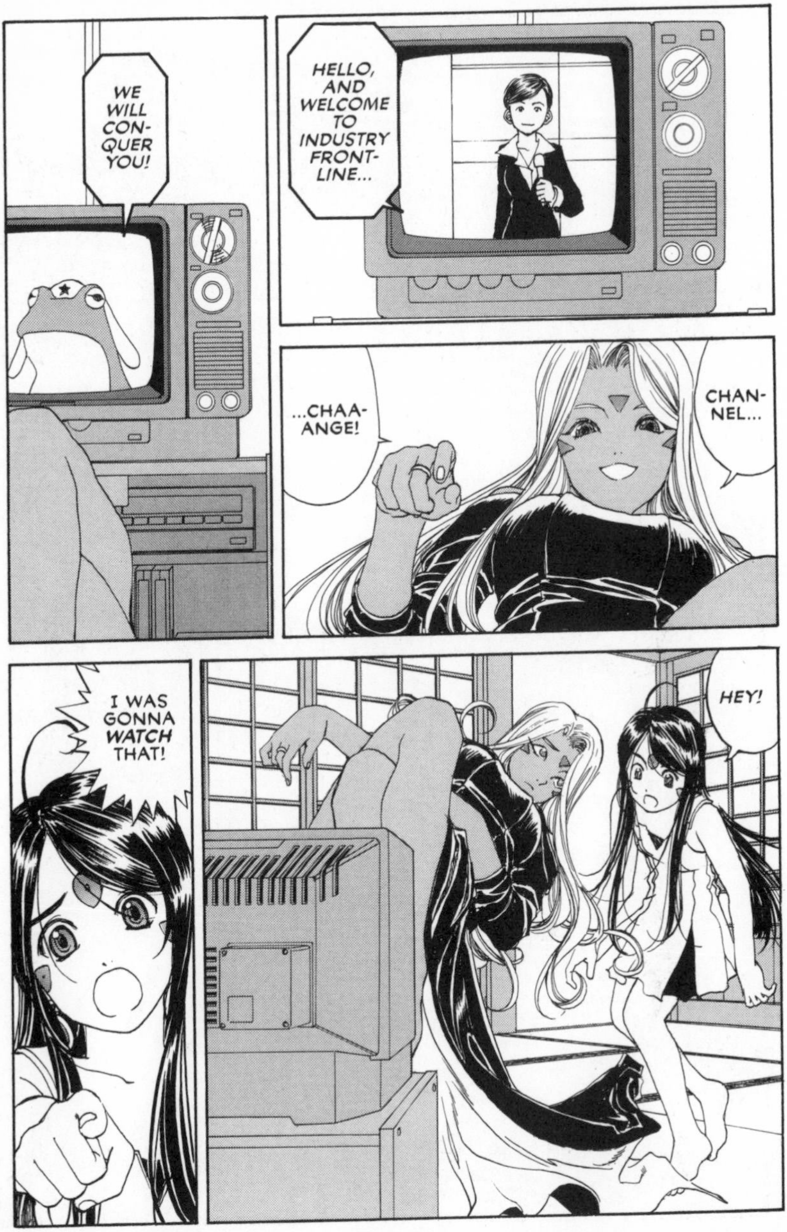
HELLO, AND WELCOME TO INDUSTRY FRONT-LINE...
CHAN-NEL...
...CHAA-ANGE!
WE WILL CON-QUER YOU!
HEY!
I WAS GONNA *WATCH* THAT!

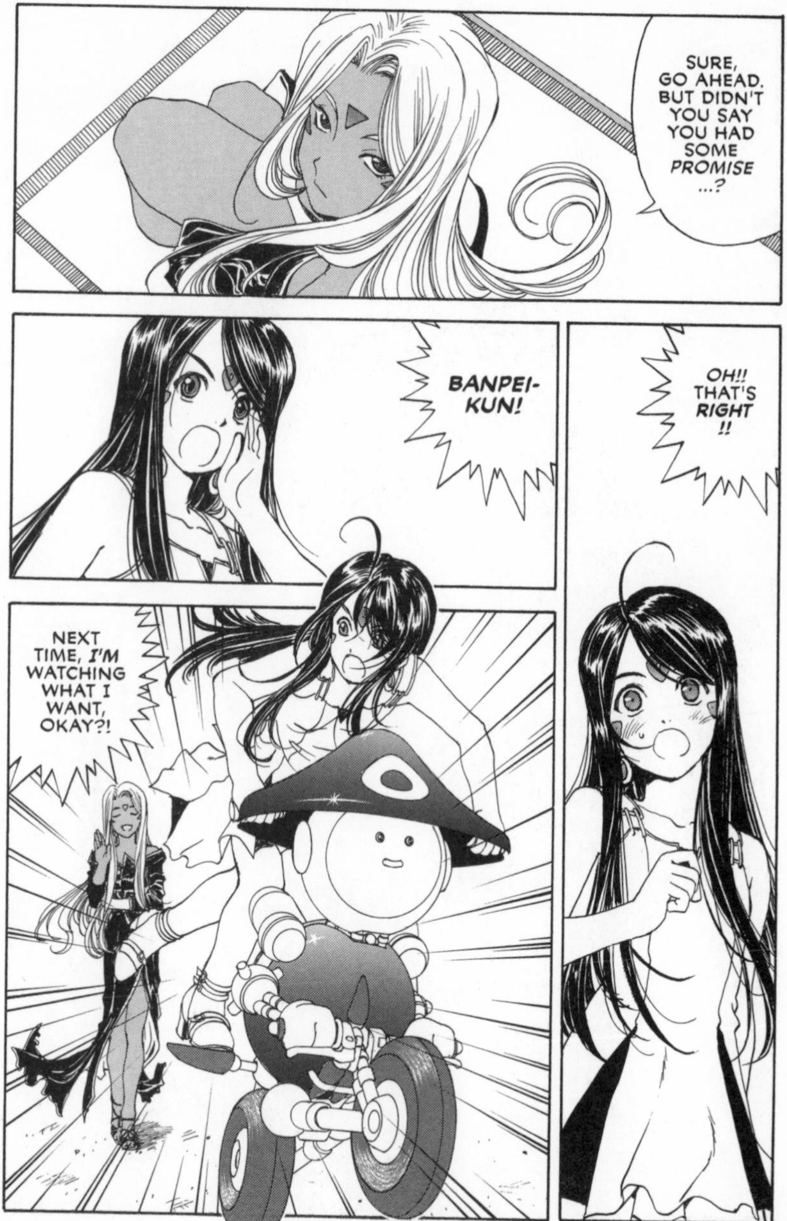
SURE, GO AHEAD. BUT DIDN'T YOU SAY YOU HAD SOME *PROMISE* ...?
OH!! THAT'S **RIGHT** !!
**BANPEI-KUN!**
NEXT TIME, *I'M* WATCHING WHAT I WANT, OKAY?!

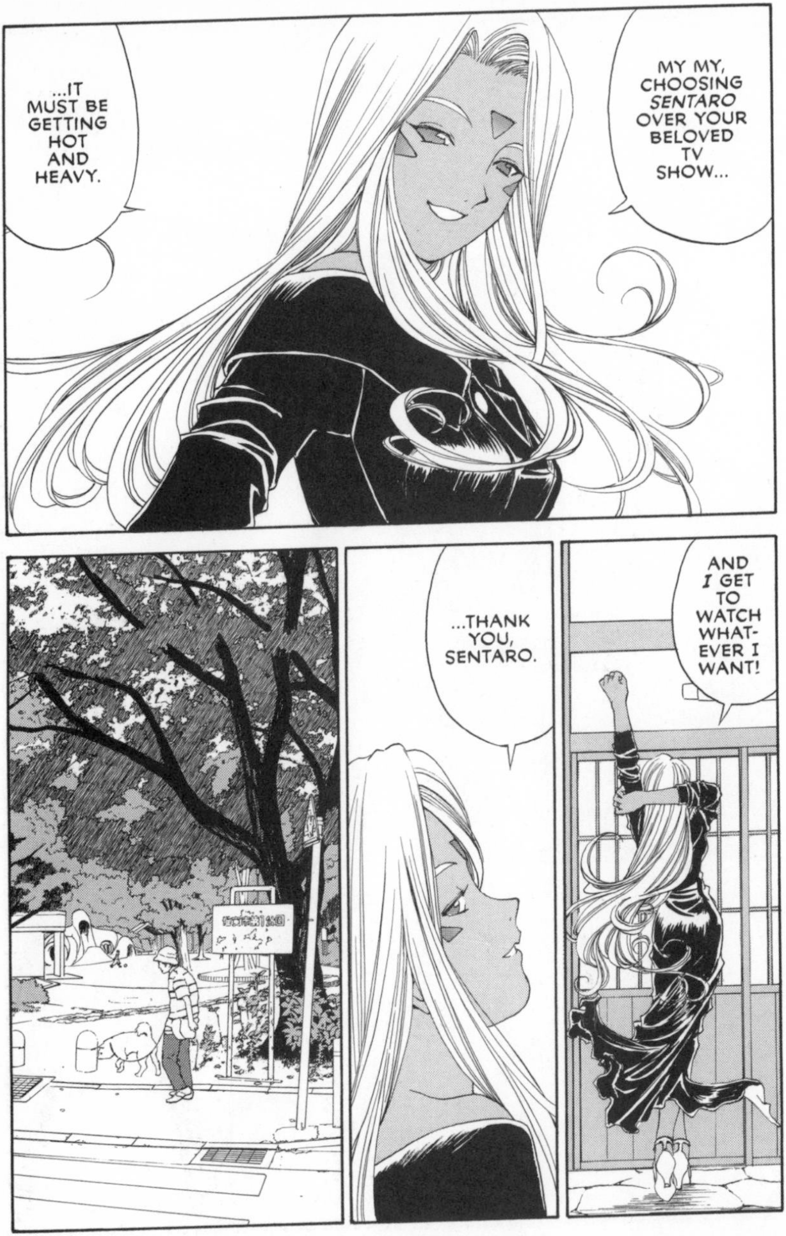
MY MY, CHOOSING *SENTARO* OVER YOUR BELOVED TV SHOW...
...IT MUST BE GETTING HOT AND HEAVY.
AND *I* GET TO WATCH WHAT-EVER I WANT!
...THANK YOU, SENTARO.

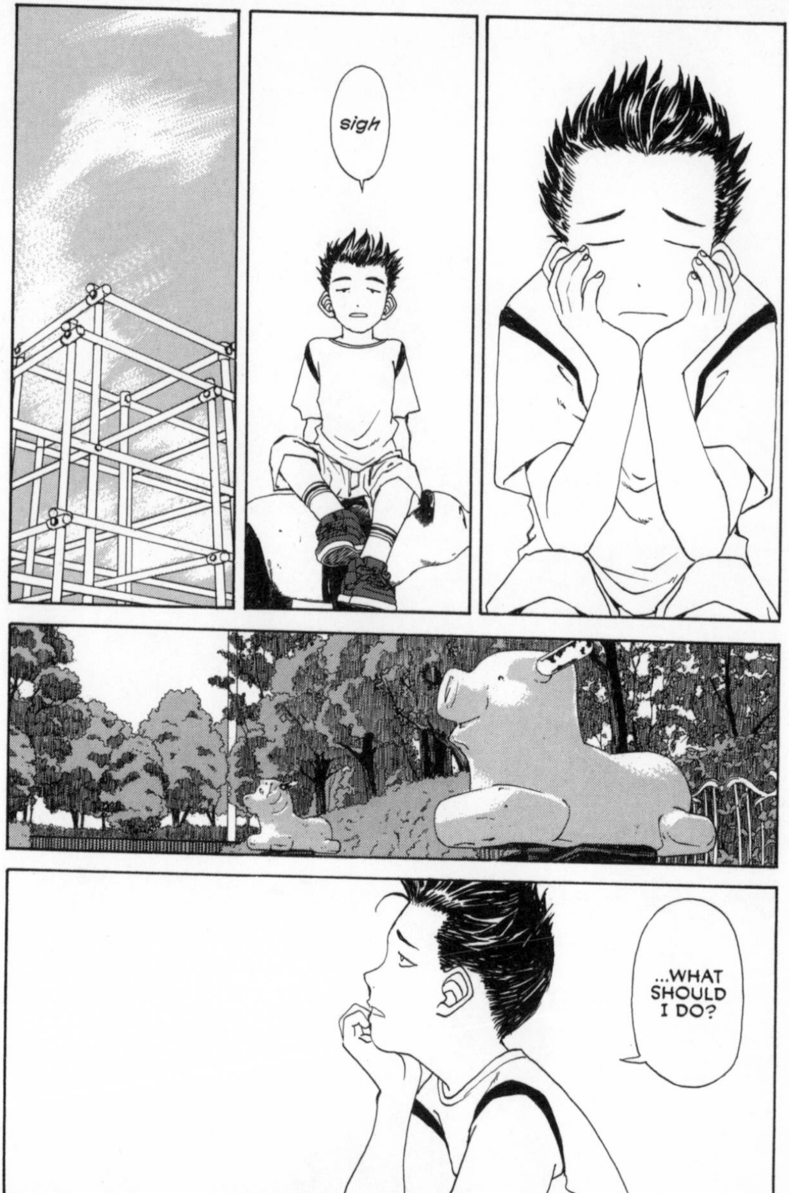
sigh
...WHAT SHOULD I DO?

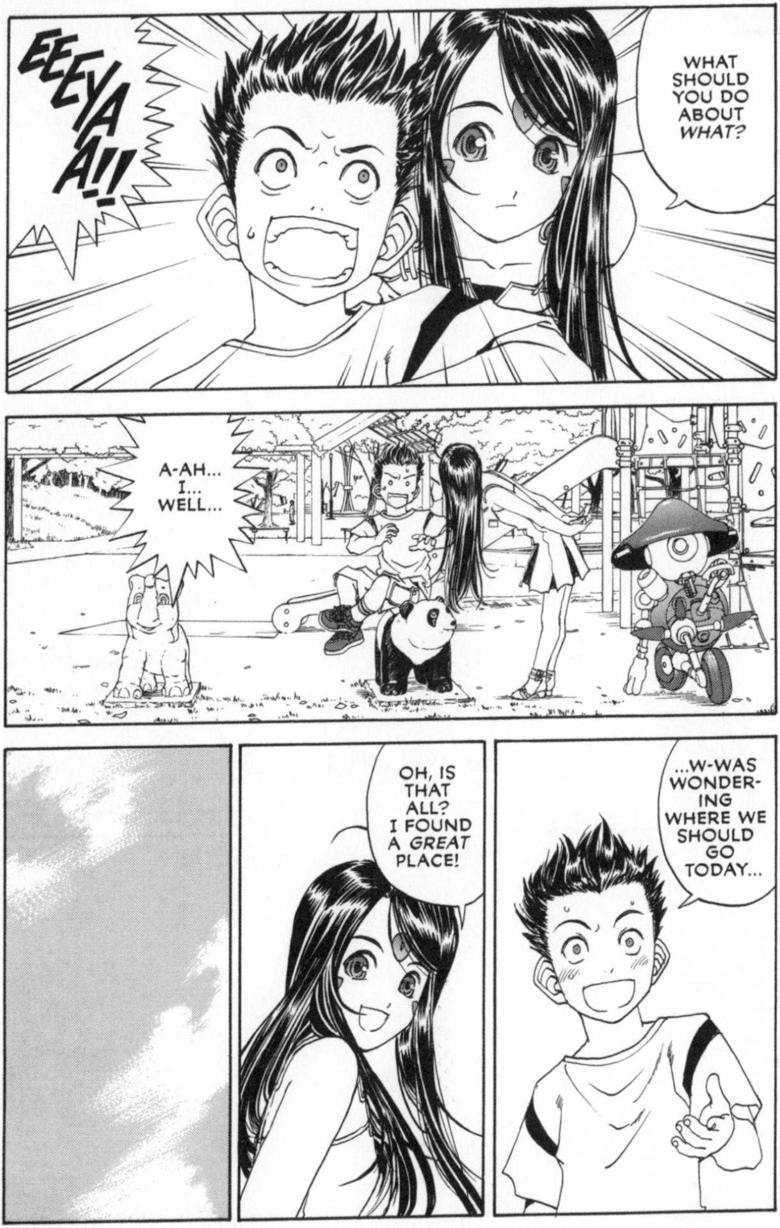
WHAT SHOULD YOU DO ABOUT *WHAT?*
EEEYAA!!
A-AH... I... WELL...
...W-WAS WONDER-ING WHERE WE SHOULD GO TODAY...
OH, IS THAT ALL? I FOUND A *GREAT* PLACE!

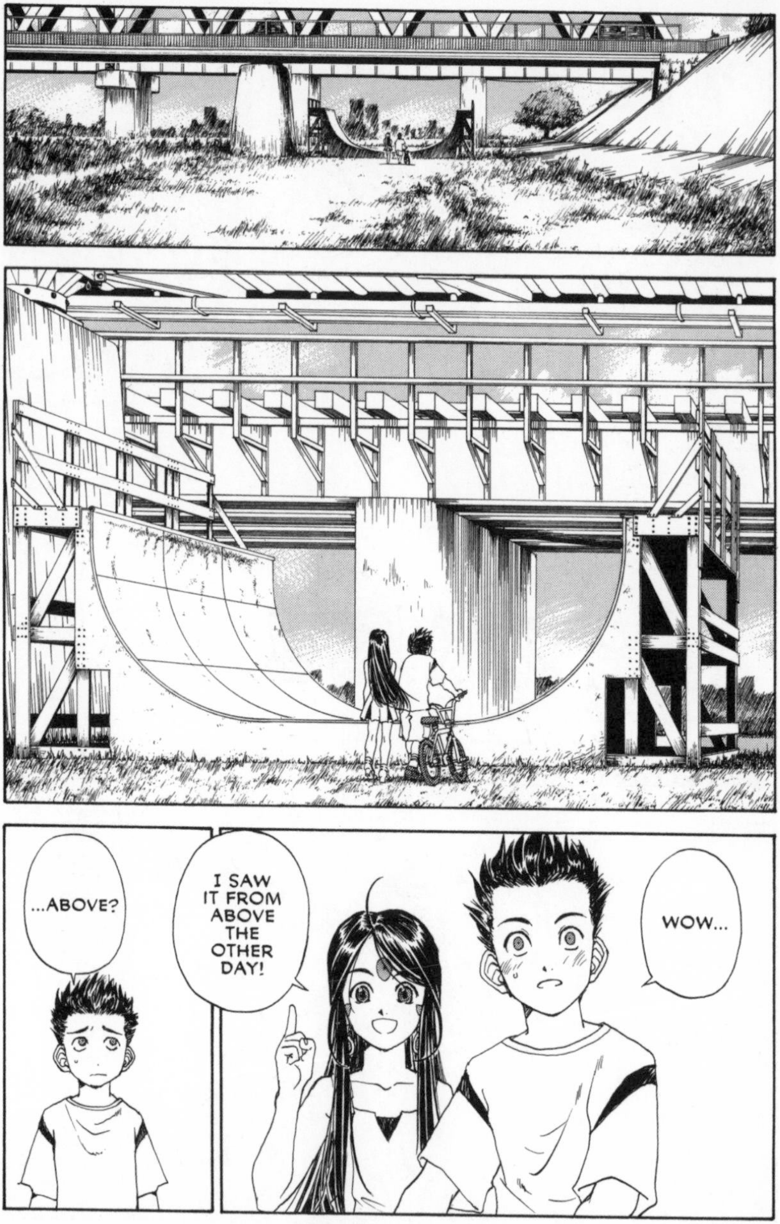
WOW...
I SAW IT FROM ABOVE THE OTHER DAY!
...ABOVE?

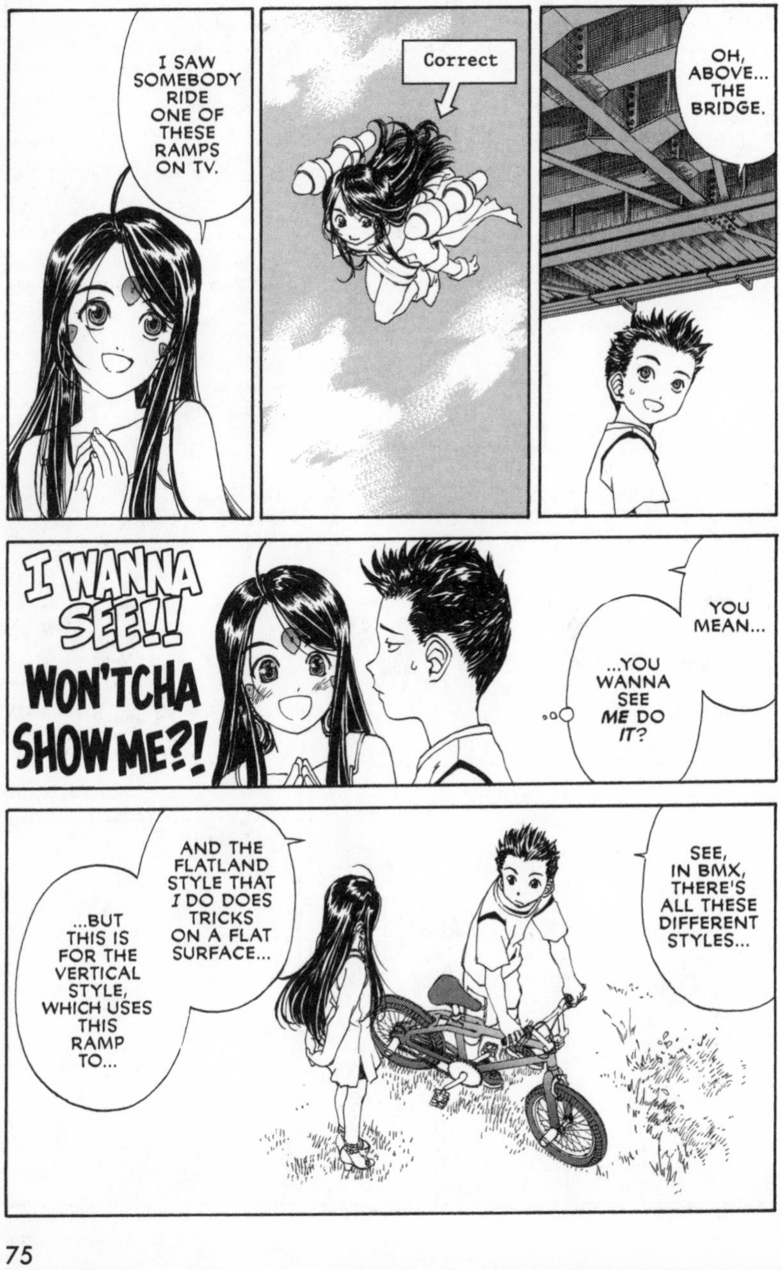
OH, ABOVE... THE BRIDGE.
Correct
I SAW SOMEBODY RIDE ONE OF THESE RAMPS ON TV.
YOU MEAN...
...YOU WANNA SEE *ME* DO *IT*?
I WANNA SEE!!
WON'TCHA SHOW ME?!
SEE, IN BMX, THERE'S ALL THESE DIFFERENT STYLES...
AND THE FLATLAND STYLE THAT *I* DO DOES TRICKS ON A FLAT SURFACE...
...BUT THIS IS FOR THE VERTICAL STYLE, WHICH USES THIS RAMP TO...

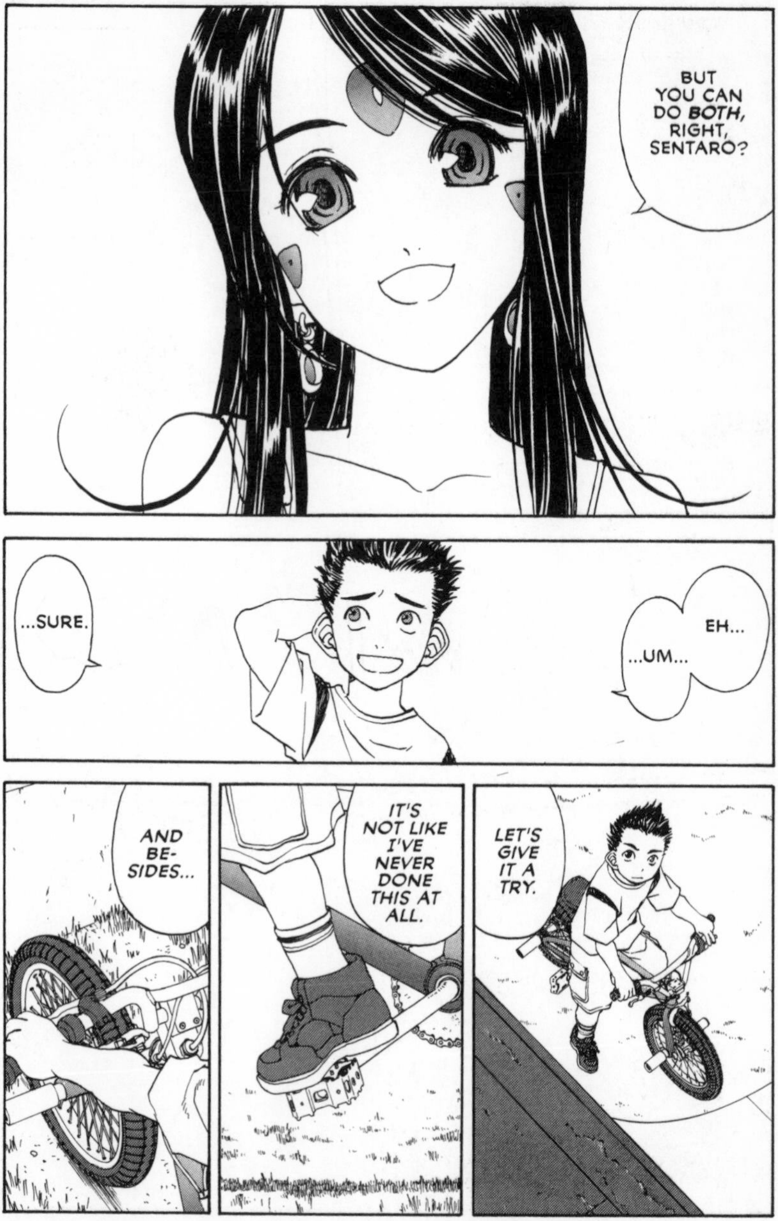
BUT YOU CAN DO *BOTH,* RIGHT, SENTARO?
EH... ...UM...
...SURE.
LET'S GIVE IT A TRY.
IT'S NOT LIKE I'VE NEVER DONE THIS AT ALL.
AND BE-SIDES...

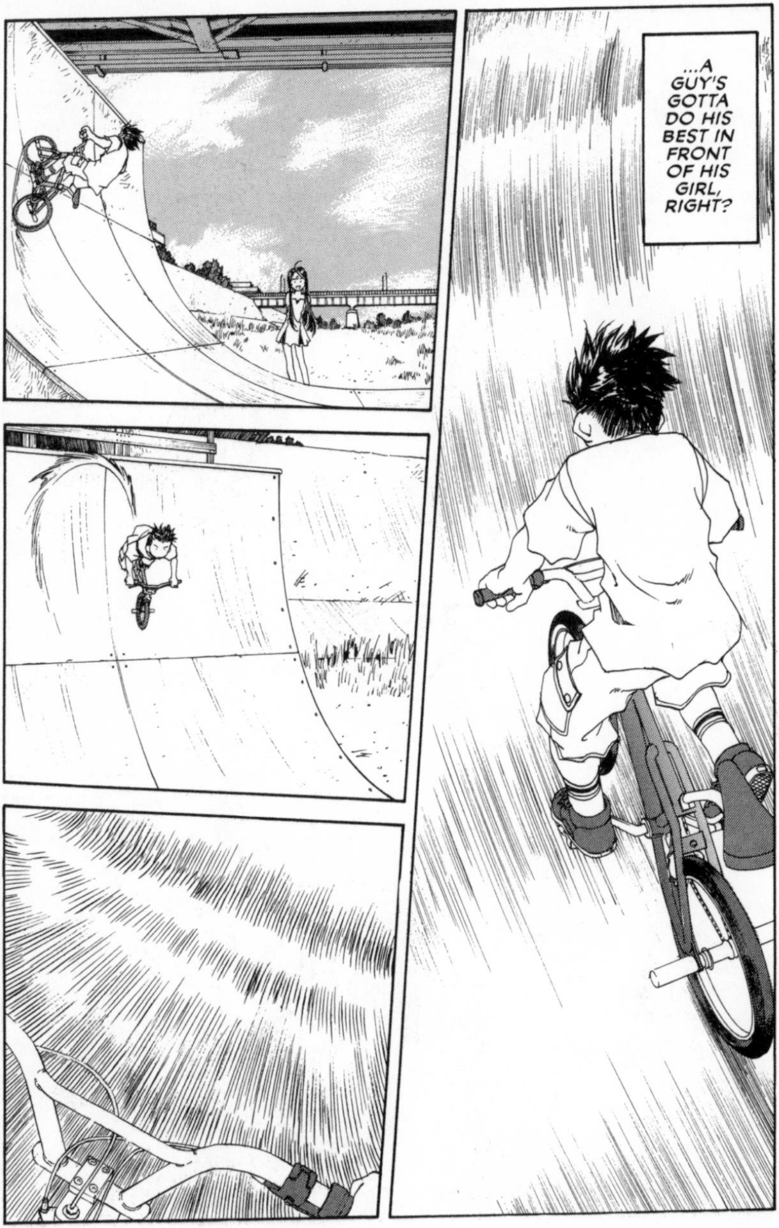
...A GUY'S GOTTA DO HIS BEST IN FRONT OF HIS GIRL, RIGHT?

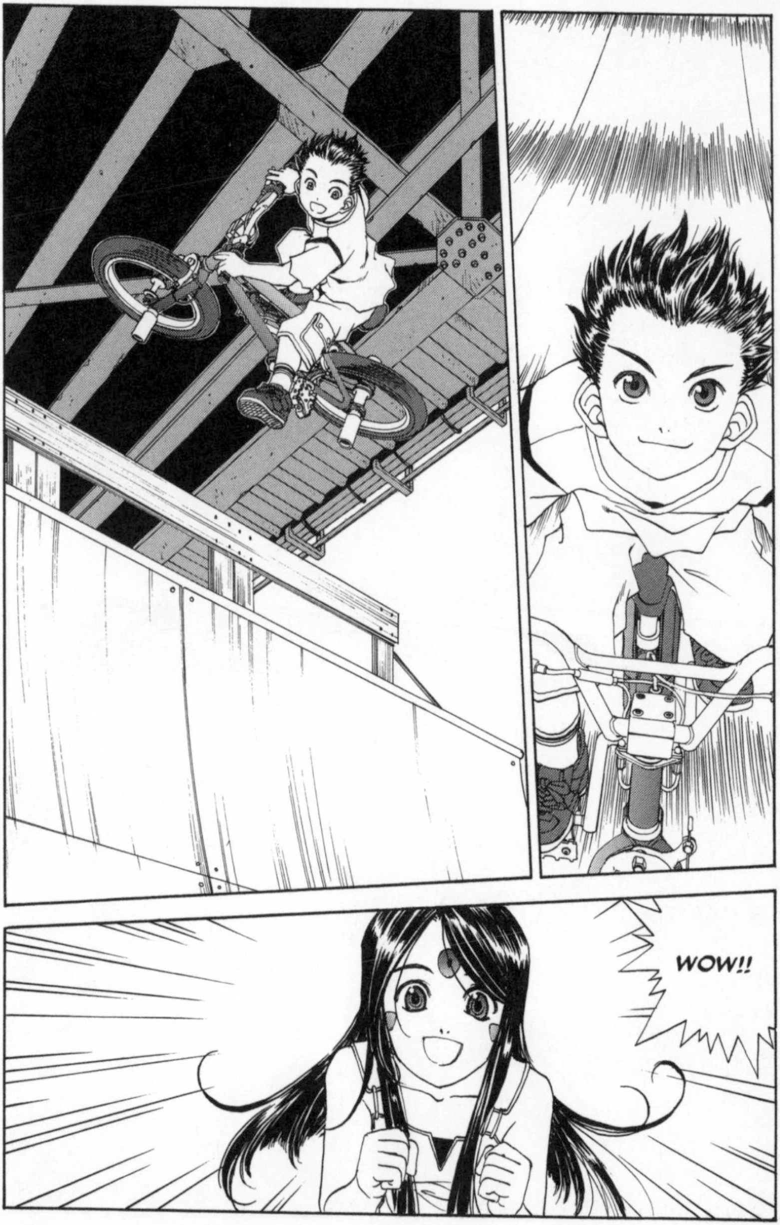
WOW!!

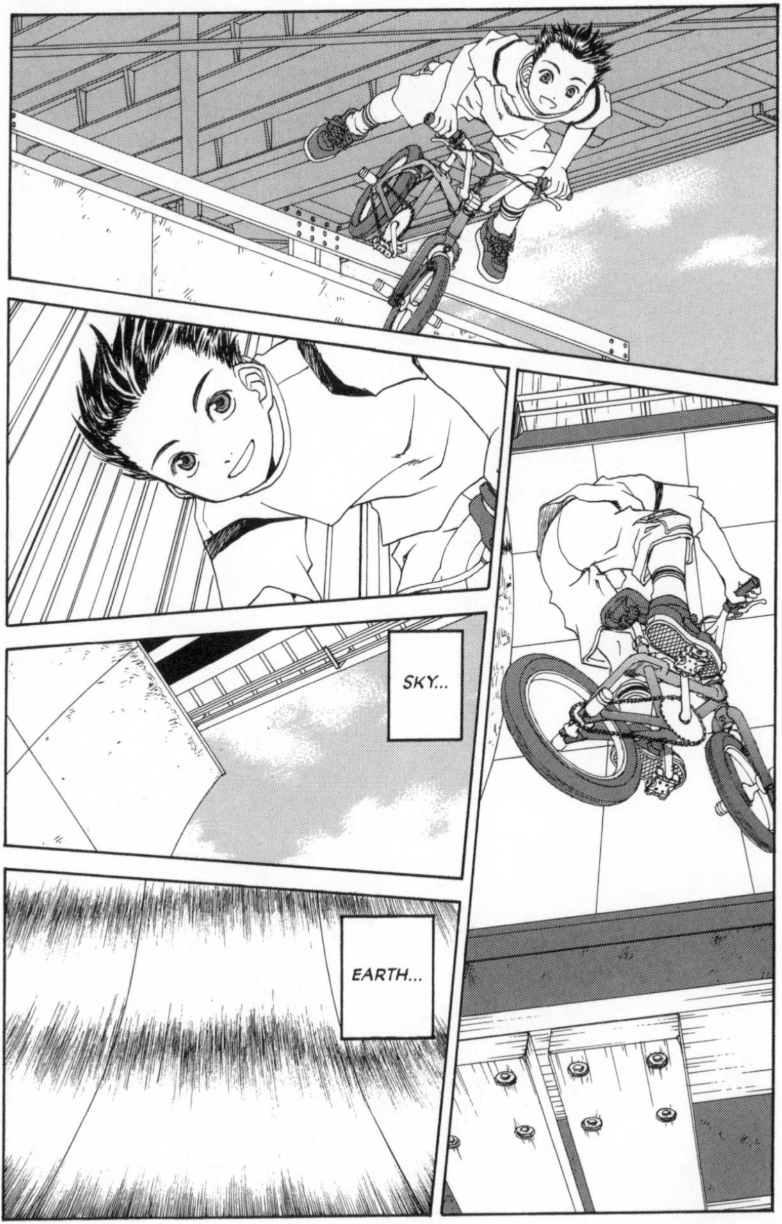
SKY...
EARTH...

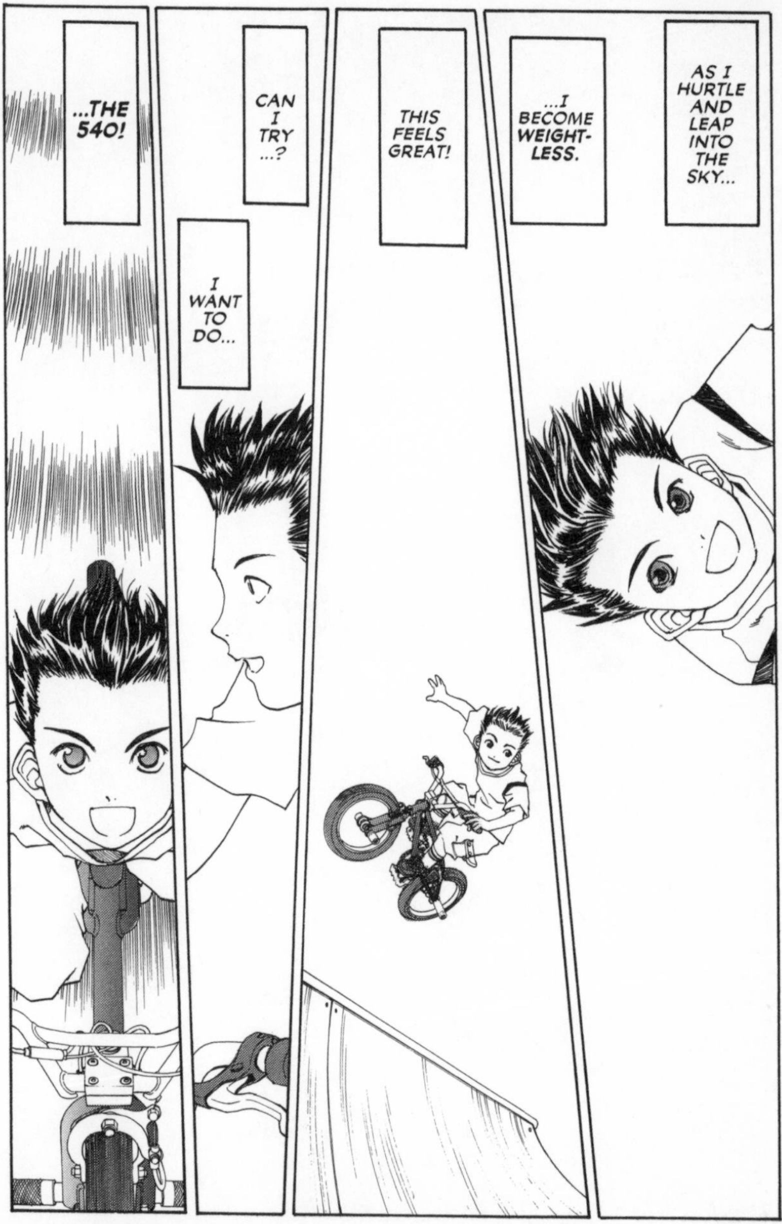
AS I HURTLE AND LEAP INTO THE SKY...
...I BECOME WEIGHT-LESS.
THIS FEELS GREAT!
CAN I TRY ...?
I WANT TO DO...
...THE 540!

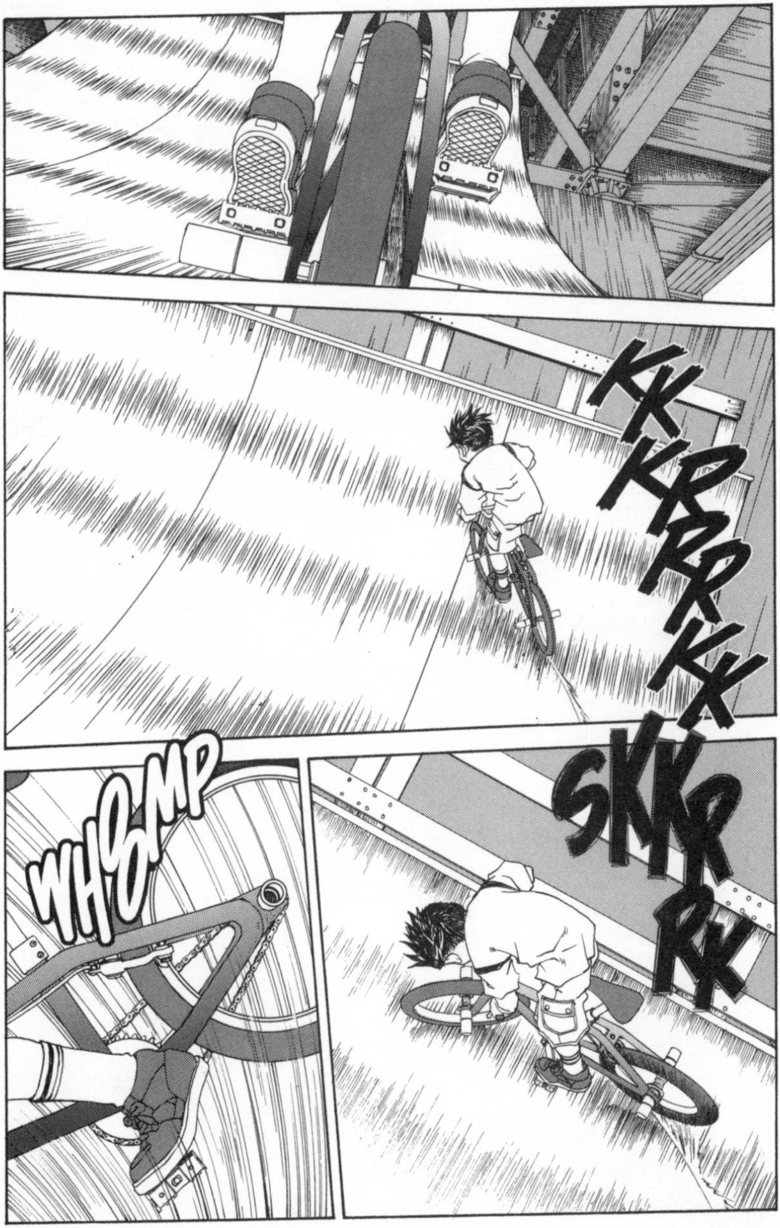
KKKRRRKK
SKKRRK
WHOMP

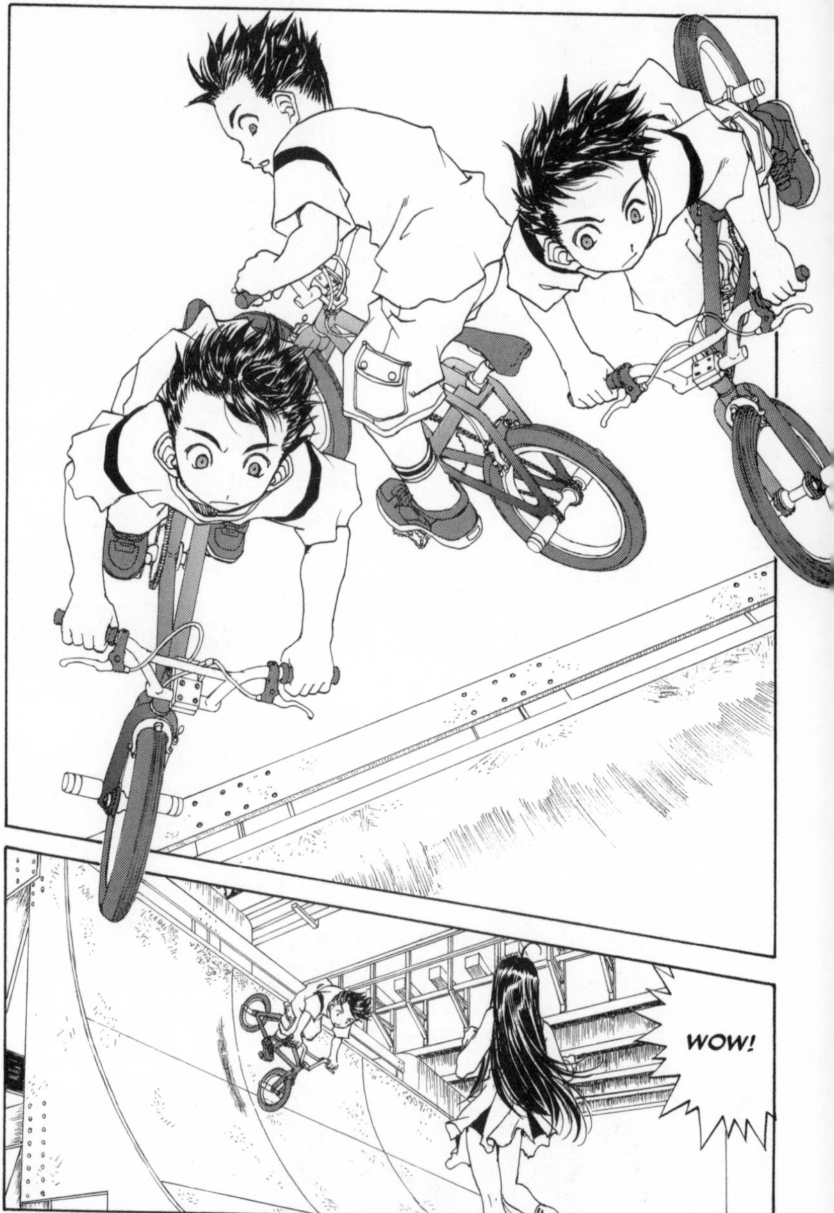
WOW!

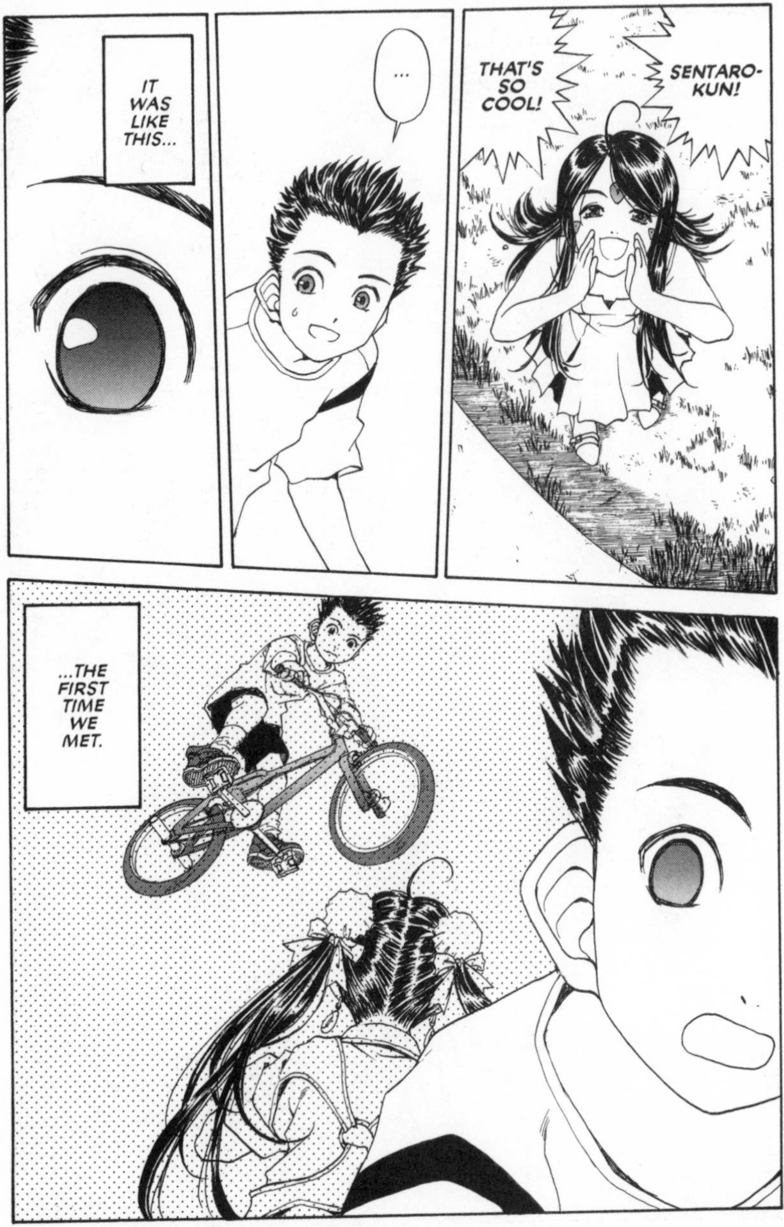
SENTARO-KUN!
THAT'S SO COOL!
...
IT WAS LIKE THIS...
...THE FIRST TIME WE MET.

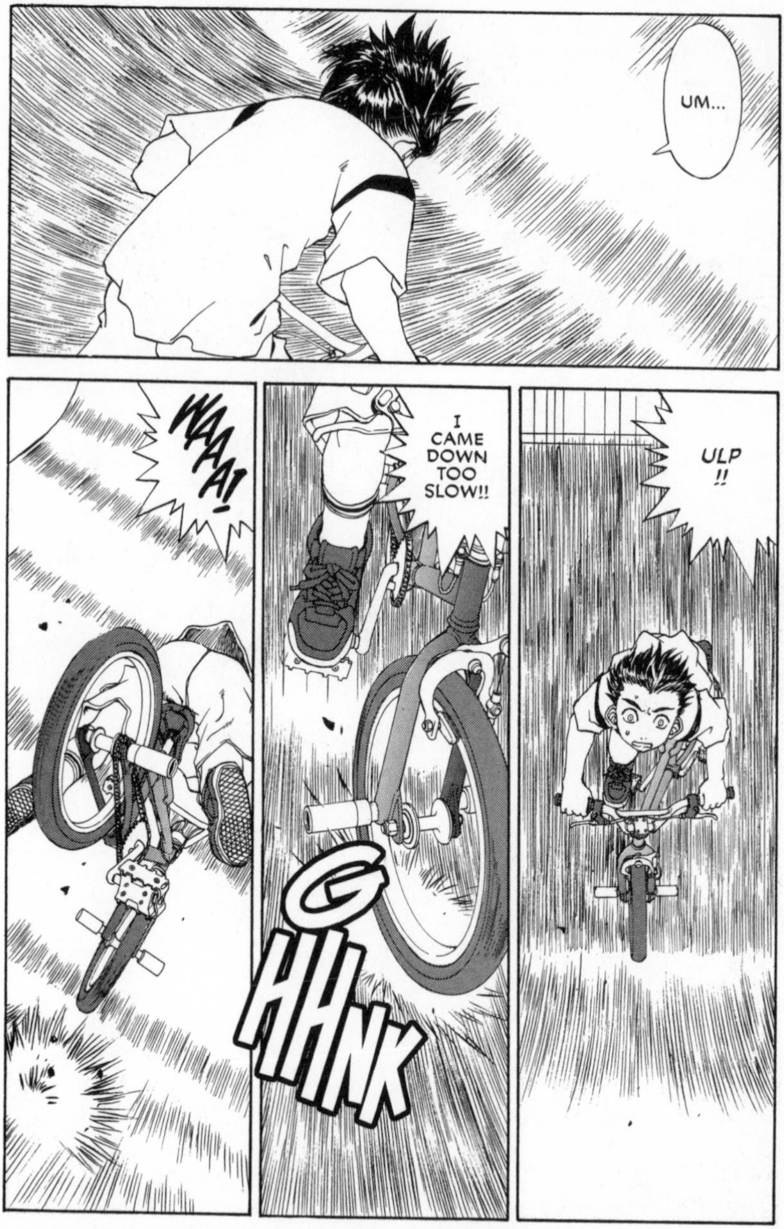
UM...
ULP !!
I CAME DOWN TOO SLOW!!
GHHNK
WAAAA!

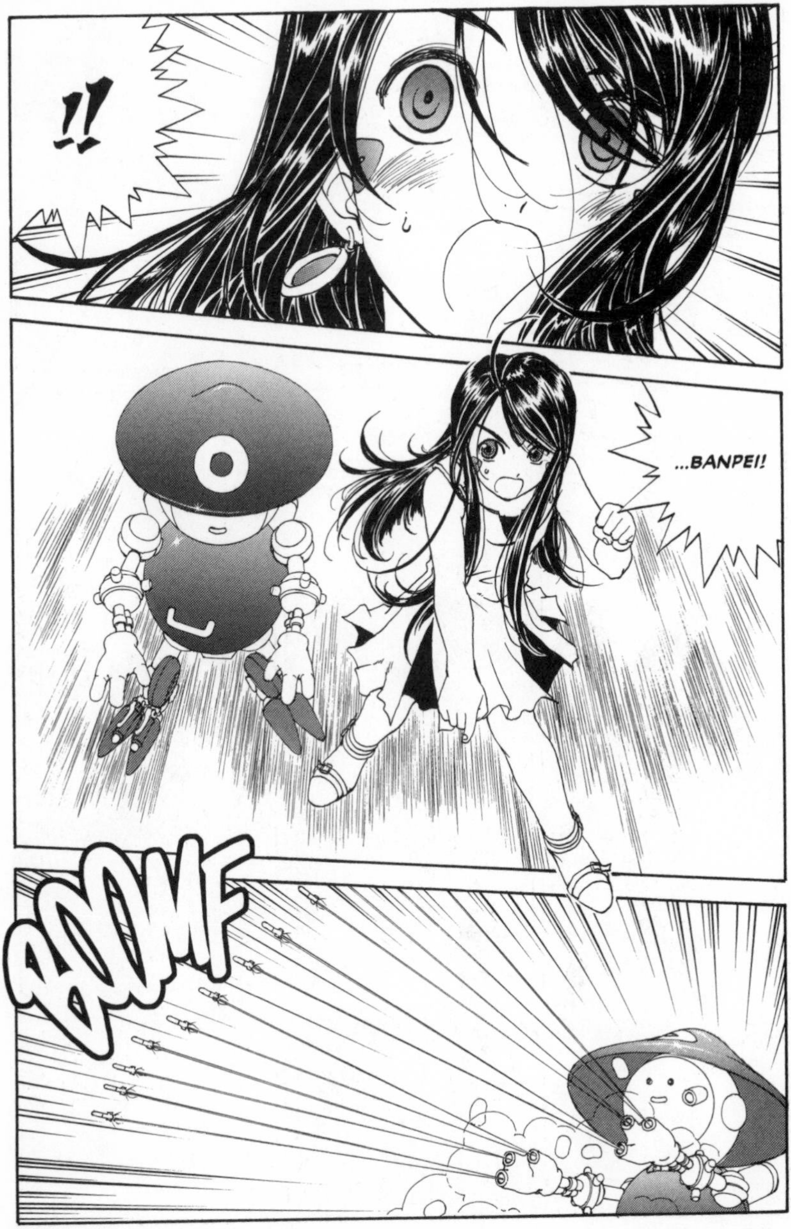

!!
...BANPEI!
BOOMF

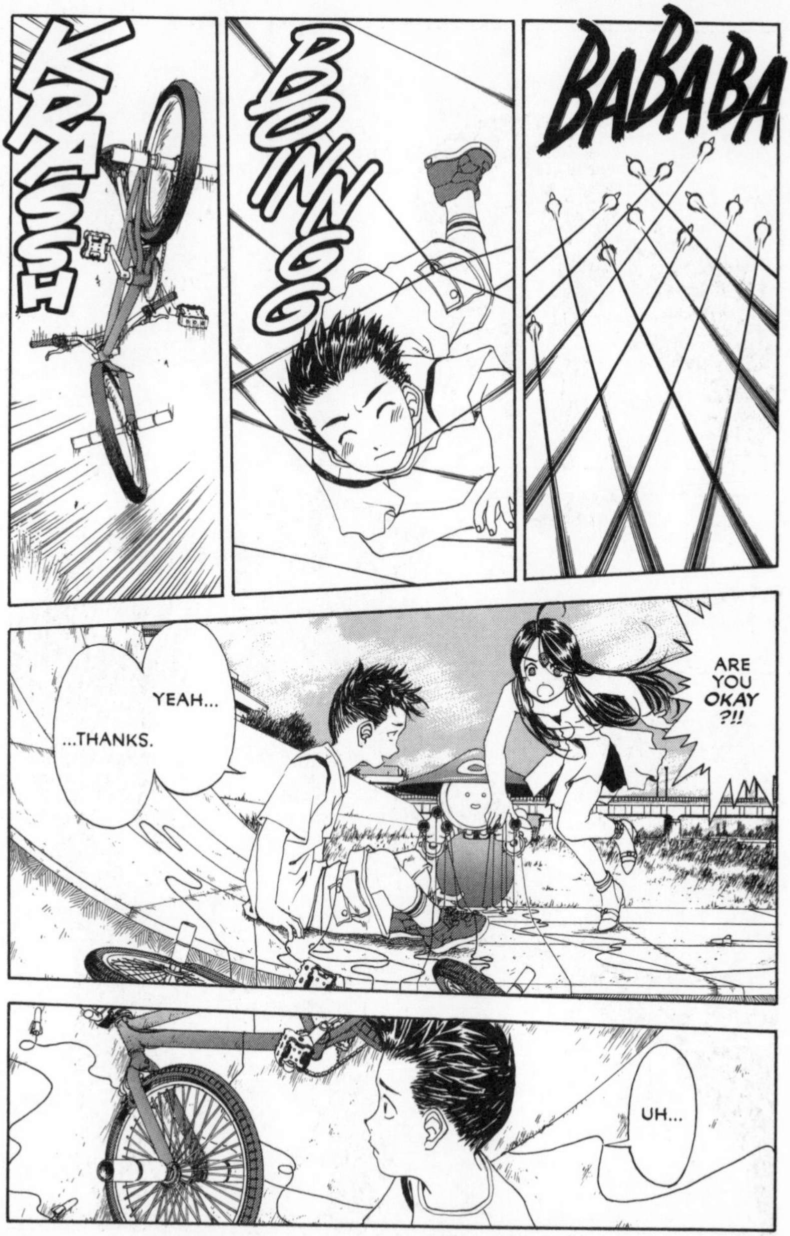
BABABA
BOINNGG
KRASSH
ARE YOU OKAY ?!!
YEAH... ...THANKS.
UH...

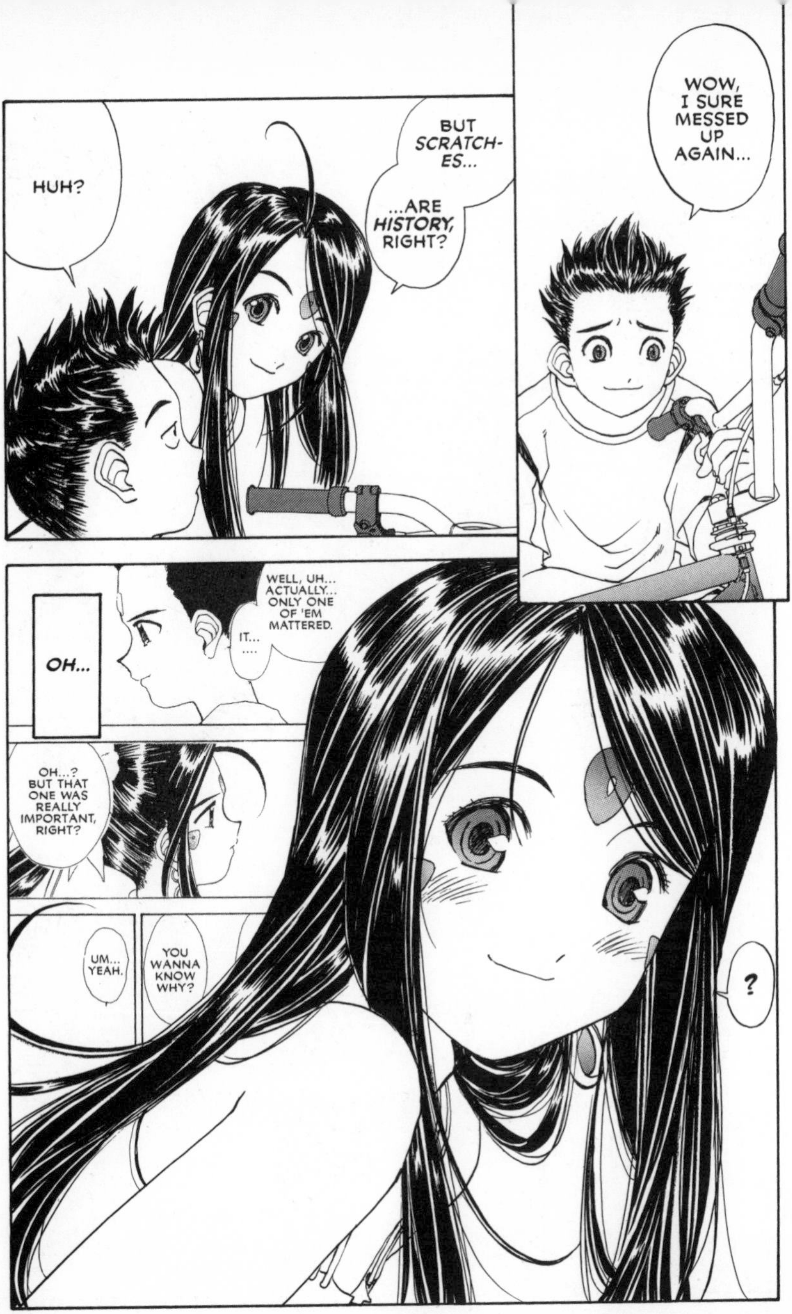
WOW, I SURE MESSED UP AGAIN...
BUT SCRATCH-ES...
...ARE HISTORY, RIGHT?
HUH?
?
WELL, UH... ACTUALLY... ONLY ONE OF 'EM MATTERED.
IT... ....
OH...
OH...? BUT THAT ONE WAS REALLY IMPORTANT, RIGHT?
YOU WANNA KNOW WHY?
UM... YEAH.

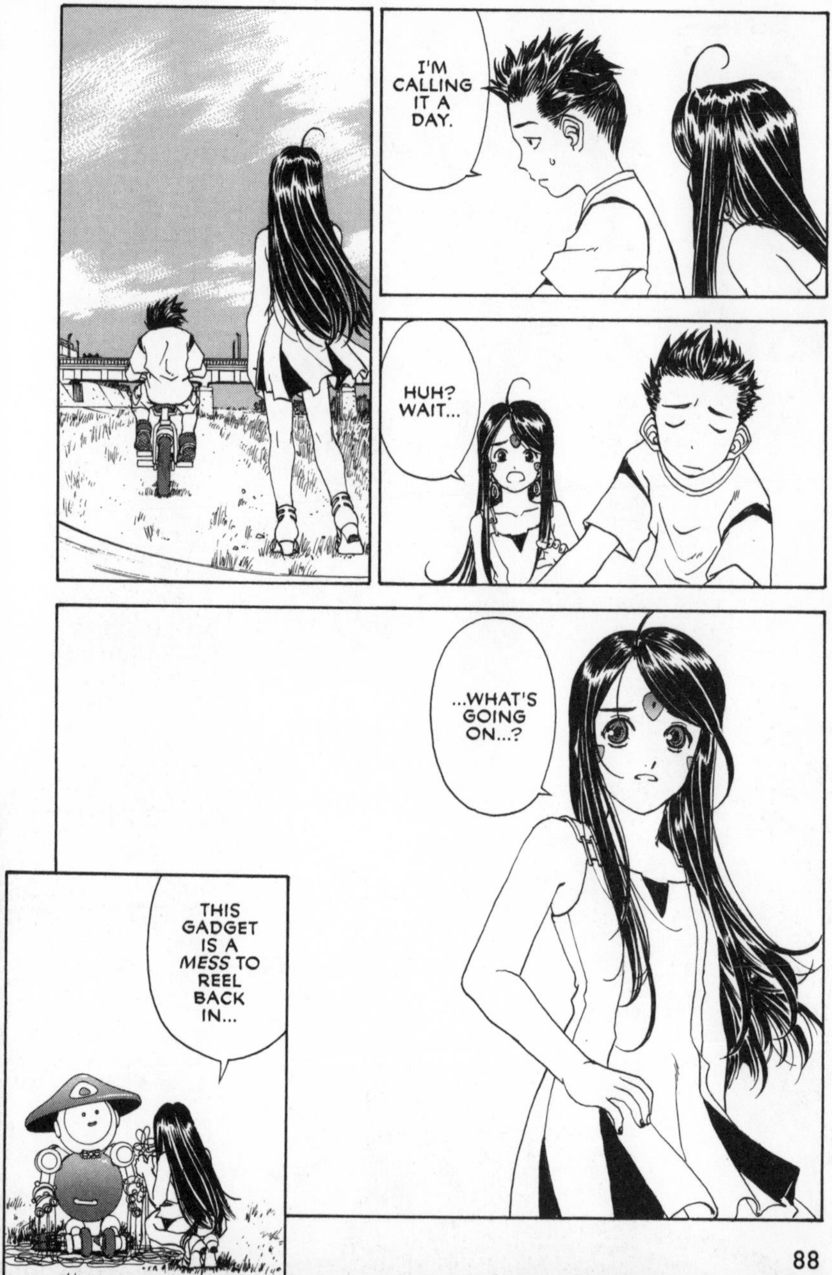
I'M CALLING IT A DAY.
HUH? WAIT...
...WHAT'S GOING ON...?
THIS GADGET IS A *MESS* TO REEL BACK IN...

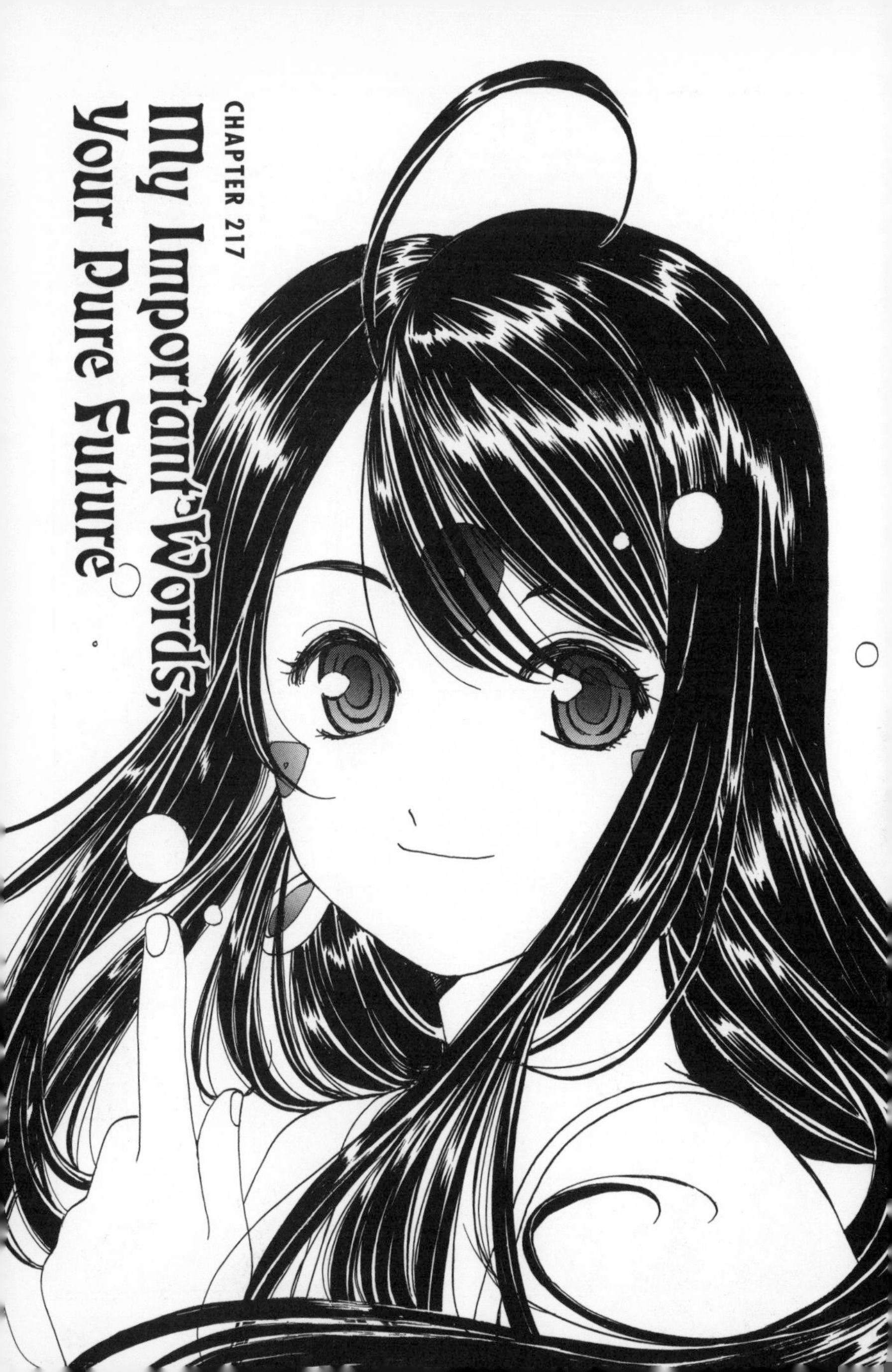
CHAPTER 217
My Important Words, Your Pure Future

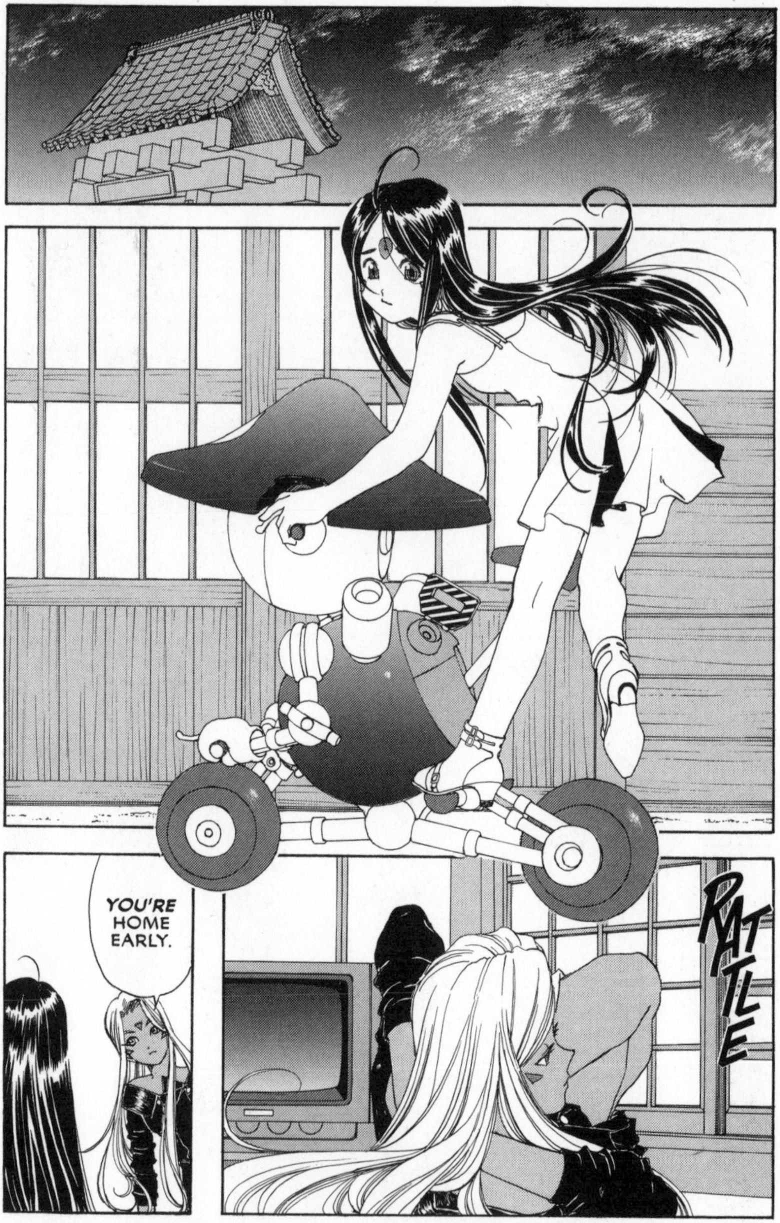
RATTLE
YOU'RE HOME EARLY.

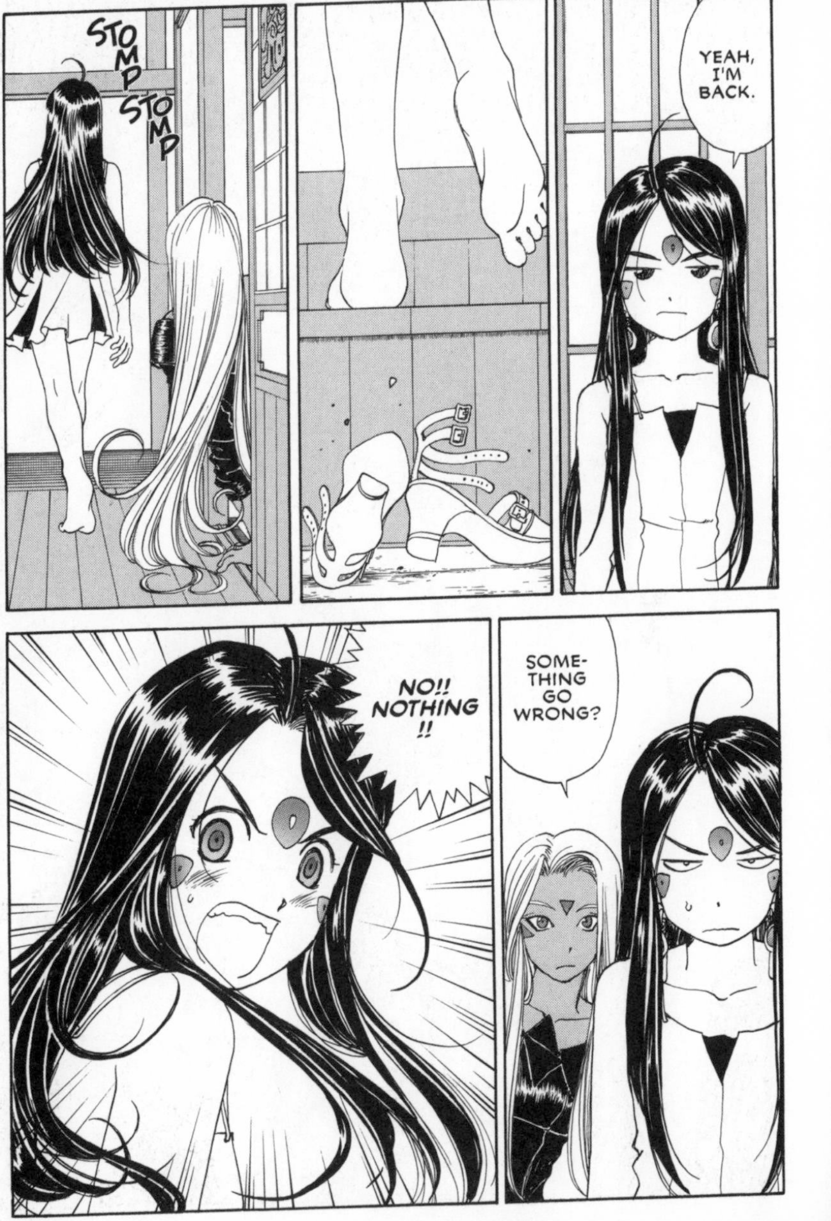
YEAH, I'M BACK.
STOMP STOMP
SOME-THING GO WRONG?
NO!! NOTHING !!

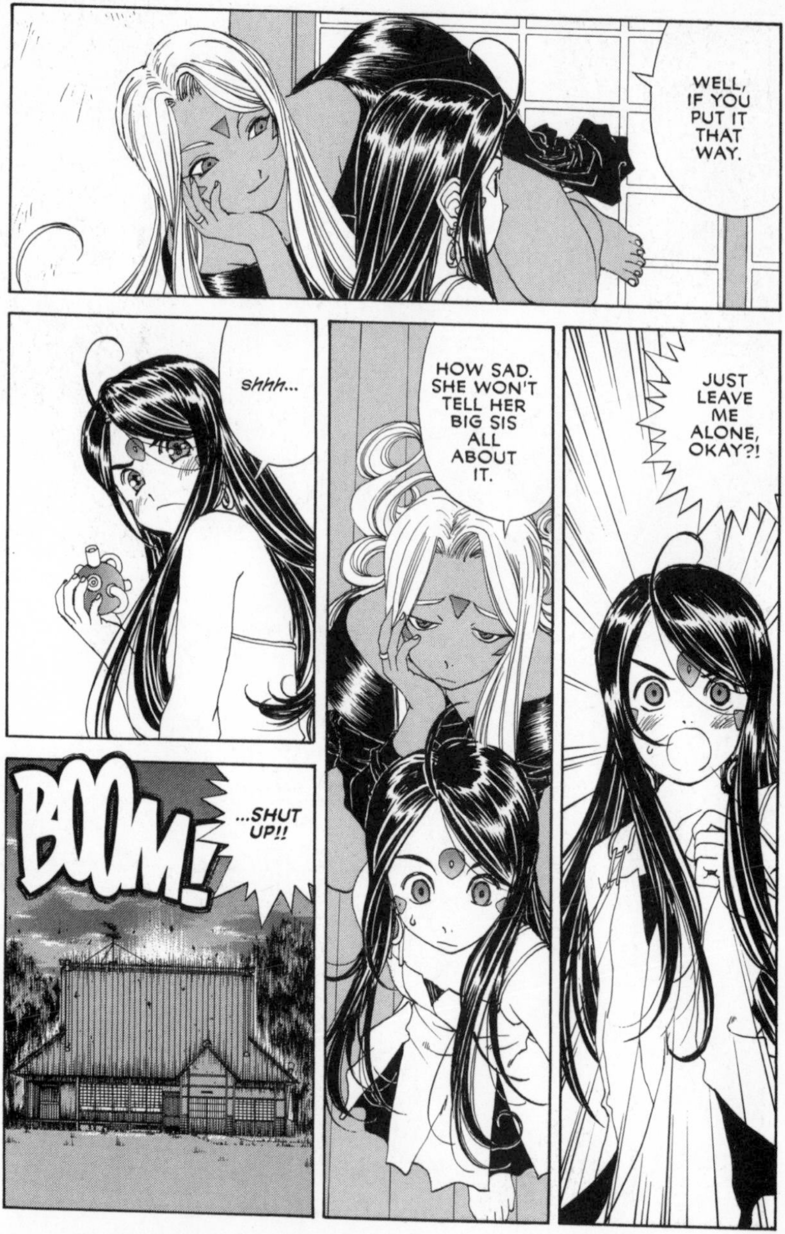
WELL, IF YOU PUT IT THAT WAY.
JUST LEAVE ME ALONE, OKAY?!
HOW SAD. SHE WON'T TELL HER BIG SIS ALL ABOUT IT.
shhh...
BOOM!
...SHUT UP!!

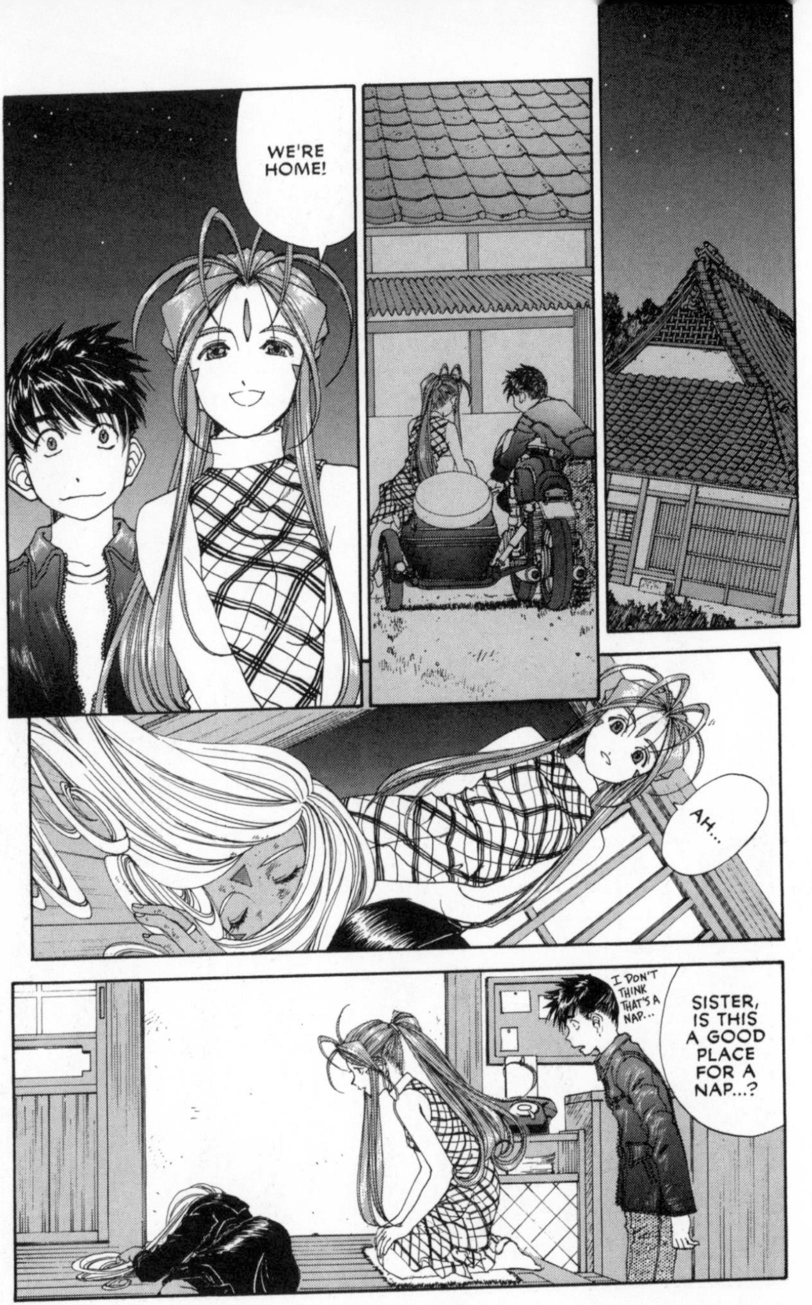
WE'RE HOME!
AH...
SISTER, IS THIS A GOOD PLACE FOR A NAP...?
I DON'T THINK THAT'S A NAP...

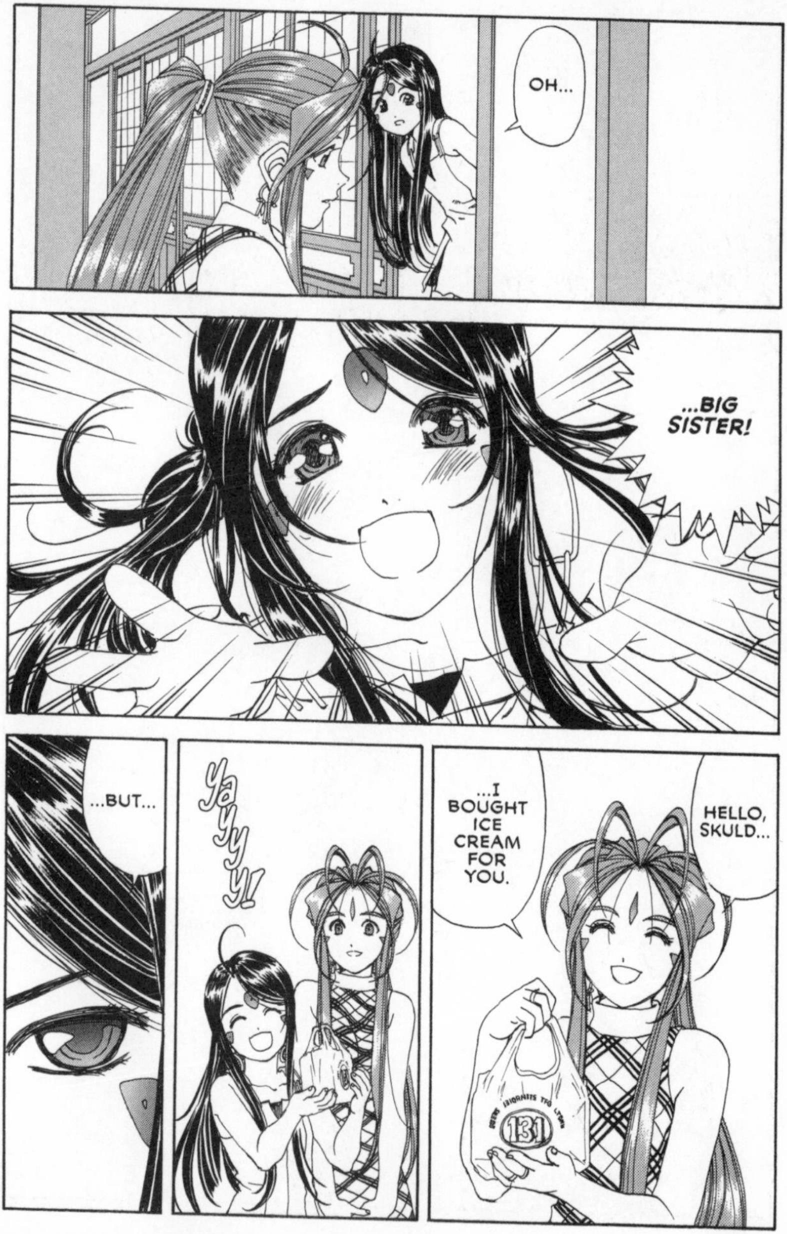
OH...
...BIG SISTER!
HELLO, SKULD...
...I BOUGHT ICE CREAM FOR YOU.
Yayyy!
...BUT...

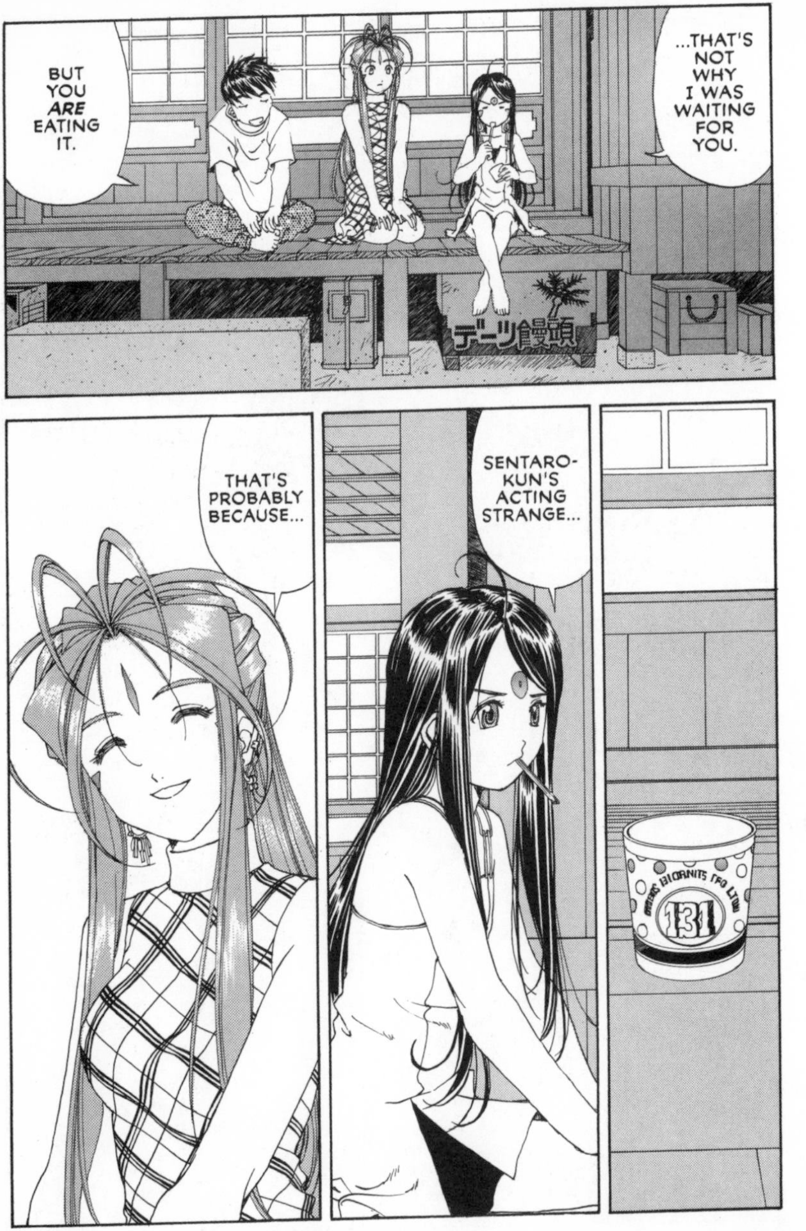
...THAT'S NOT WHY I WAS WAITING FOR YOU.
BUT YOU *ARE* EATING IT.
デーツ饅頭
SENTARO-KUN'S ACTING STRANGE...
THAT'S PROBABLY BECAUSE...

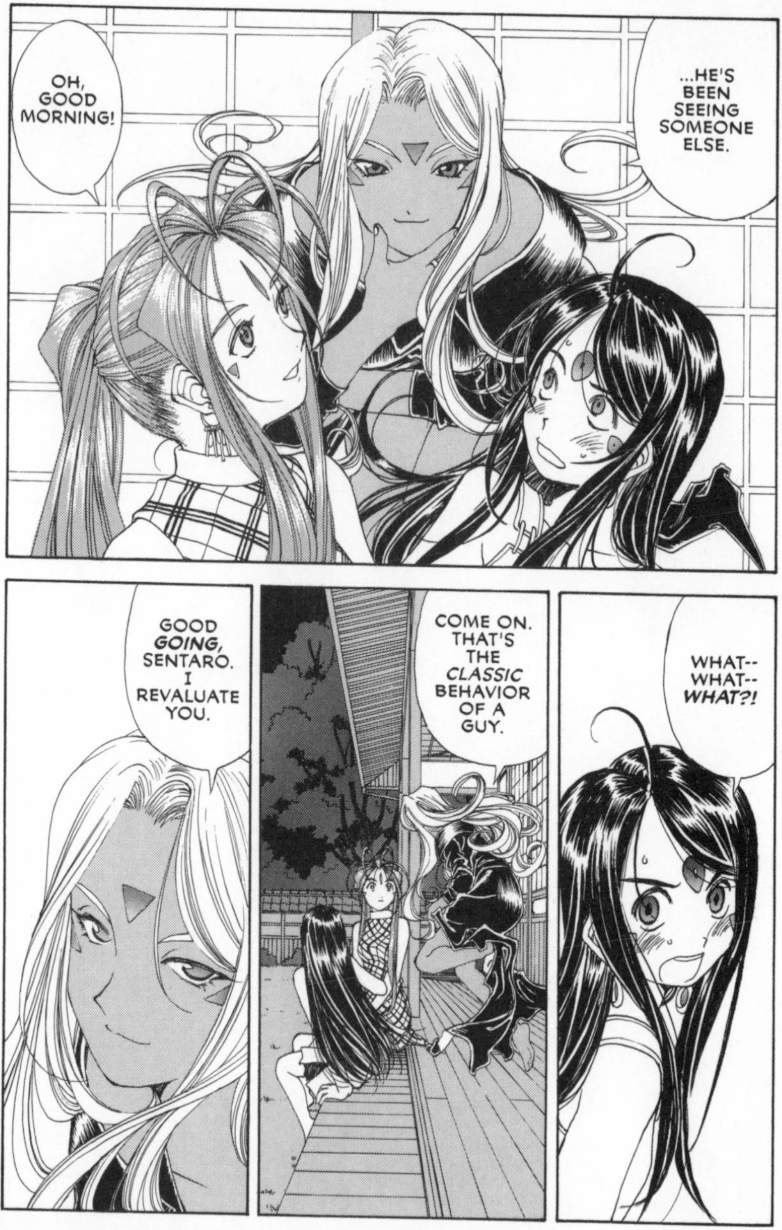
...HE'S BEEN SEEING SOMEONE ELSE.
OH, GOOD MORNING!
WHAT-- WHAT-- *WHAT?!*
COME ON. THAT'S THE *CLASSIC* BEHAVIOR OF A GUY.
GOOD *GOING,* SENTARO. I REVALUATE YOU.

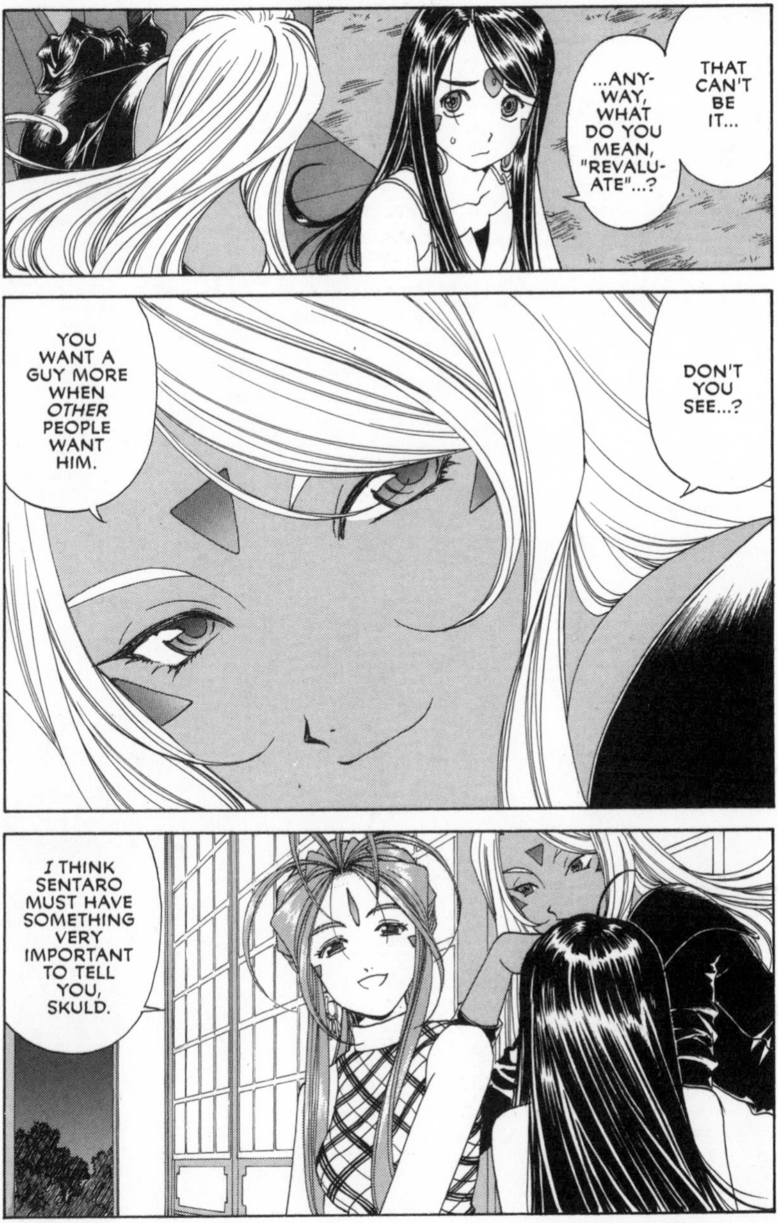
THAT CAN'T BE IT...
...ANYWAY, WHAT DO YOU MEAN, "REVALUATE"...?
DON'T YOU SEE...?
YOU WANT A GUY MORE WHEN *OTHER* PEOPLE WANT HIM.
*I* THINK SENTARO MUST HAVE SOMETHING VERY IMPORTANT TO TELL YOU, SKULD.

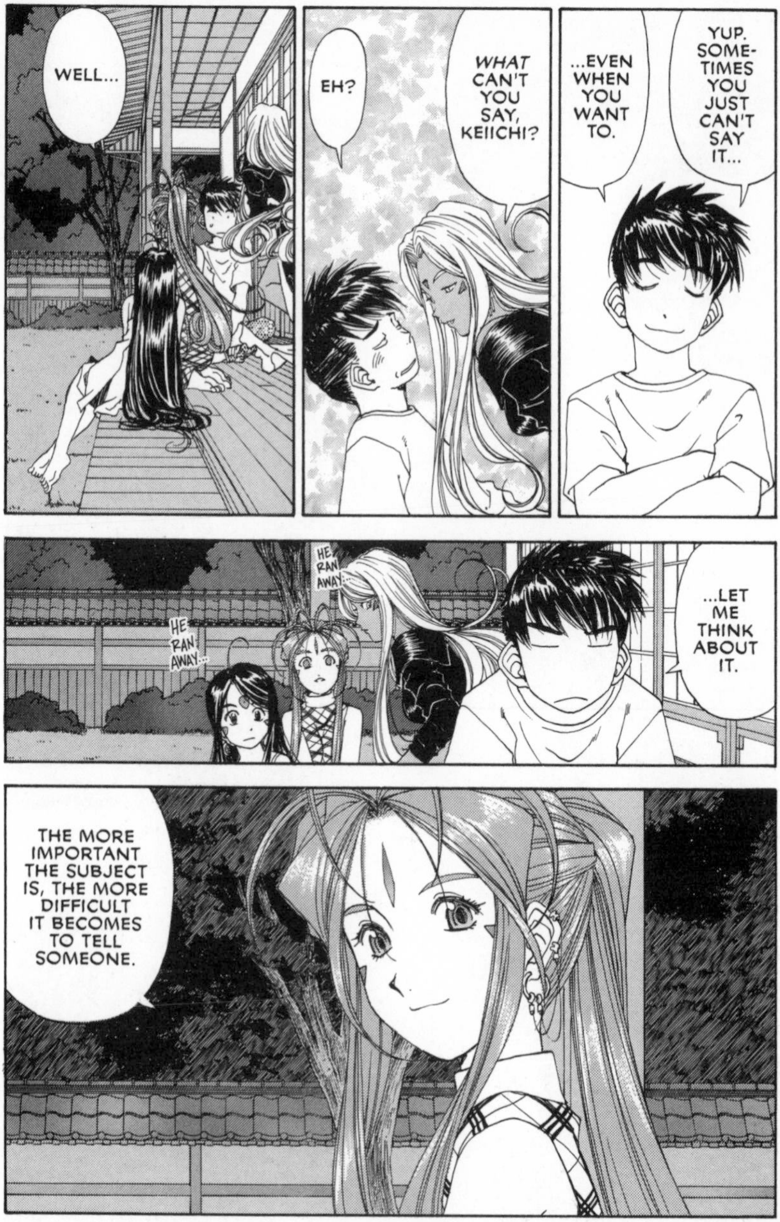
YUP. SOME-TIMES YOU JUST CAN'T SAY IT...
...EVEN WHEN YOU WANT TO.
*WHAT* CAN'T YOU SAY, KEIICHI?
EH?
WELL...
...LET ME THINK ABOUT IT.
HE RAN AWAY...
HE RAN AWAY...
THE MORE IMPORTANT THE SUBJECT IS, THE MORE DIFFICULT IT BECOMES TO TELL SOMEONE.

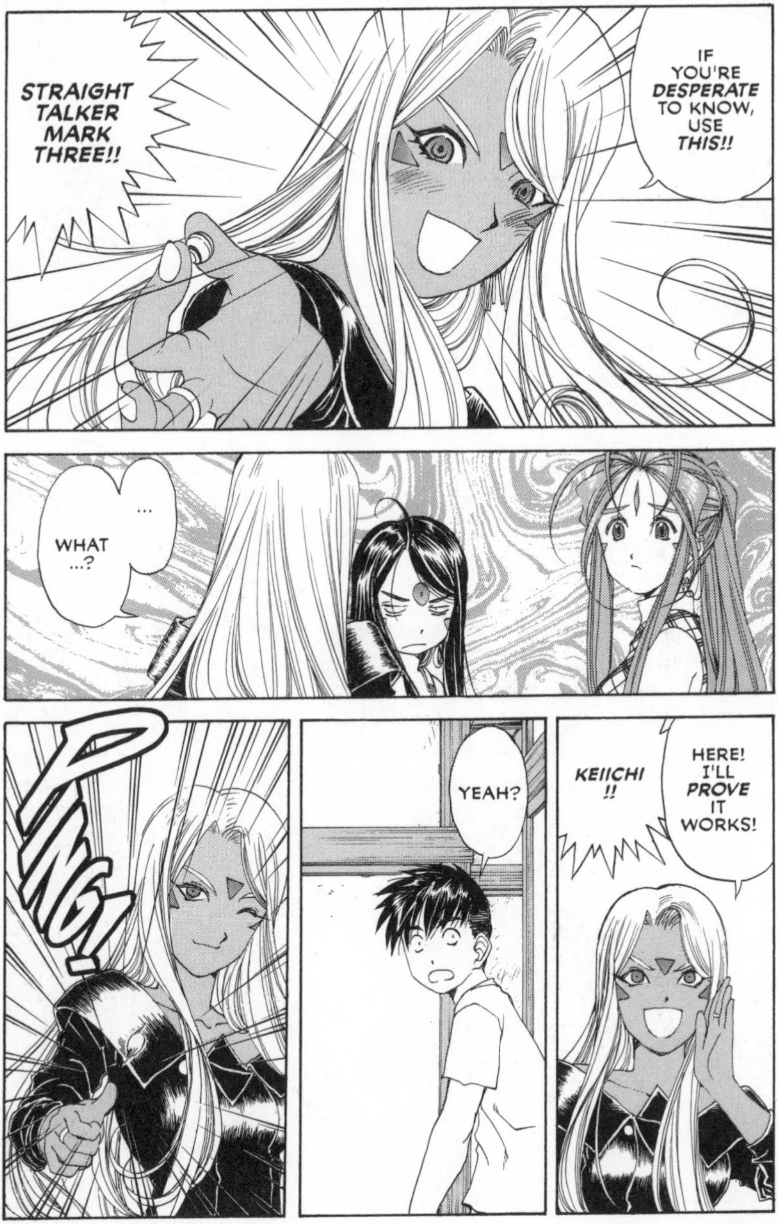
IF YOU'RE DESPERATE TO KNOW, USE THIS!!
STRAIGHT TALKER MARK THREE!!
... WHAT ...?
HERE! I'LL PROVE IT WORKS!
KEIICHI !!
YEAH?
PING!

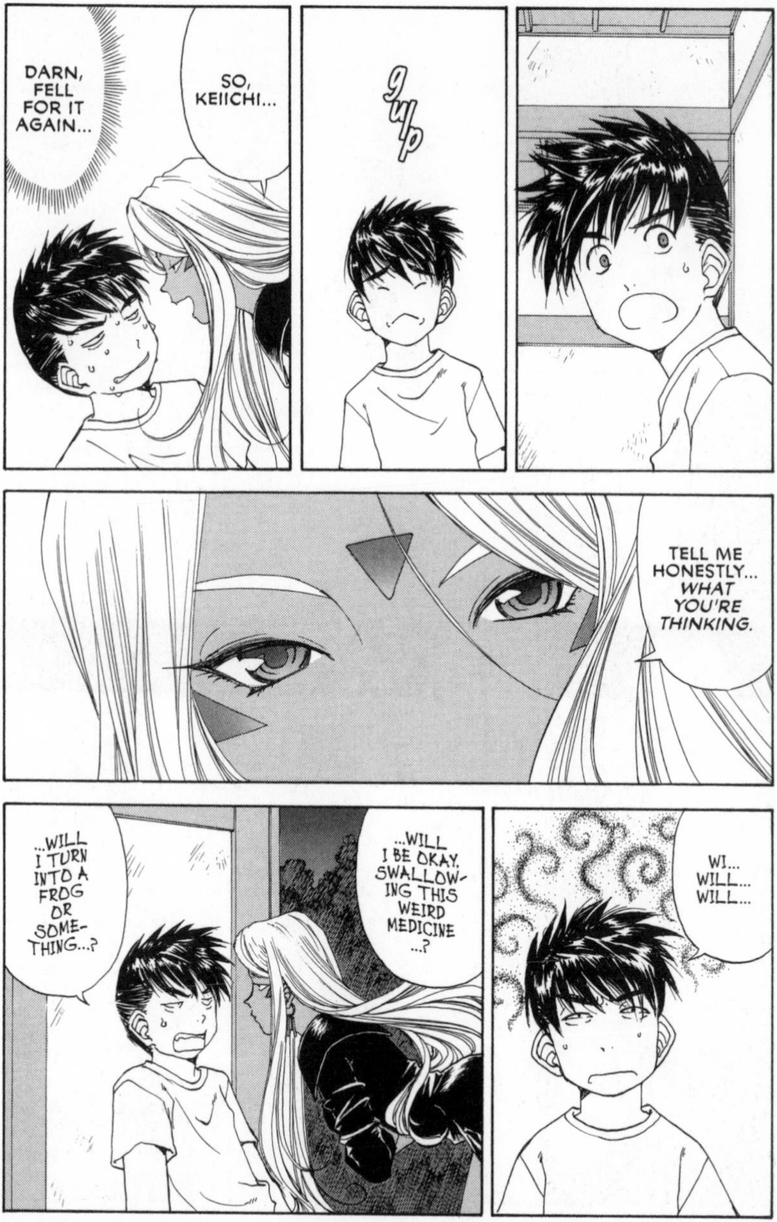
gulp
SO, KEIICHI...
DARN, FELL FOR IT AGAIN...
TELL ME HONESTLY... *WHAT YOU'RE THINKING.*
WI... WILL... WILL...
...WILL I BE OKAY, SWALLOWING THIS WEIRD MEDICINE ...?
...WILL I TURN INTO A FROG OR SOMETHING...?

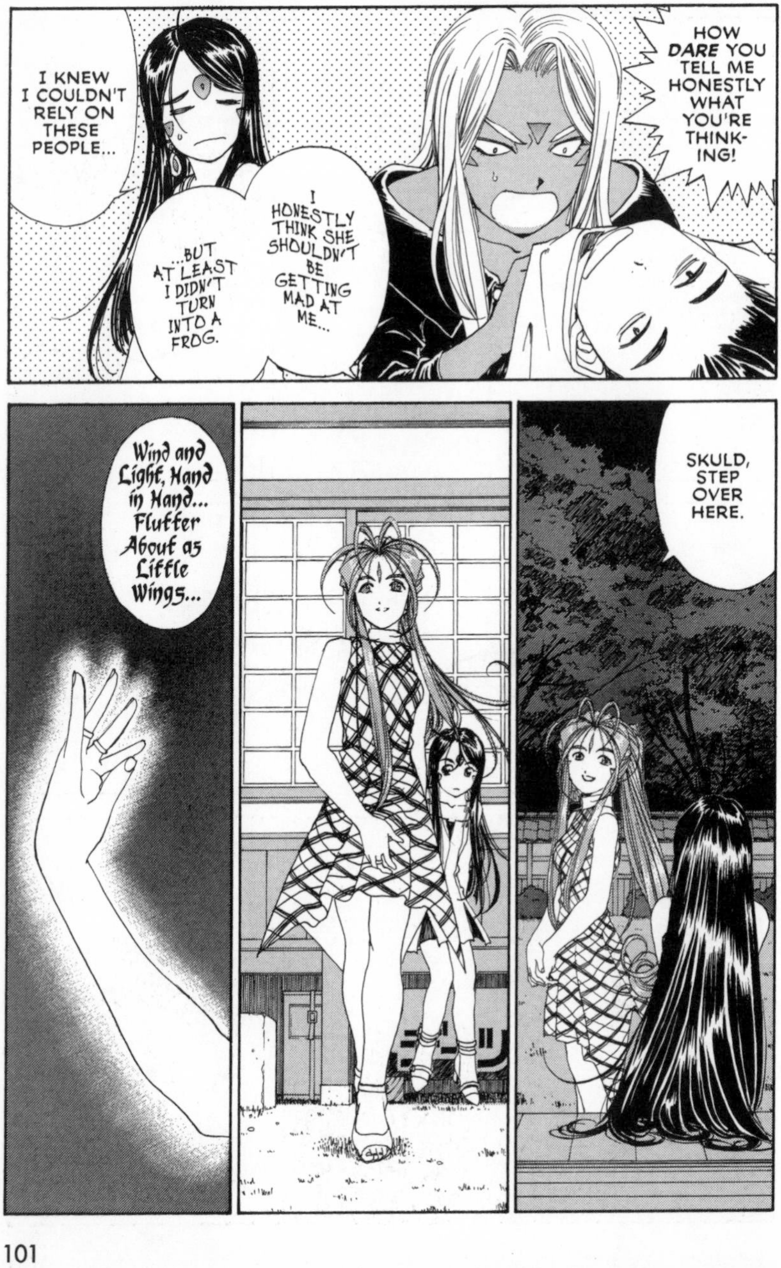
HOW DARE YOU TELL ME HONESTLY WHAT YOU'RE THINKING!
I HONESTLY THINK SHE SHOULDN'T BE GETTING MAD AT ME...
I KNEW I COULDN'T RELY ON THESE PEOPLE...
...BUT AT LEAST I DIDN'T TURN INTO A FROG.
SKULD, STEP OVER HERE.
Wind and Light, Hand in Hand... Flutter About as Little Wings...

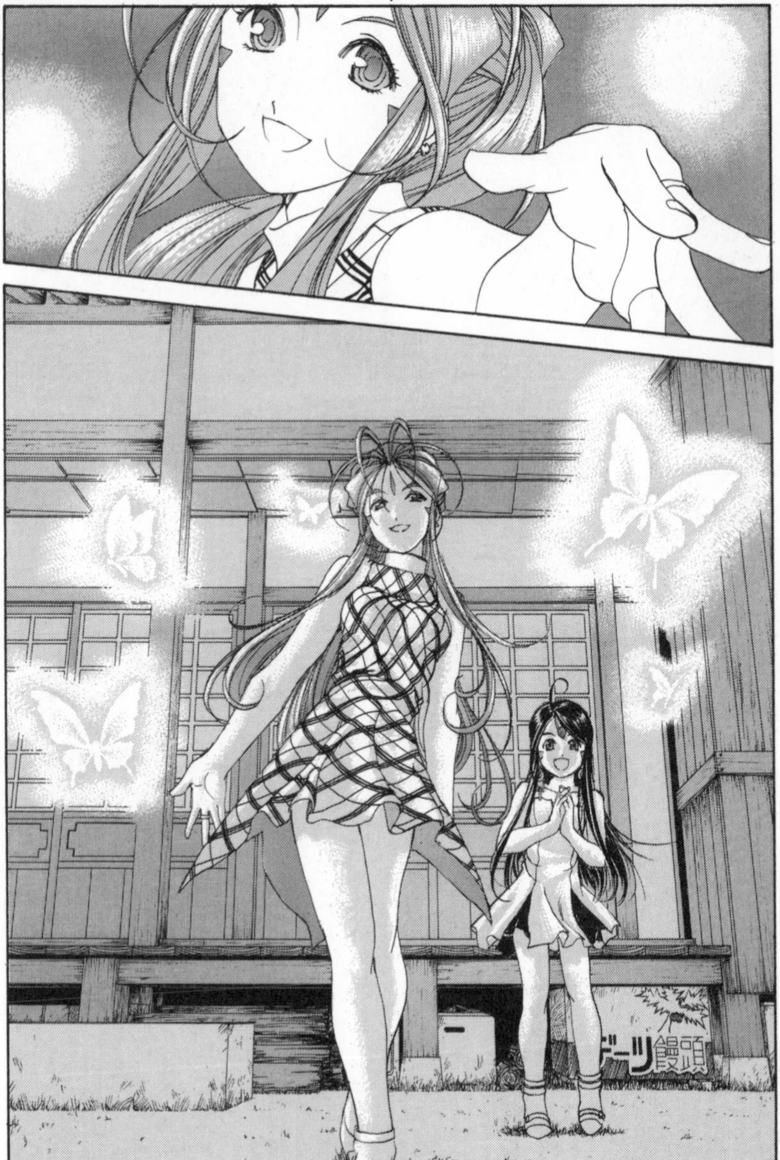
ーツ饅頭

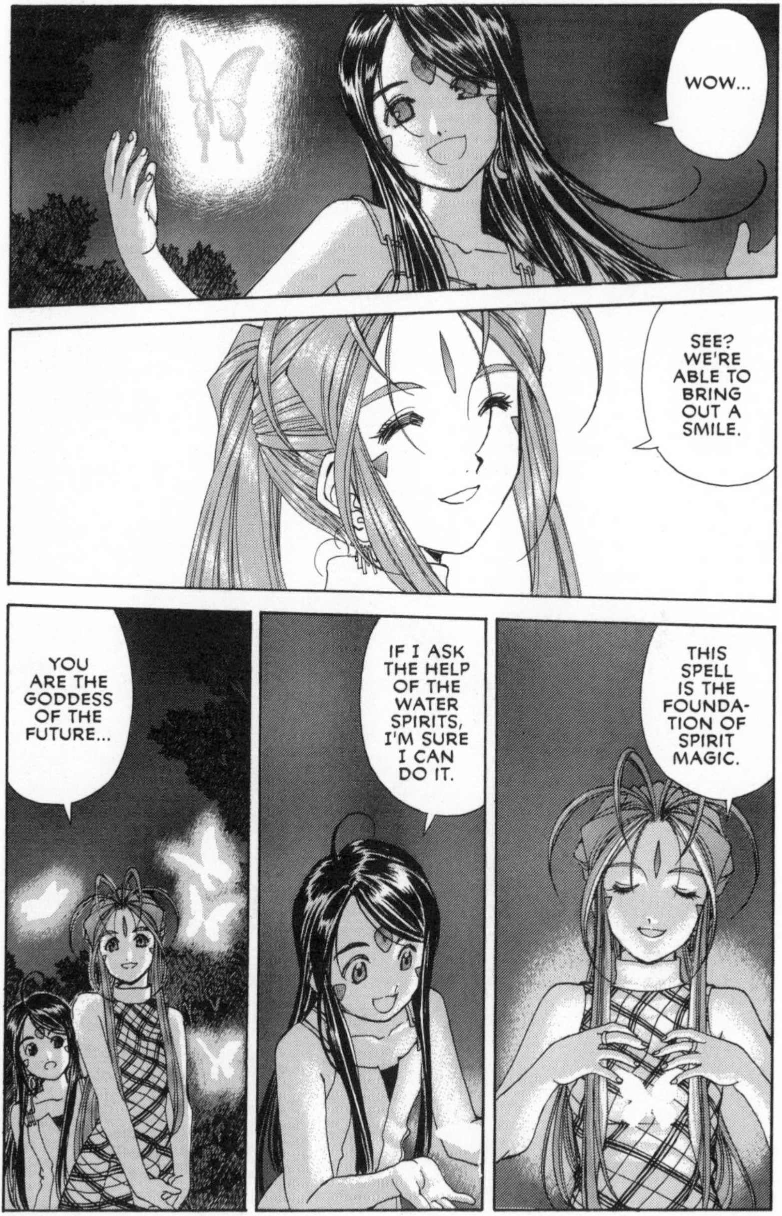
WOW...
SEE? WE'RE ABLE TO BRING OUT A SMILE.
THIS SPELL IS THE FOUNDATION OF SPIRIT MAGIC.
IF I ASK THE HELP OF THE WATER SPIRITS, I'M SURE I CAN DO IT.
YOU ARE THE GODDESS OF THE FUTURE...

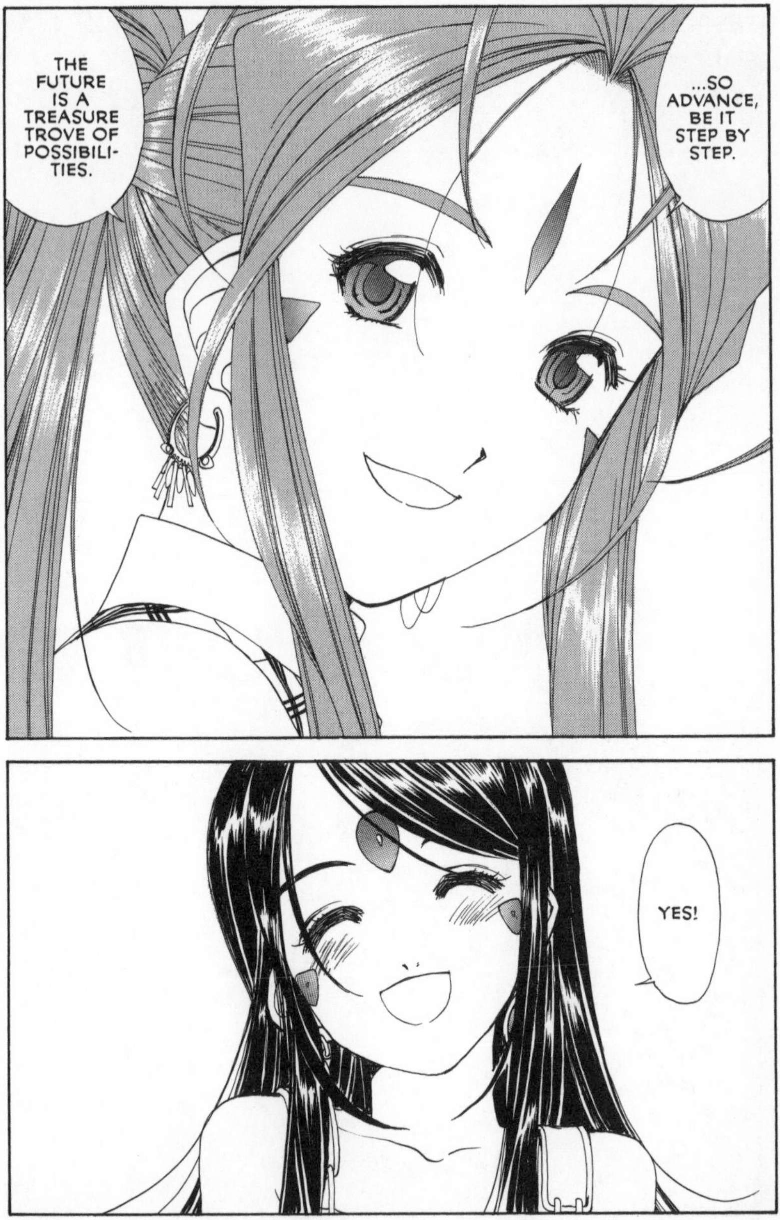
...SO ADVANCE, BE IT STEP BY STEP.
THE FUTURE IS A TREASURE TROVE OF POSSIBILI-TIES.
YES!

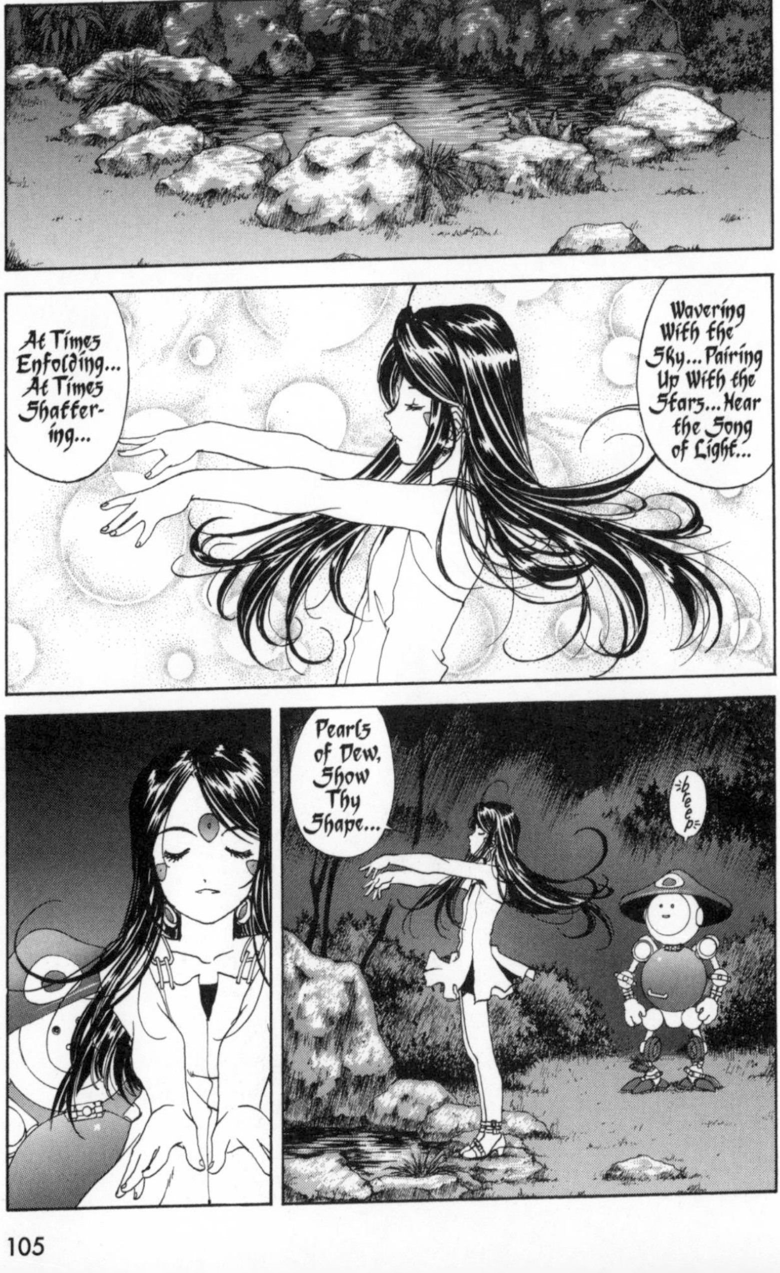
Wavering With the Sky... Pairing Up With the Stars... Hear the Song of Light...
At Times Enfolding... At Times Shattering...
Pearls of Dew, Show Thy Shape...
beep

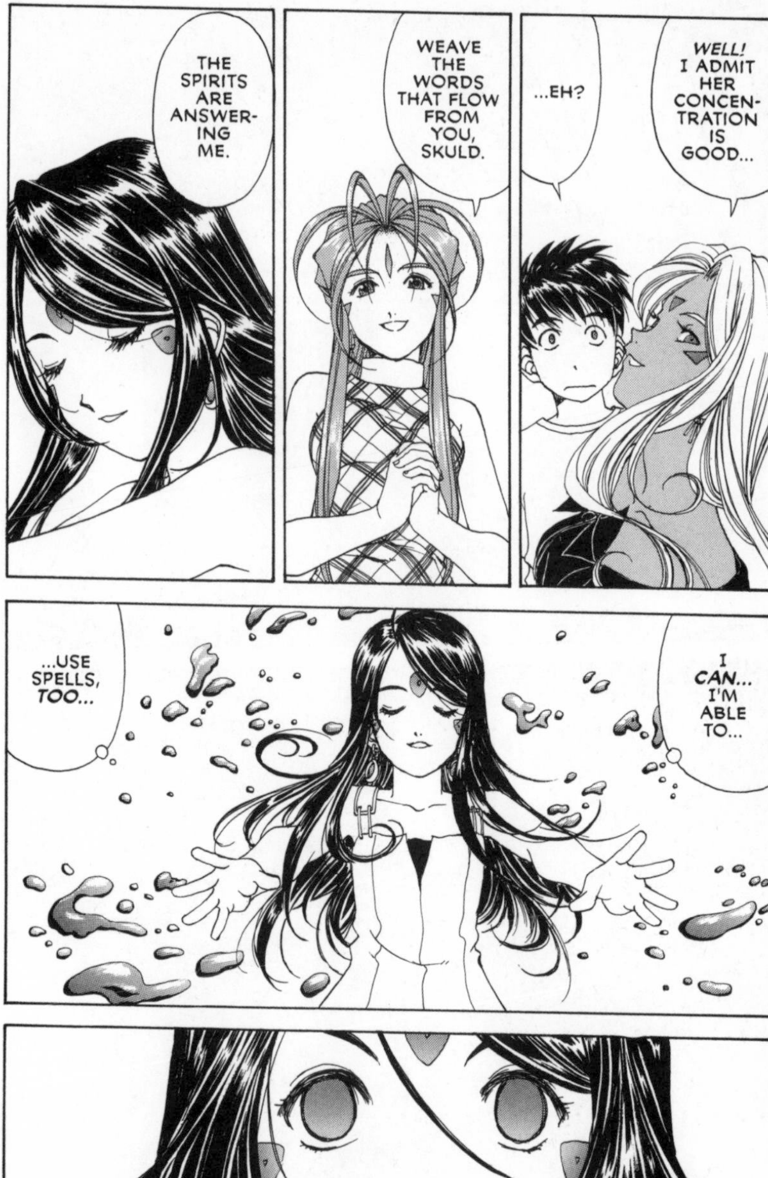
*WELL!* I ADMIT HER CONCENTRATION IS GOOD...
...EH?
WEAVE THE WORDS THAT FLOW FROM YOU, SKULD.
THE SPIRITS ARE ANSWERING ME.
I *CAN*... I'M ABLE TO...
...USE SPELLS, *TOO*...

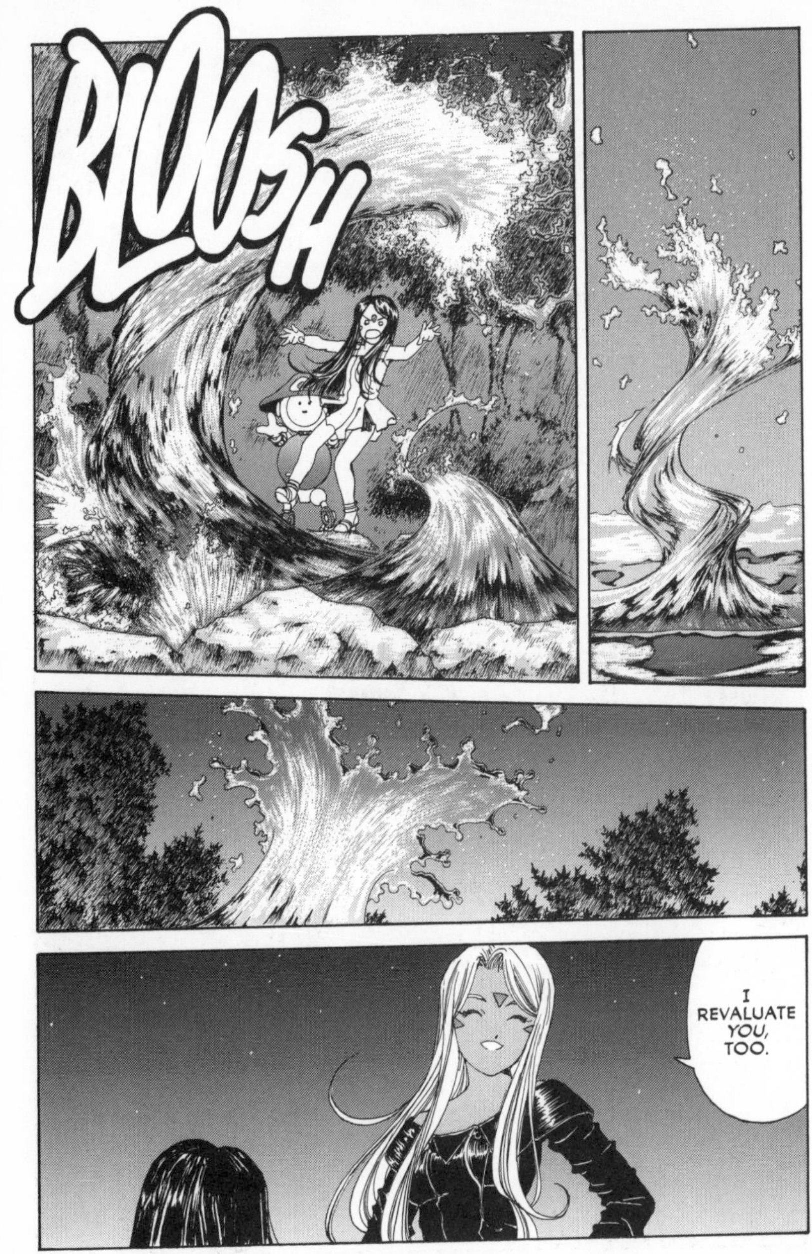
BLOOSH
I REVALUATE YOU, TOO.

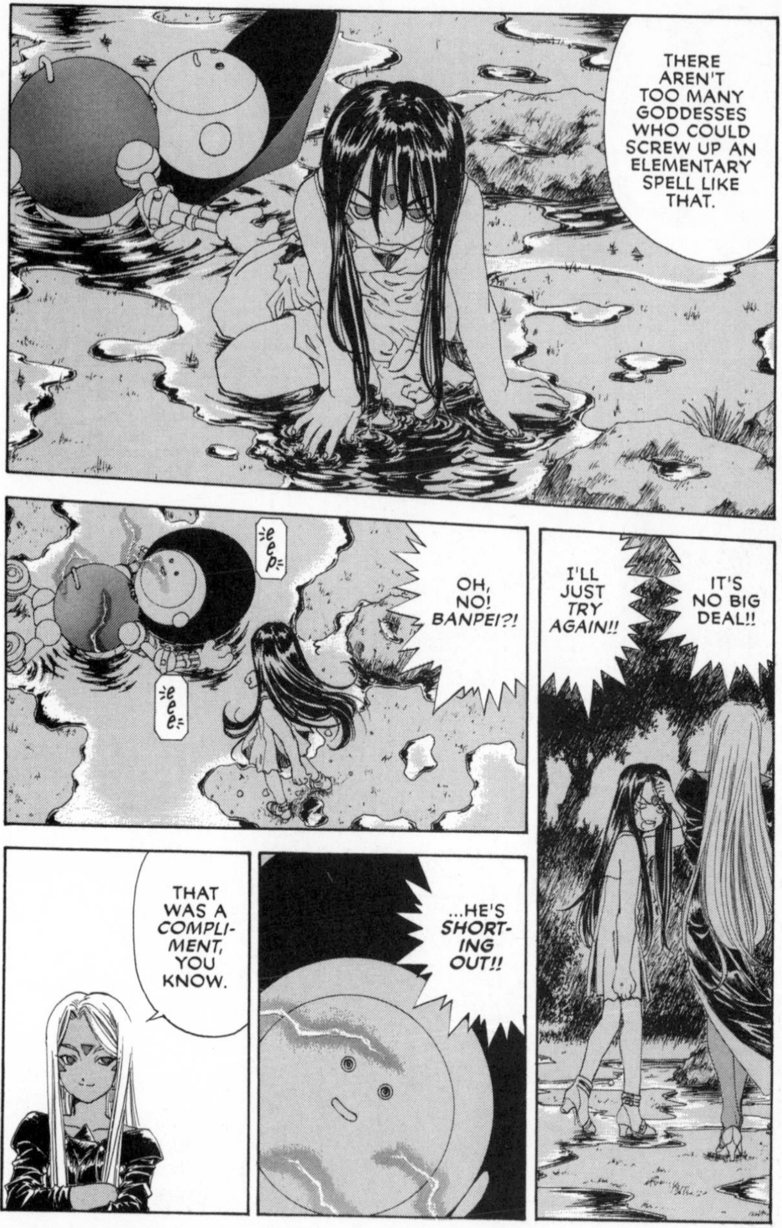
THERE AREN'T TOO MANY GODDESSES WHO COULD SCREW UP AN ELEMENTARY SPELL LIKE THAT.
IT'S NO BIG DEAL!!
I'LL JUST *TRY* AGAIN!!
eep
OH, NO! *BANPEI?!*
eee
...HE'S *SHORT-ING OUT!!*
THAT WAS A *COMPLI-MENT,* YOU KNOW.

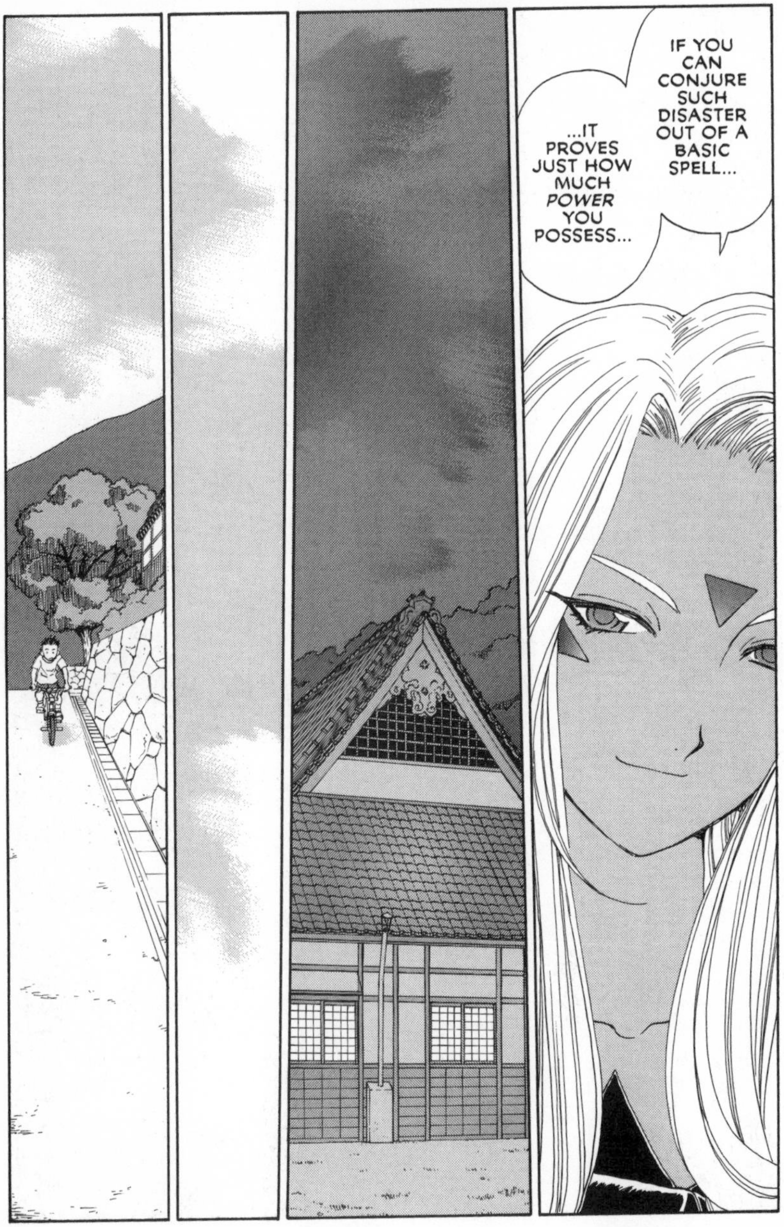
IF YOU CAN CONJURE SUCH DISASTER OUT OF A BASIC SPELL...
...IT PROVES JUST HOW MUCH *POWER* YOU POSSESS...

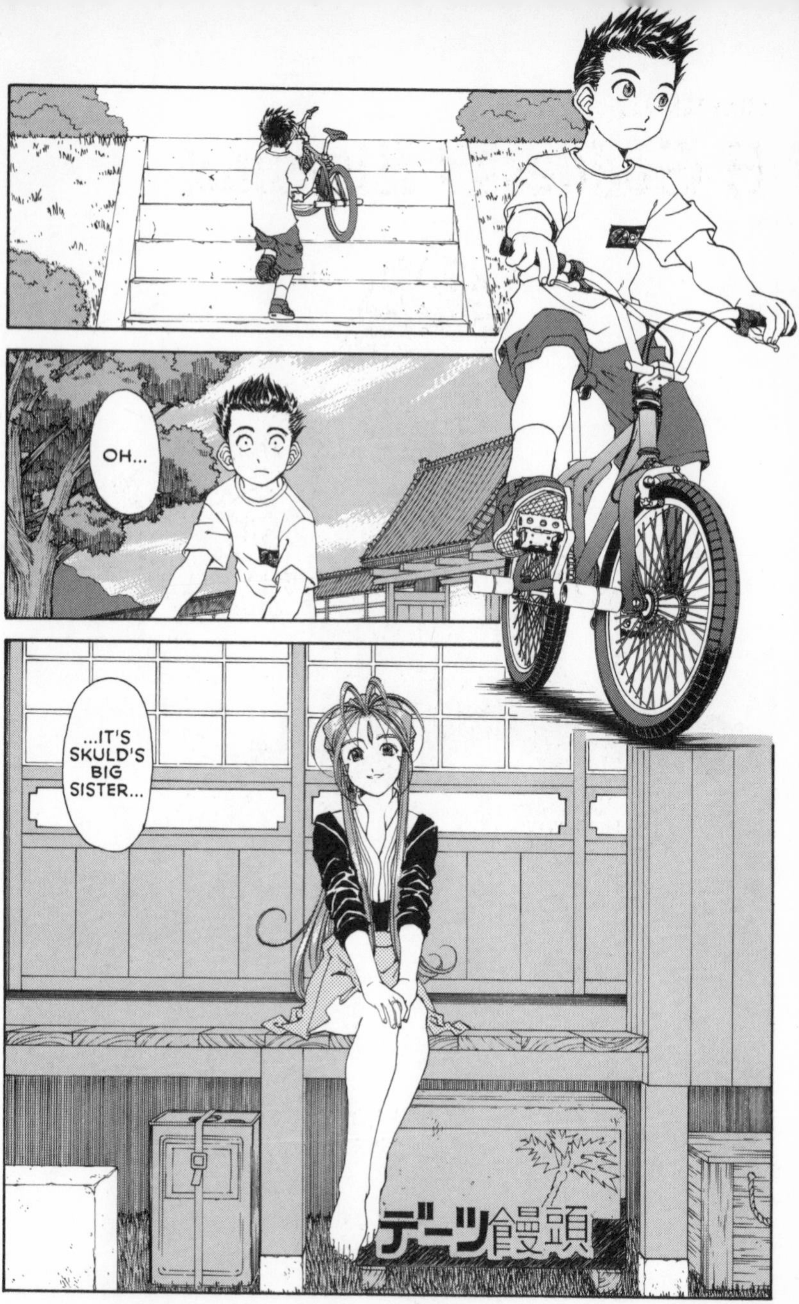
OH...
...IT'S SKULD'S BIG SISTER...
デーツ饅頭

CHAPTER 218

# A Goddess's Blessing

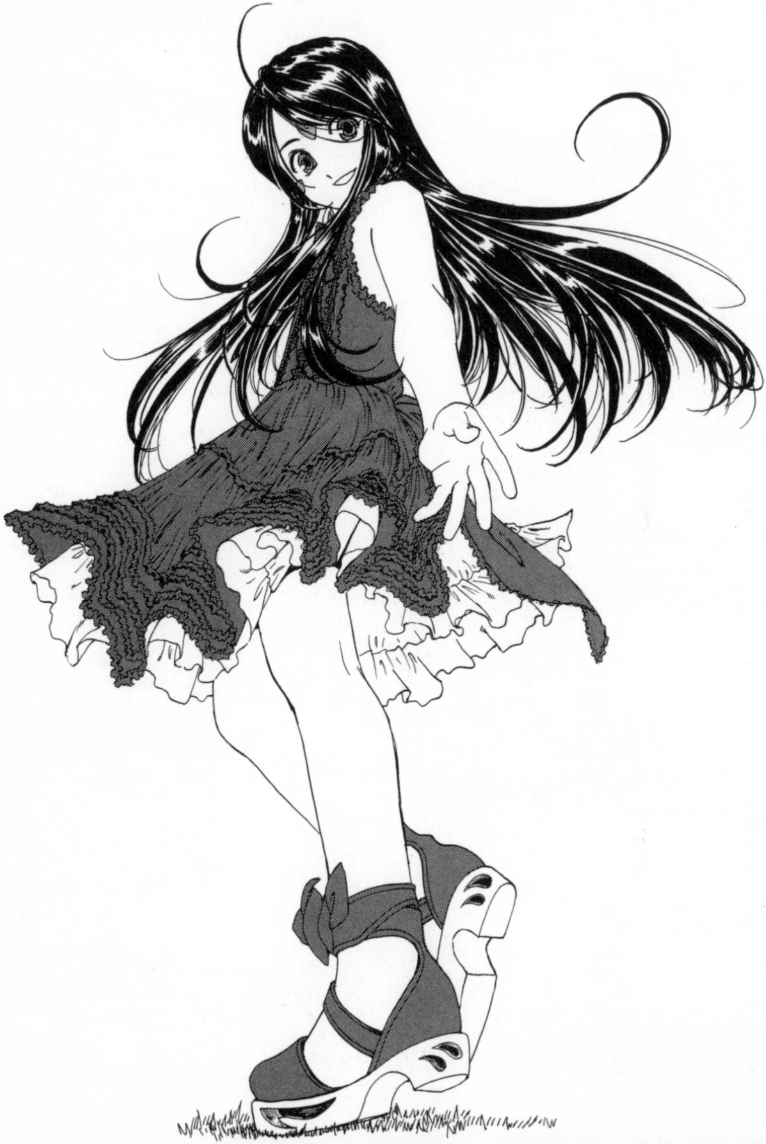

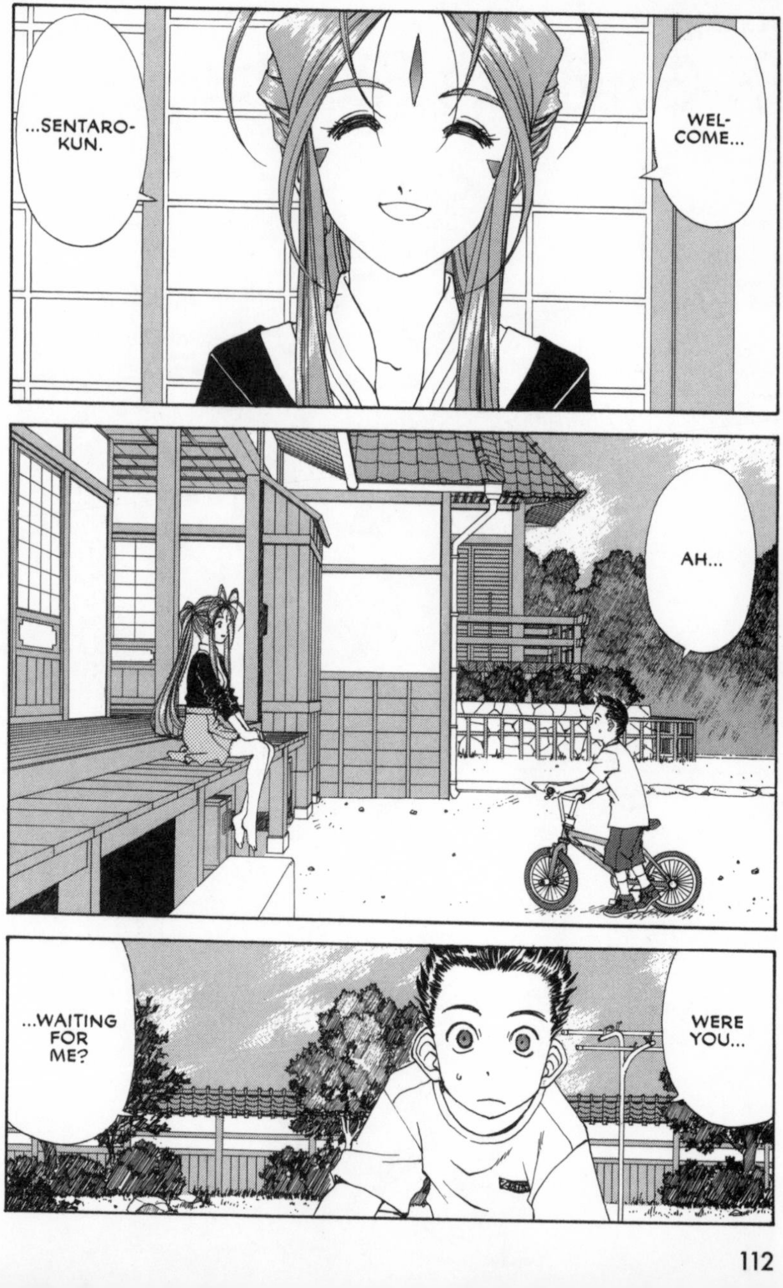
WEL-COME...
...SENTARO-KUN.
AH...
WERE YOU...
...WAITING FOR ME?

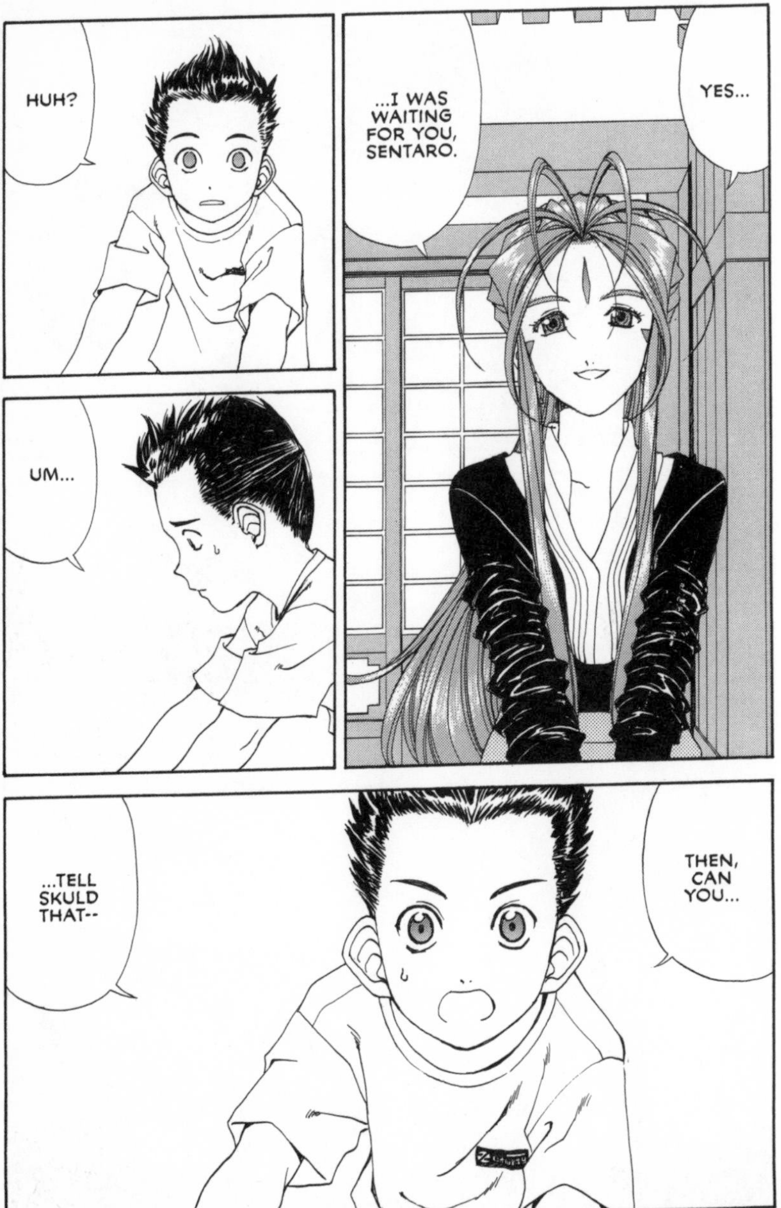
YES...
...I WAS WAITING FOR YOU, SENTARO.
HUH?
UM...
THEN, CAN YOU...
...TELL SKULD THAT--

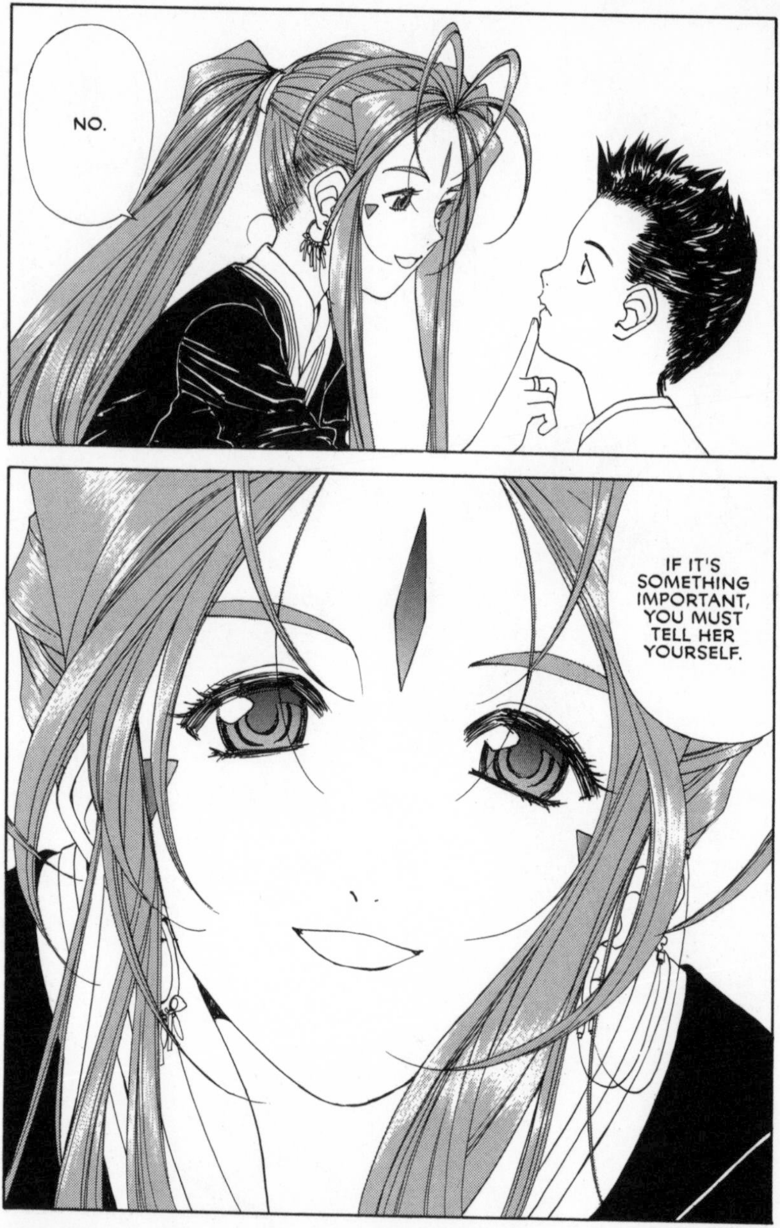
NO.
IF IT'S SOMETHING IMPORTANT, YOU MUST TELL HER YOURSELF.

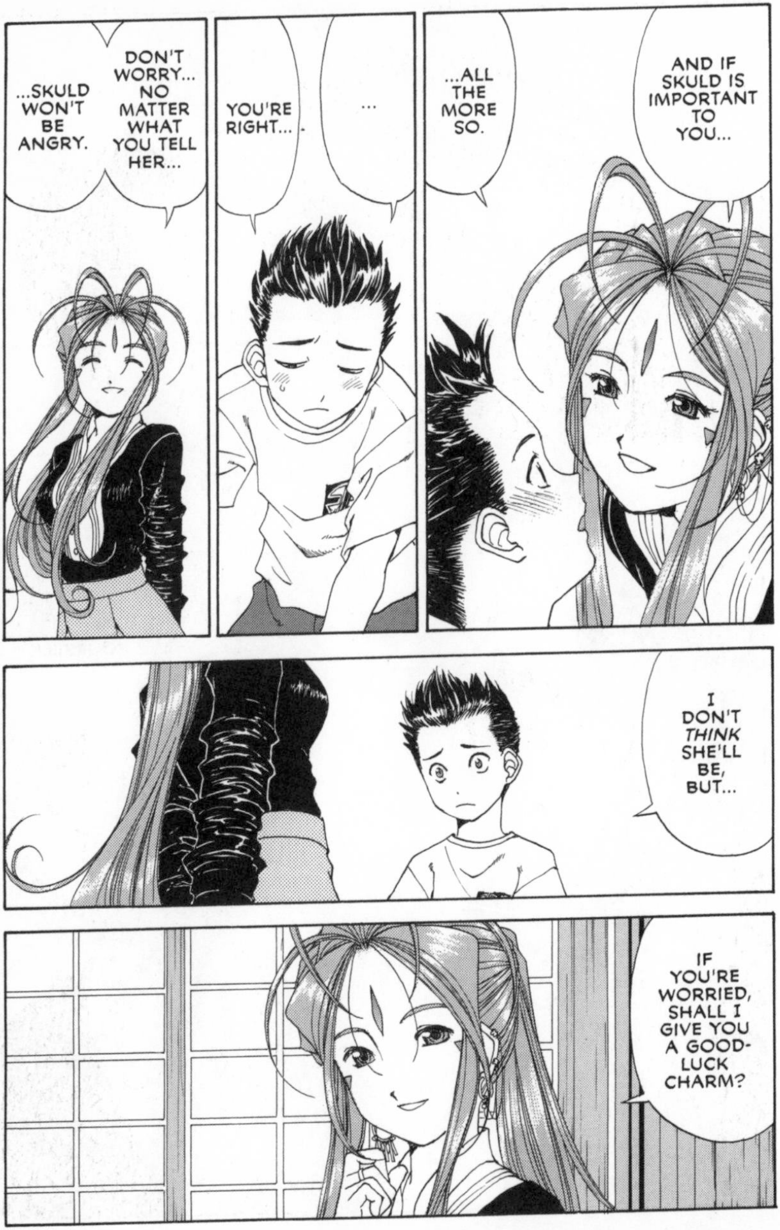
AND IF SKULD IS IMPORTANT TO YOU...
...ALL THE MORE SO.
...
YOU'RE RIGHT...
DON'T WORRY... NO MATTER WHAT YOU TELL HER...
...SKULD WON'T BE ANGRY.
I DON'T *THINK* SHE'LL BE, BUT...
IF YOU'RE WORRIED, SHALL I GIVE YOU A GOOD-LUCK CHARM?

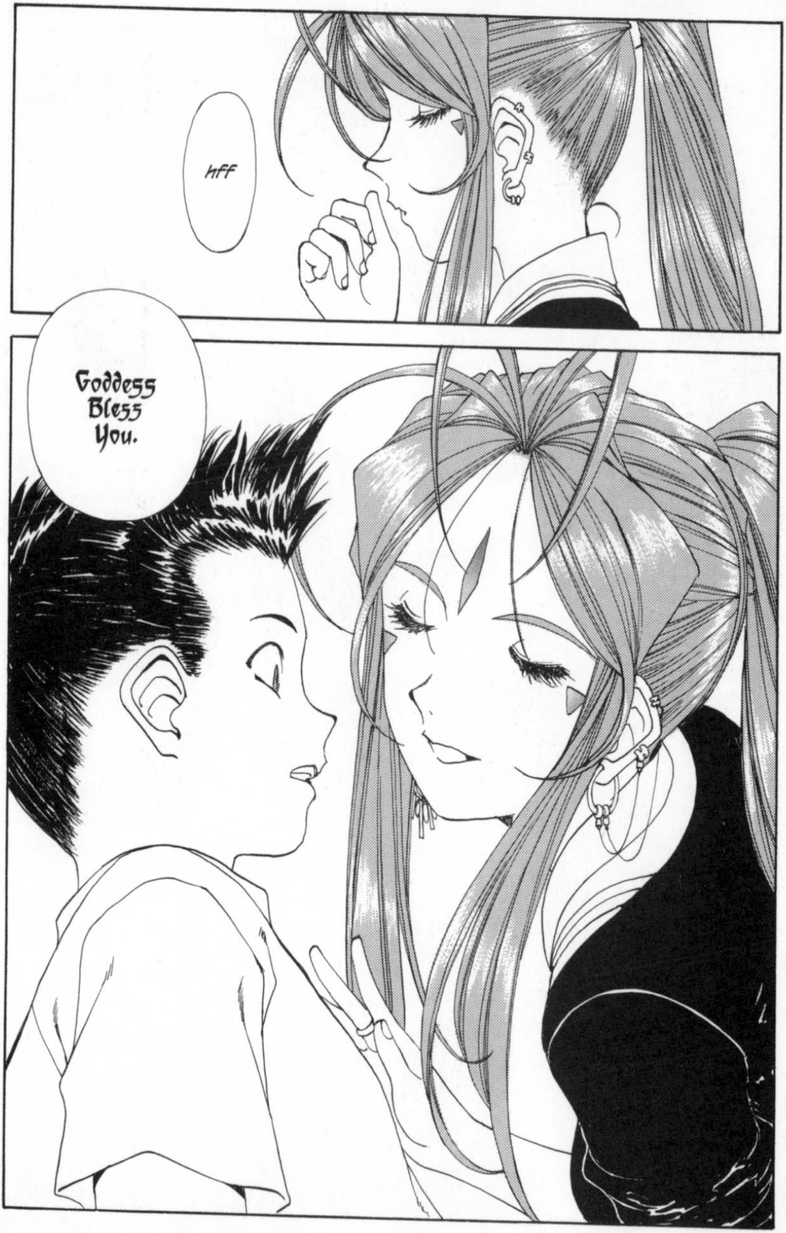
hff
Goddess Bless You.

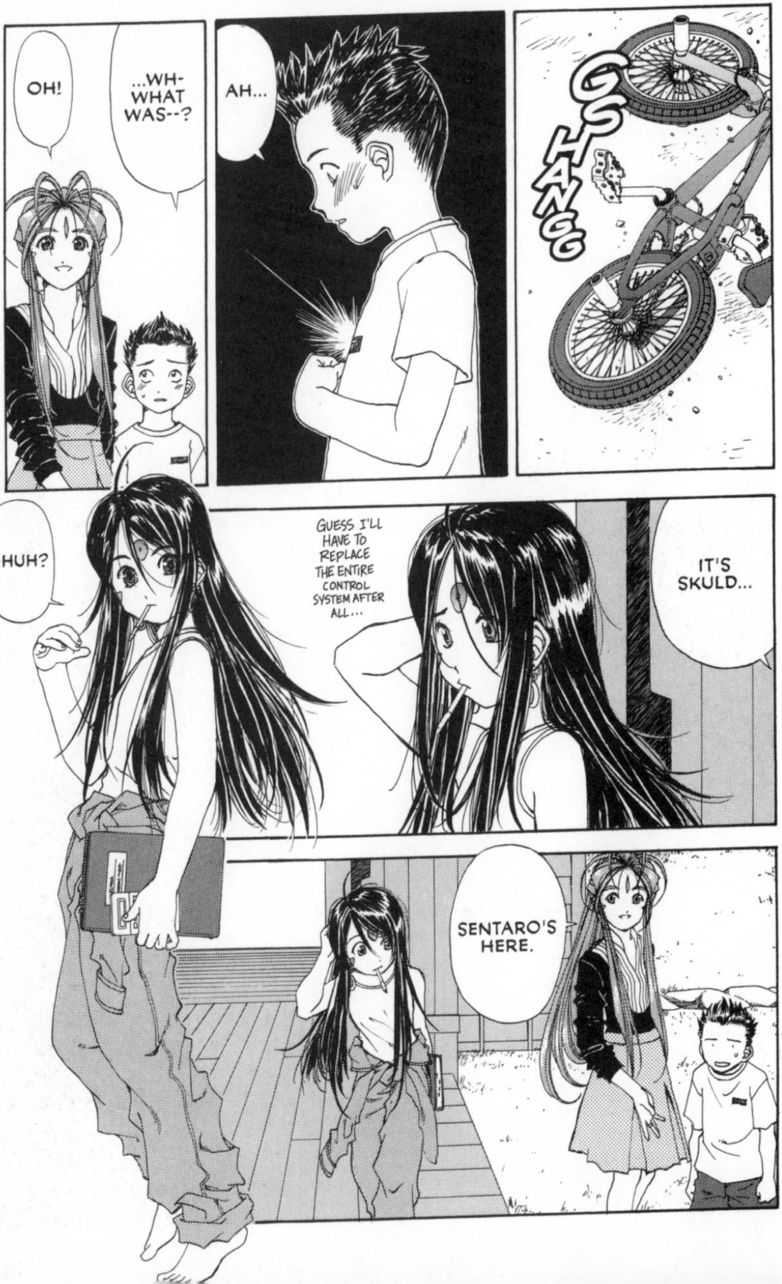
GSHANGG
AH...
...WH- WHAT WAS--?
OH!
IT'S SKULD...
GUESS I'LL HAVE TO REPLACE THE ENTIRE CONTROL SYSTEM AFTER ALL...
SENTARO'S HERE.
--HUH?

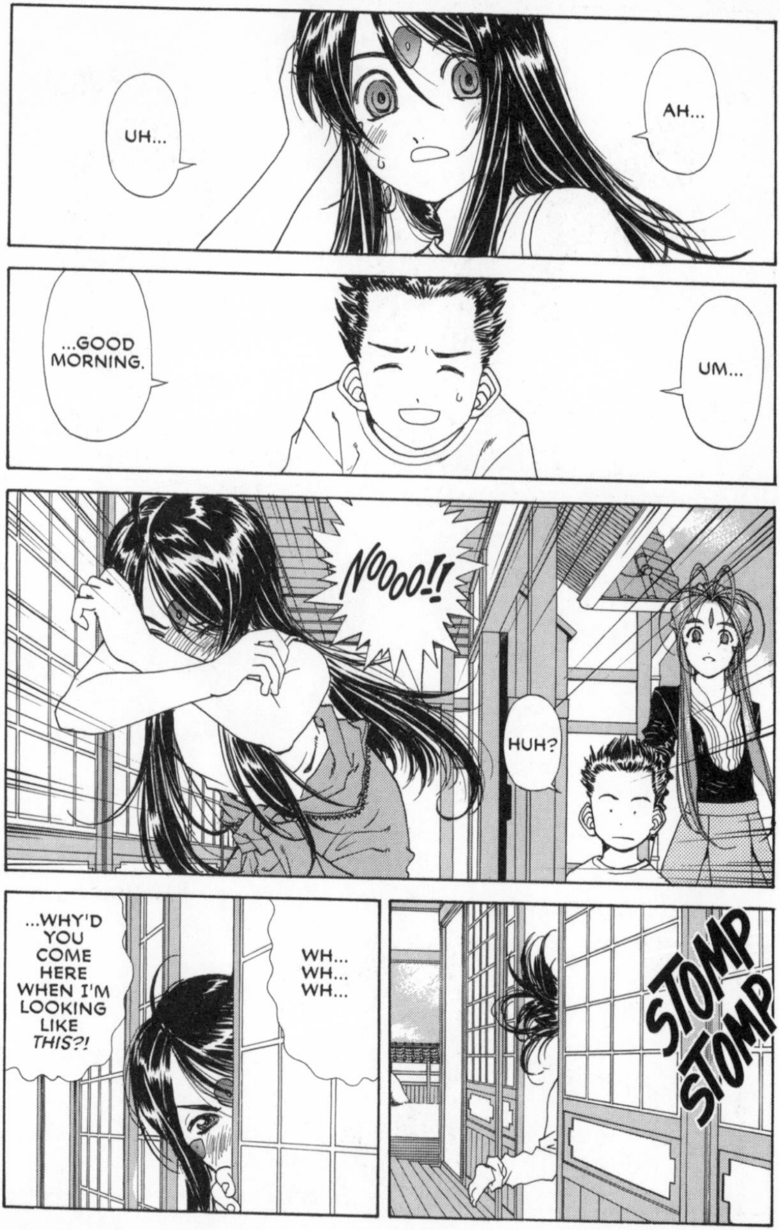
AH...
UH...
UM...
...GOOD MORNING.
NOOOO!!
HUH?
STOMP STOMP
WH... WH... WH...
...WHY'D YOU COME HERE WHEN I'M LOOKING LIKE *THIS?!*

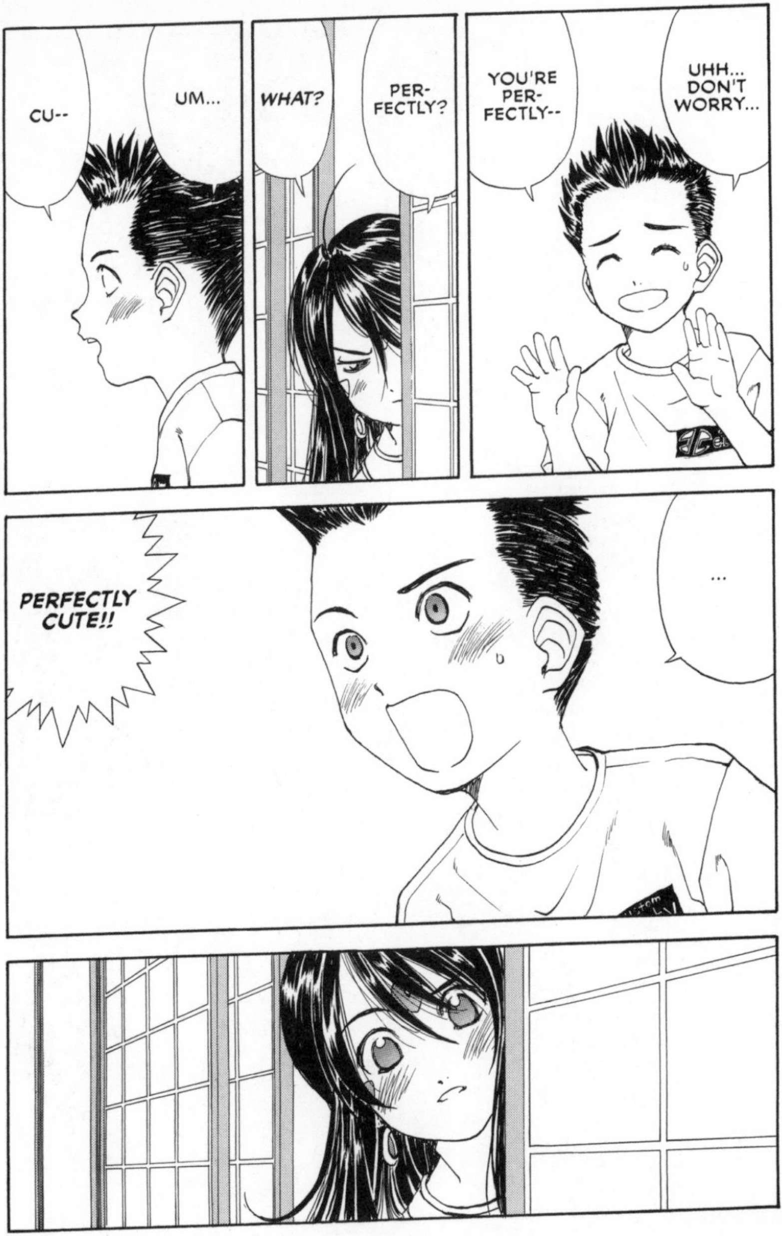
UHH... DON'T WORRY...
YOU'RE PER-FECTLY--
PER-FECTLY?
WHAT?
UM...
CU--
...
PERFECTLY CUTE!!

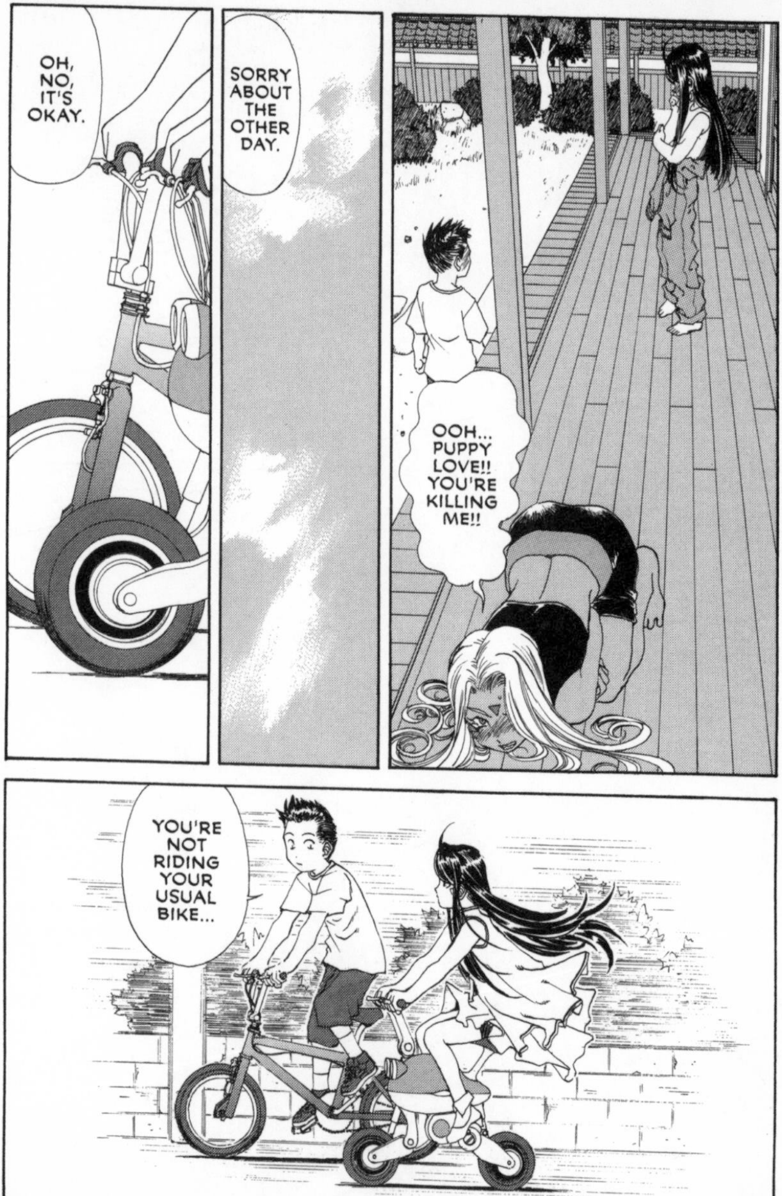
OOH... PUPPY LOVE!! YOU'RE KILLING ME!!
SORRY ABOUT THE OTHER DAY.
OH, NO, IT'S OKAY.
YOU'RE NOT RIDING YOUR USUAL BIKE...

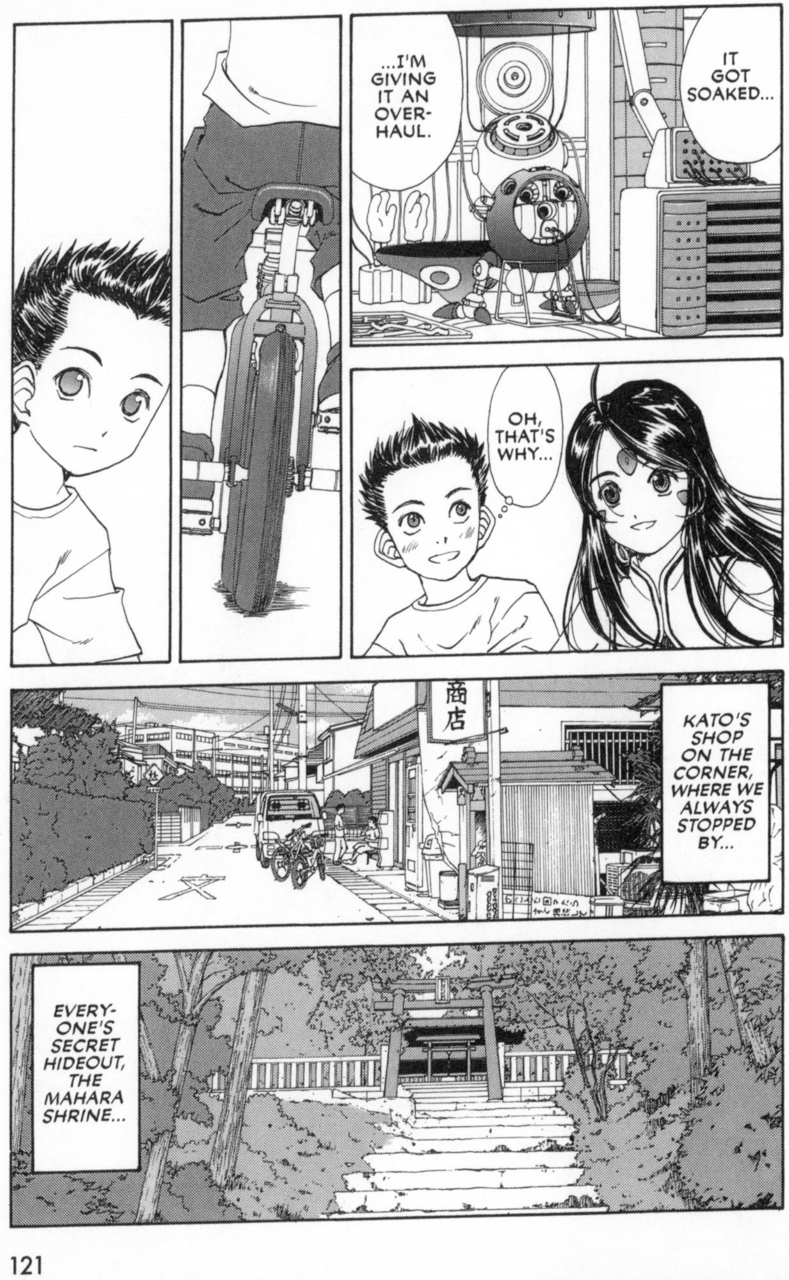
IT GOT SOAKED...
...I'M GIVING IT AN OVER-HAUL.
OH, THAT'S WHY...
KATO'S SHOP ON THE CORNER, WHERE WE ALWAYS STOPPED BY...
商店
EVERY-ONE'S SECRET HIDEOUT, THE MAHARA SHRINE...

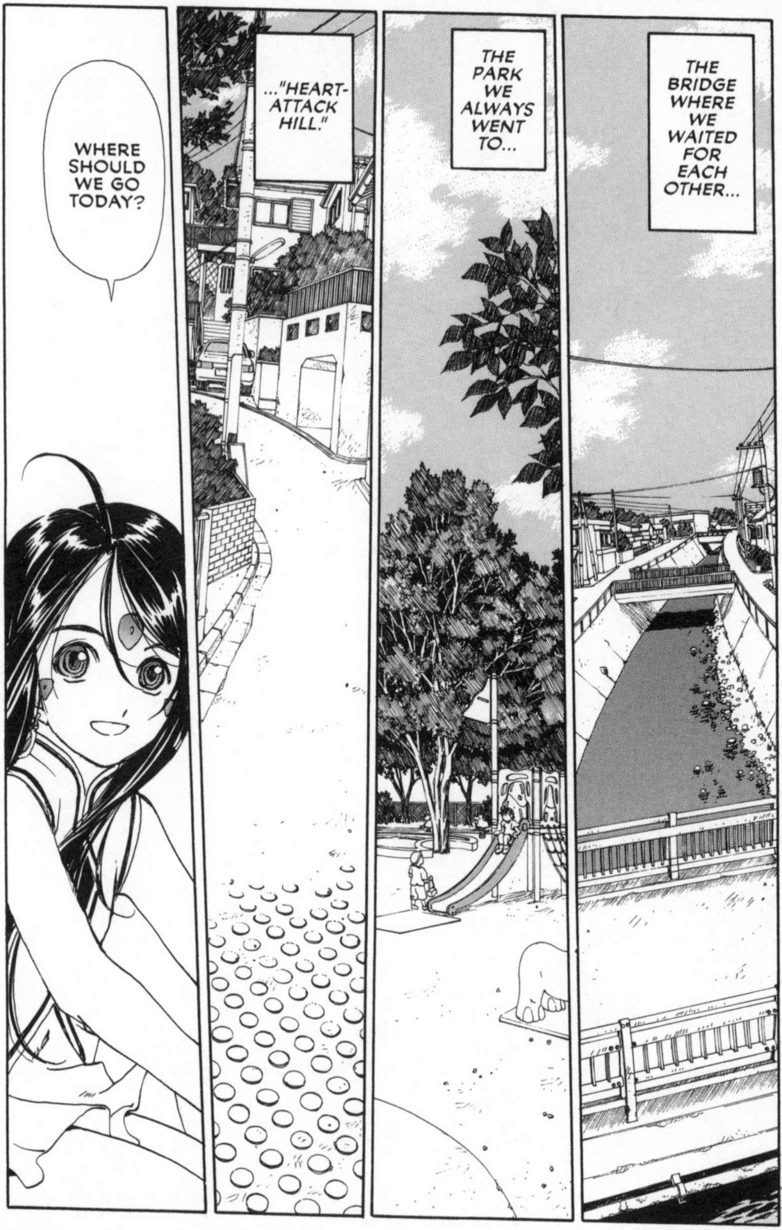
THE BRIDGE WHERE WE WAITED FOR EACH OTHER...
THE PARK WE ALWAYS WENT TO...
..."HEART-ATTACK HILL."
WHERE SHOULD WE GO TODAY?

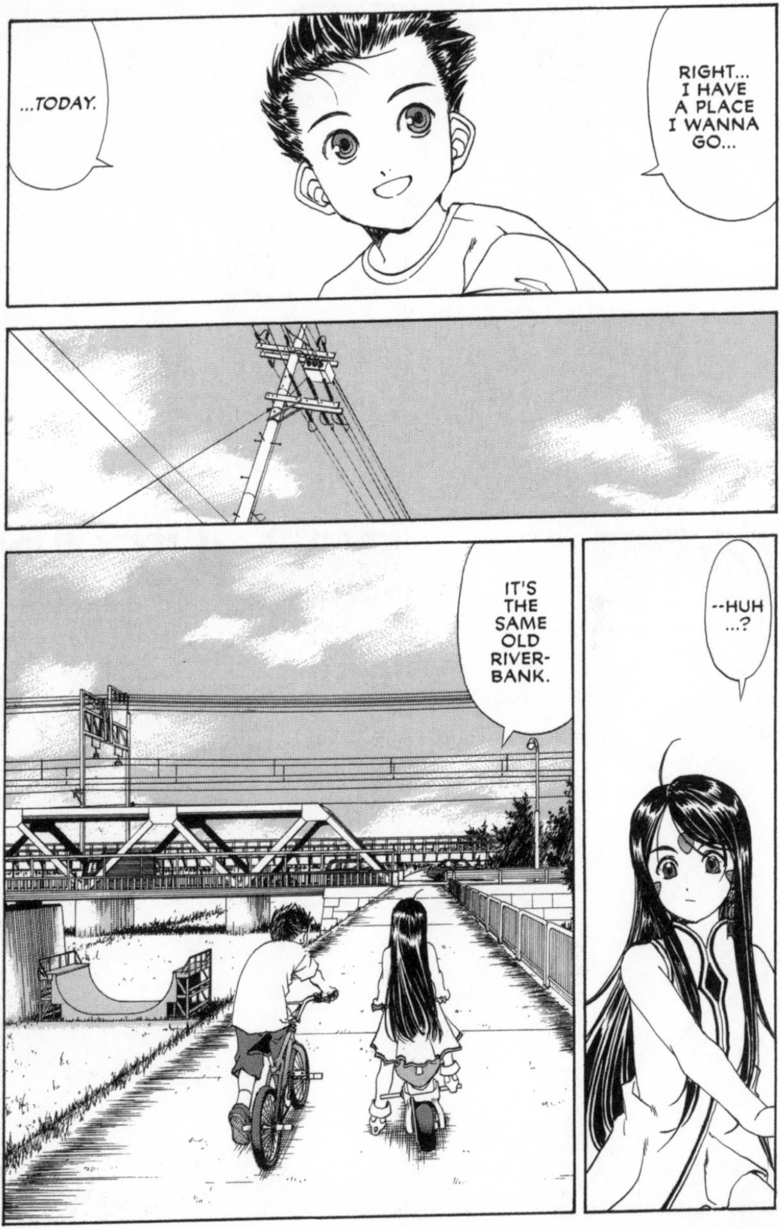
RIGHT... I HAVE A PLACE I WANNA GO...
...TODAY.
--HUH ...?
IT'S THE SAME OLD RIVER-BANK.

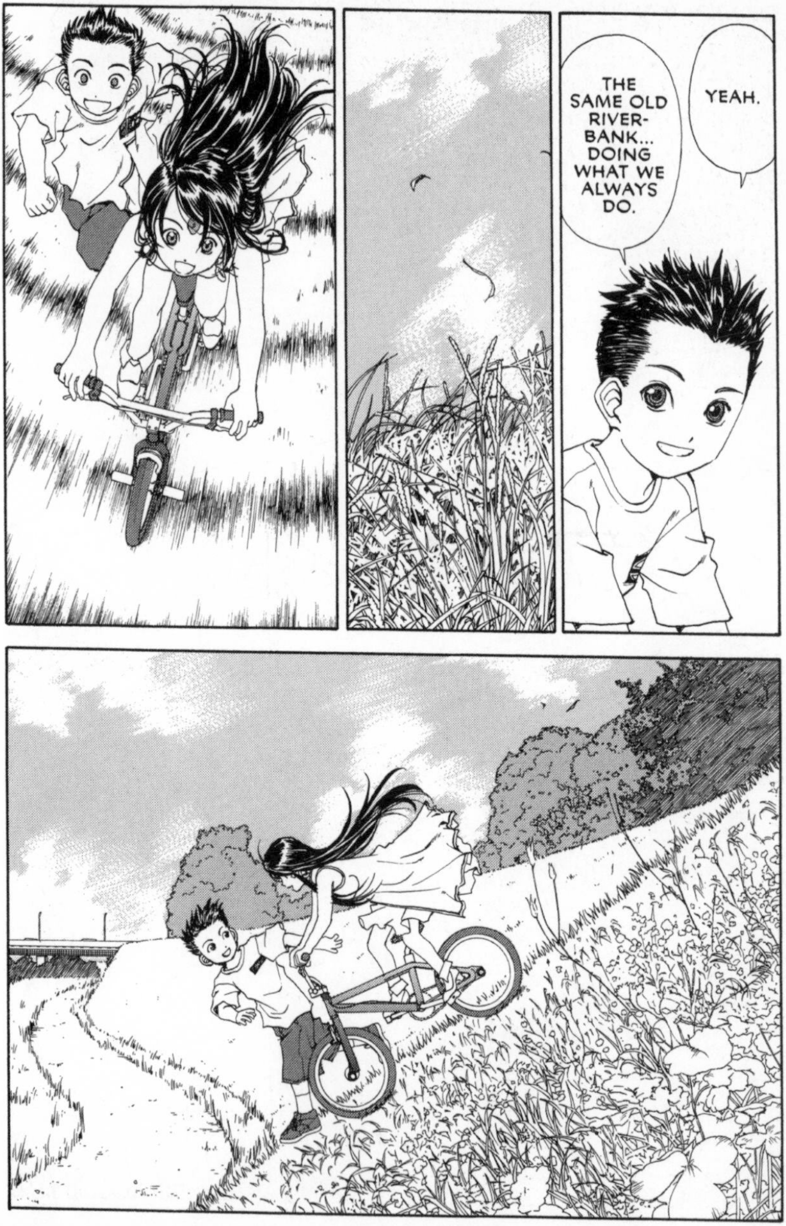
YEAH.
THE SAME OLD RIVER-BANK... DOING WHAT WE ALWAYS DO.

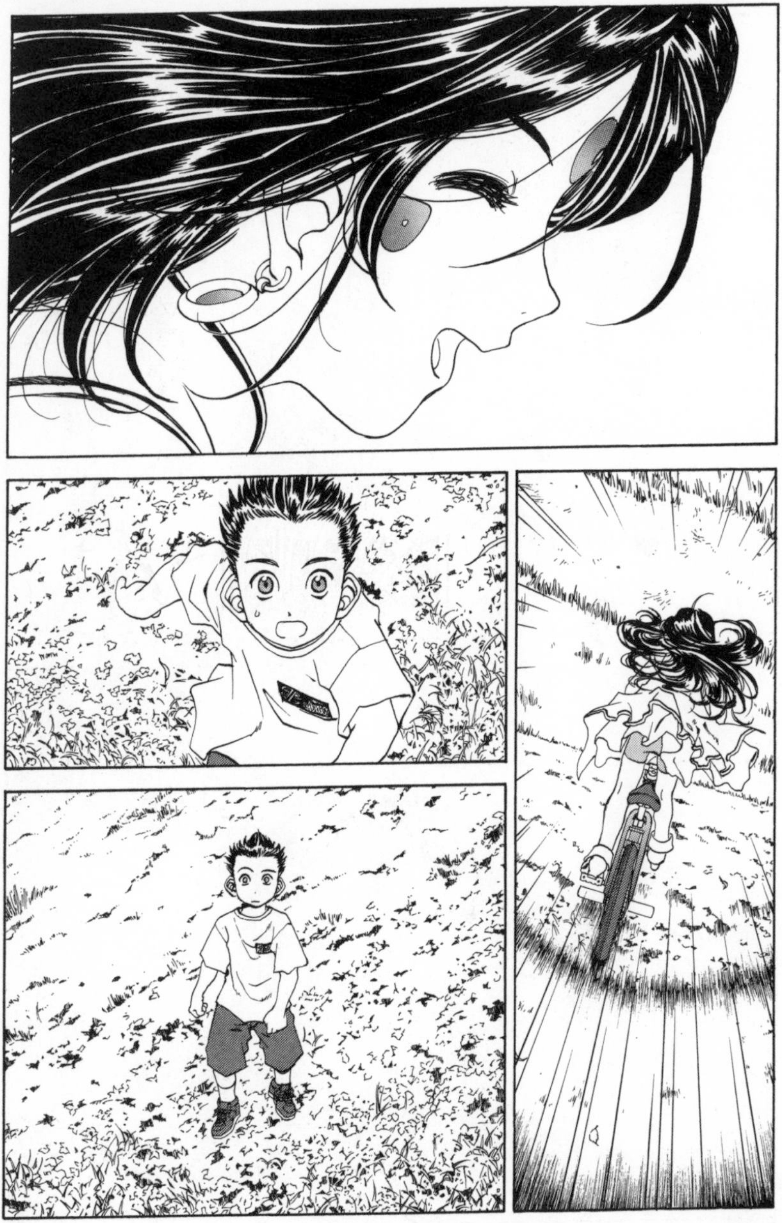

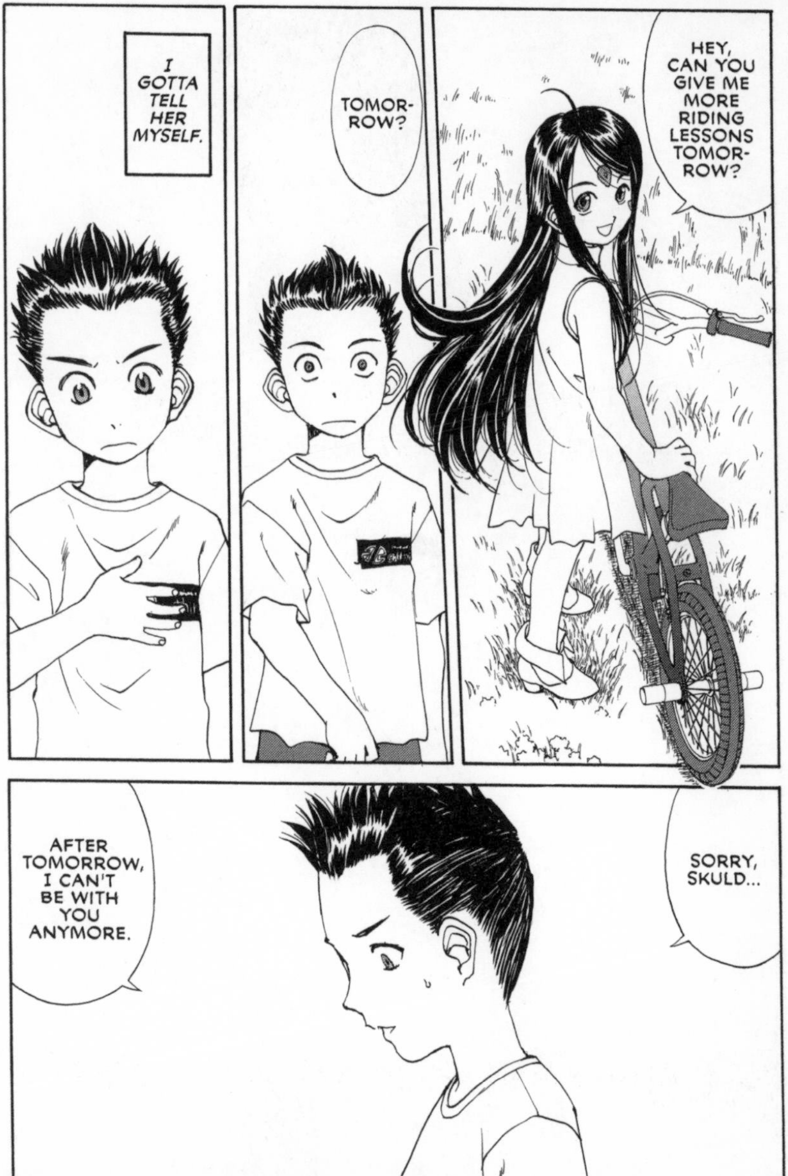
HEY, CAN YOU GIVE ME MORE RIDING LESSONS TOMORROW?
TOMORROW?
I GOTTA TELL HER MYSELF.
SORRY, SKULD...
AFTER TOMORROW, I CAN'T BE WITH YOU ANYMORE.

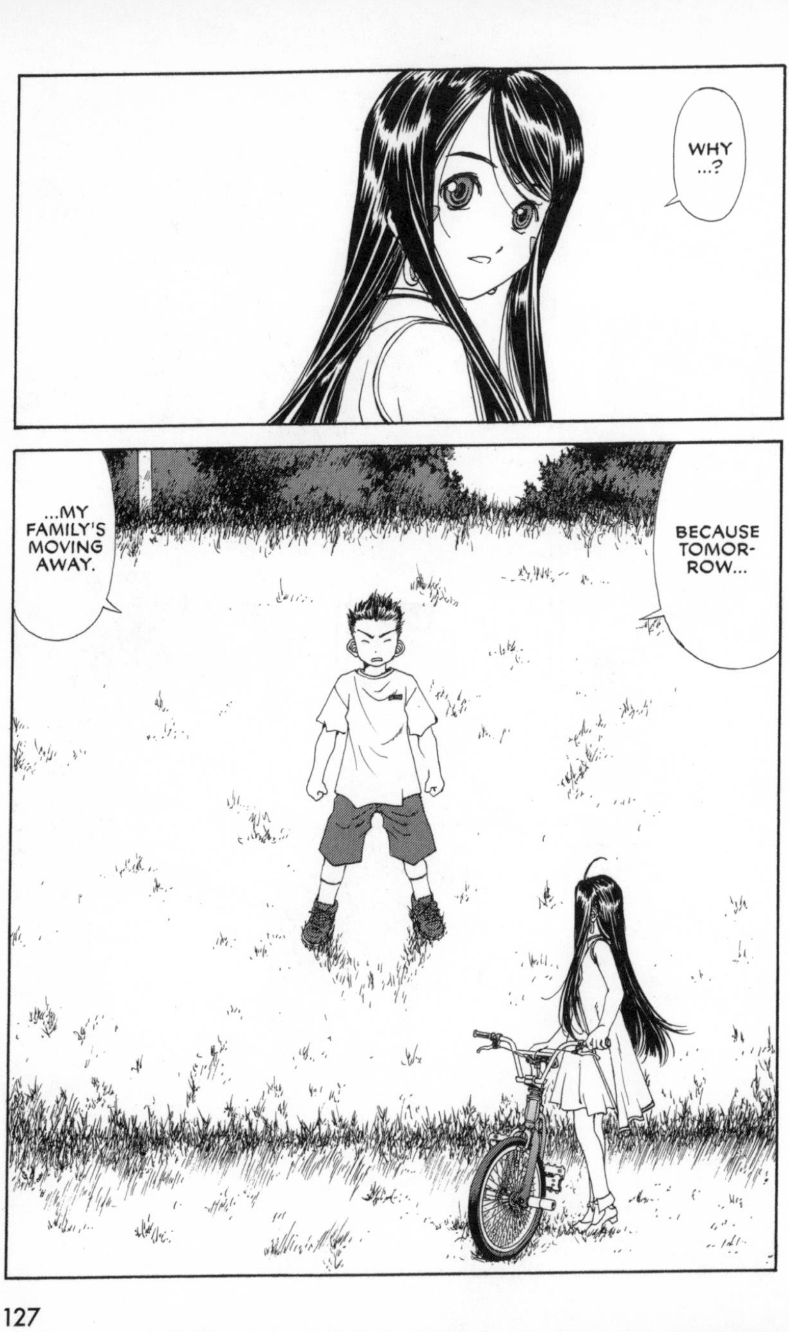
WHY ...?
BECAUSE TOMOR-ROW...
...MY FAMILY'S MOVING AWAY.

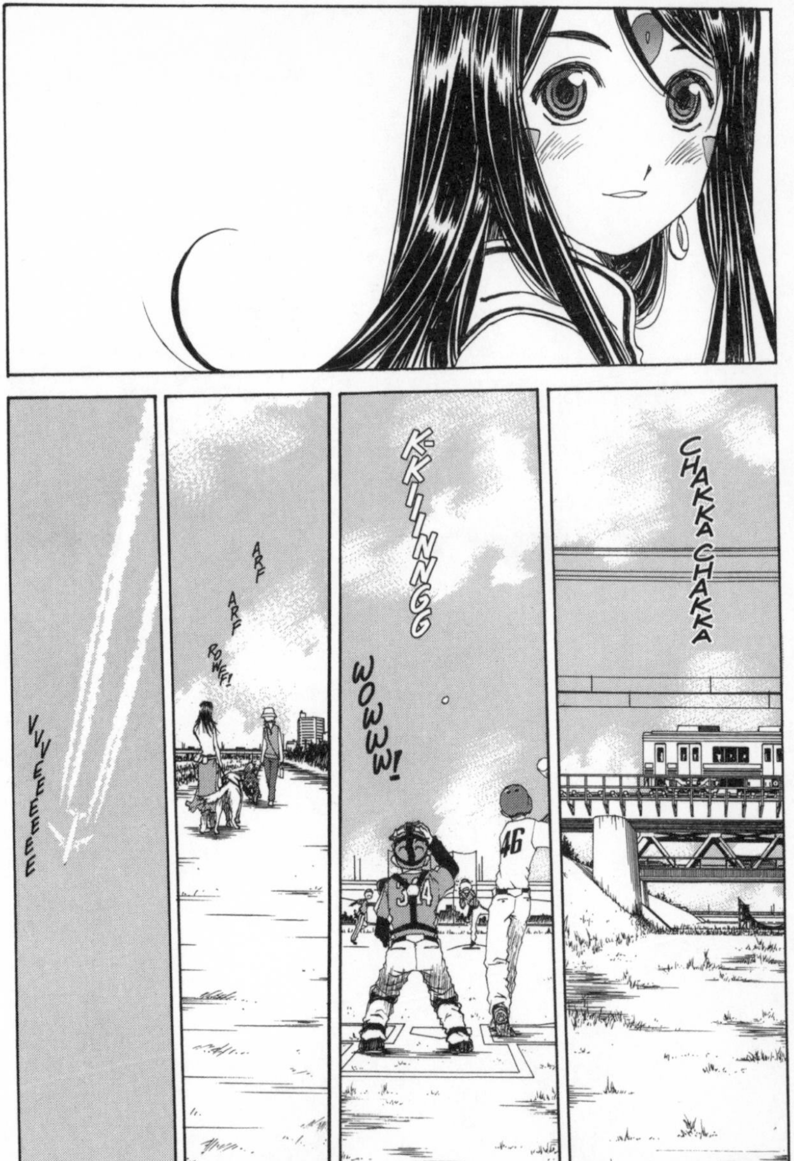
CHAKKA CHAKKA
K-KIIINNGG
WOWWW!
ARF
ARF
ROWFF!
VVVEEEEEEE

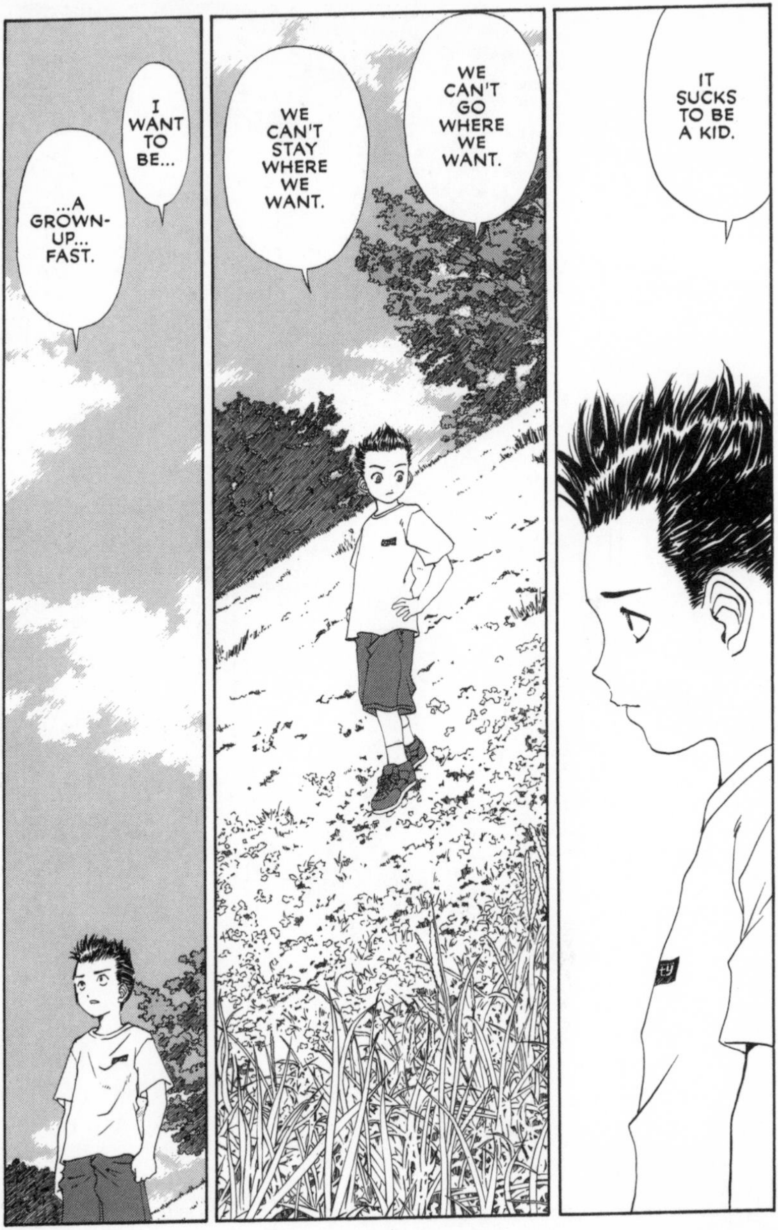
IT SUCKS TO BE A KID.
WE CAN'T GO WHERE WE WANT.
WE CAN'T STAY WHERE WE WANT.
I WANT TO BE...
...A GROWN-UP... FAST.

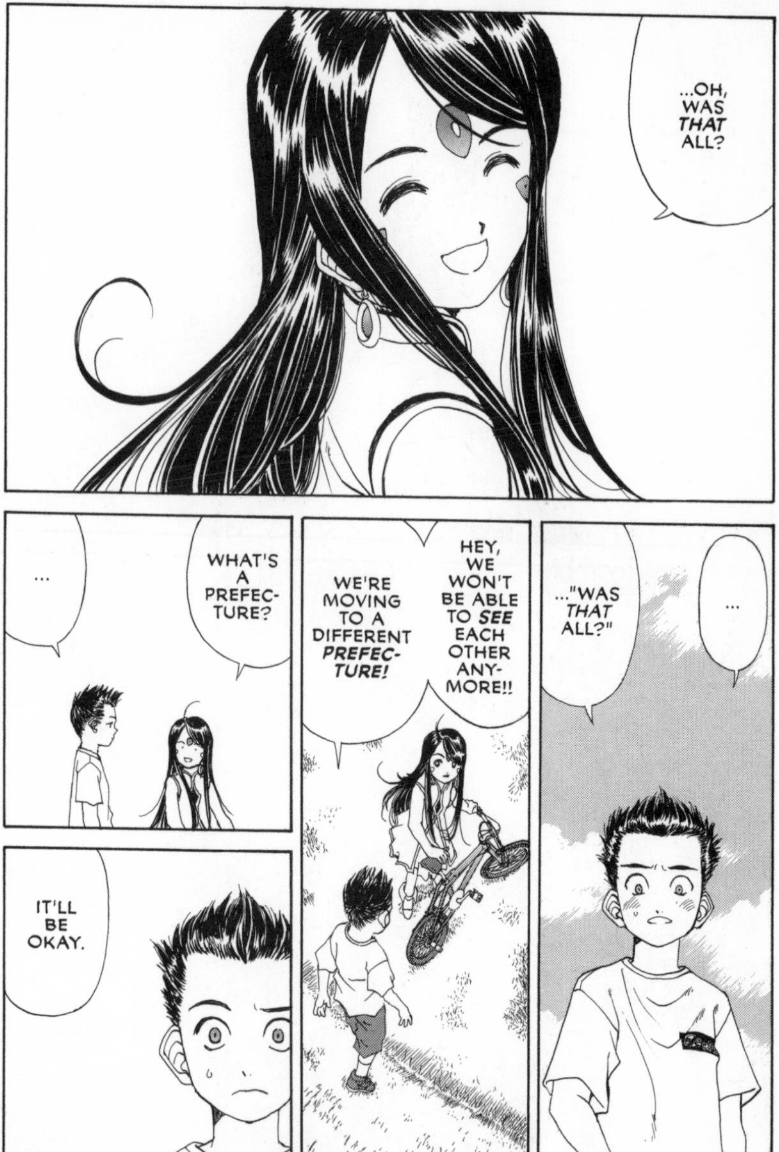
...OH, WAS *THAT* ALL?
...
..."WAS *THAT* ALL?"
HEY, WE WON'T BE ABLE TO *SEE* EACH OTHER ANY-MORE!!
WE'RE MOVING TO A DIFFERENT *PREFEC-TURE!*
WHAT'S A PREFEC-TURE?
...
IT'LL BE OKAY.

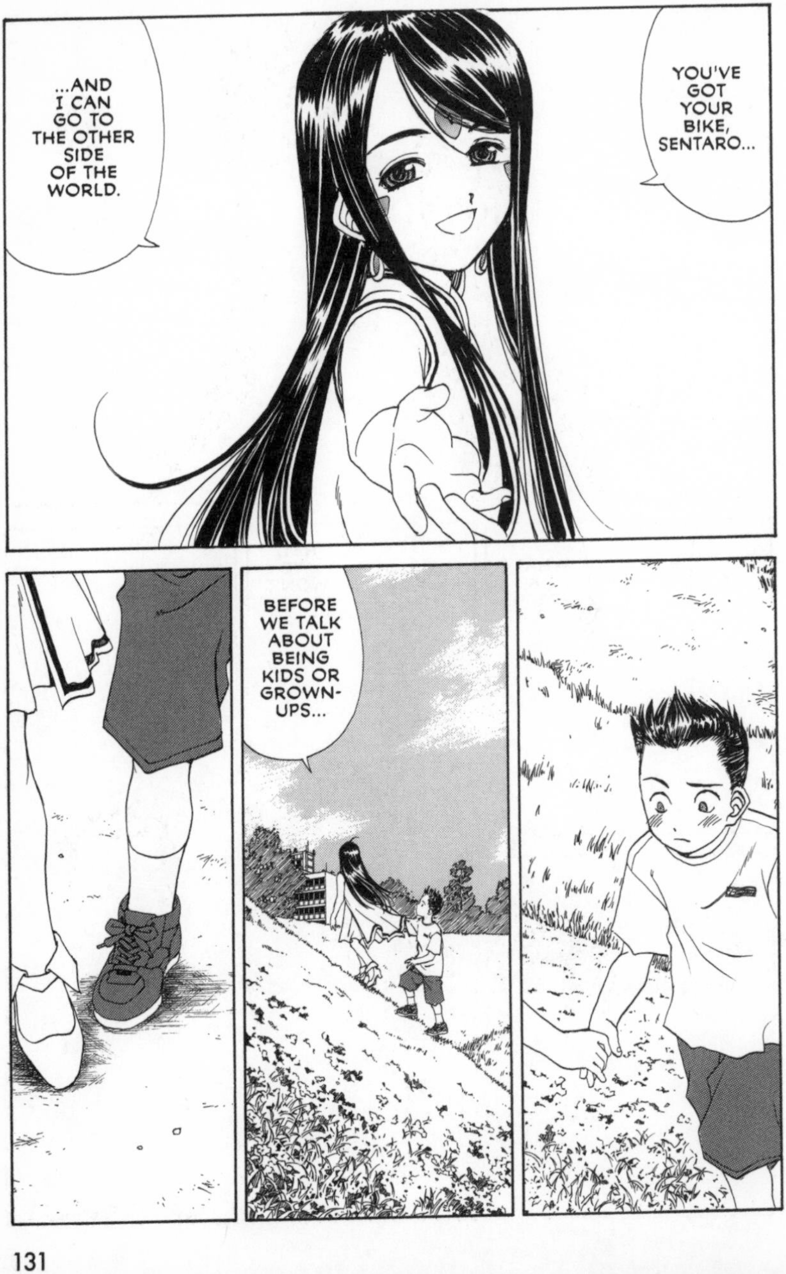
YOU'VE GOT YOUR BIKE, SENTARO...
...AND I CAN GO TO THE OTHER SIDE OF THE WORLD.
BEFORE WE TALK ABOUT BEING KIDS OR GROWN-UPS...

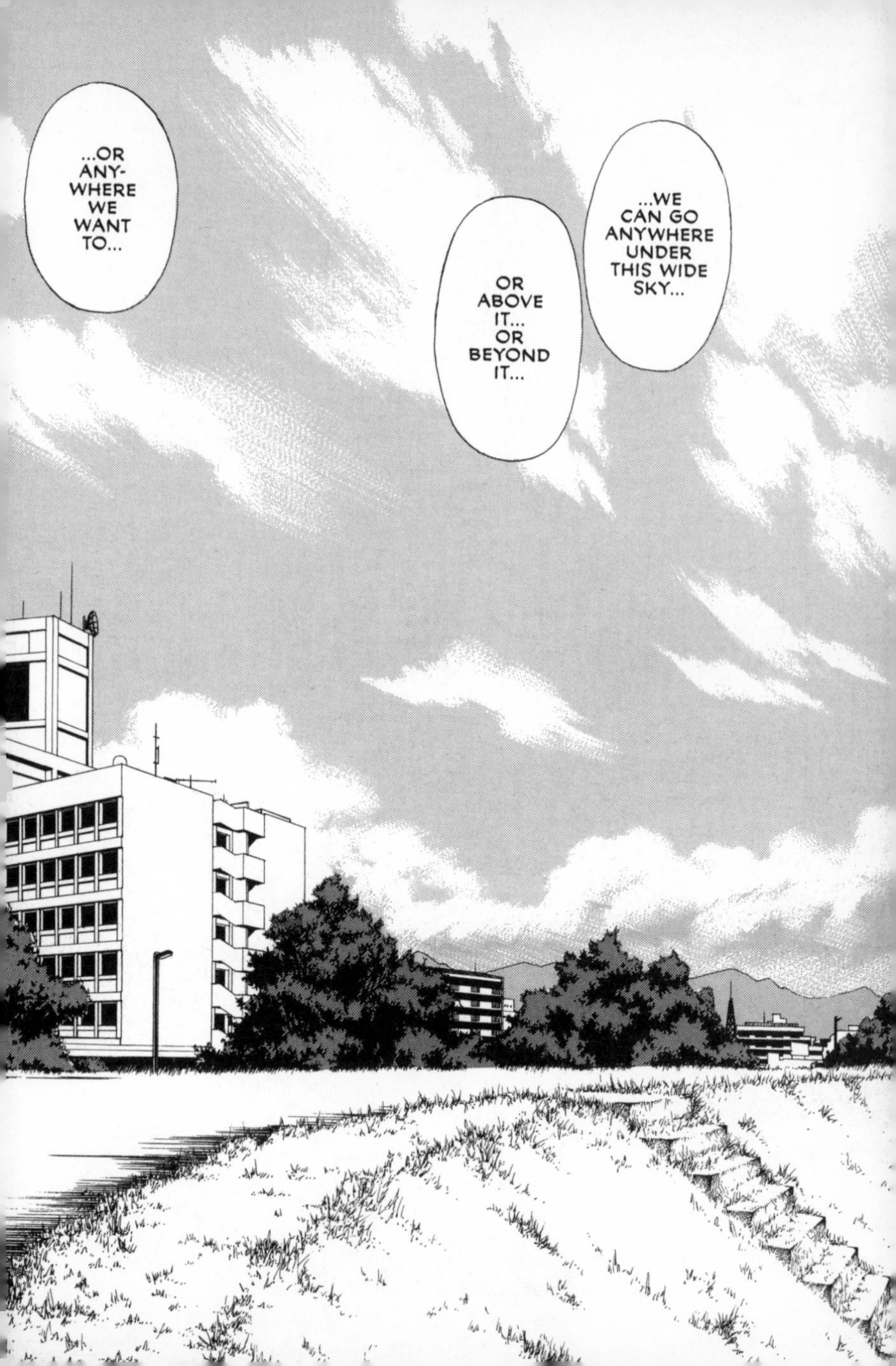
...WE CAN GO ANYWHERE UNDER THIS WIDE SKY...
OR ABOVE IT... OR BEYOND IT...
...OR ANY-WHERE WE WANT TO...

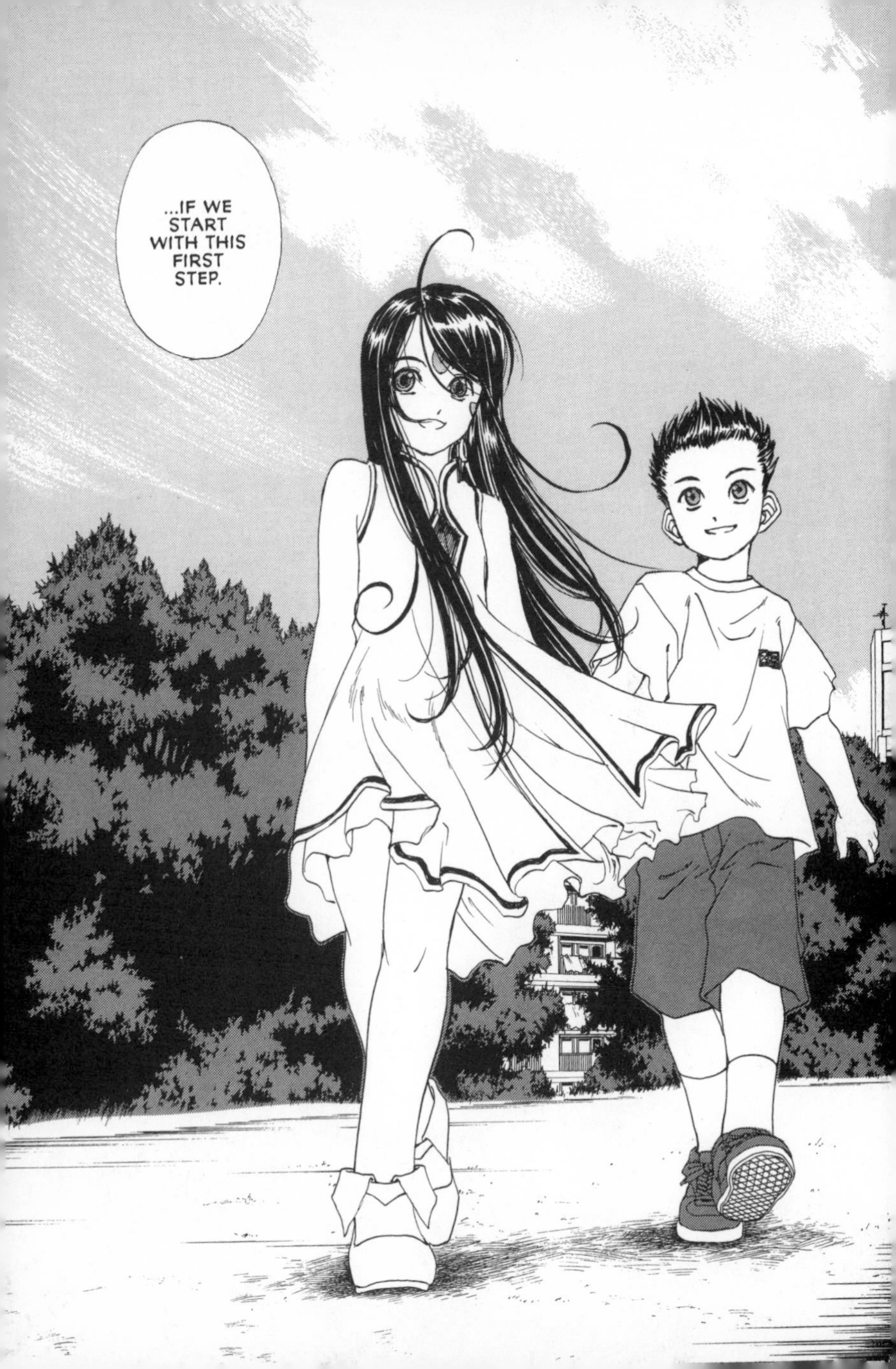
...IF WE START WITH THIS FIRST STEP.

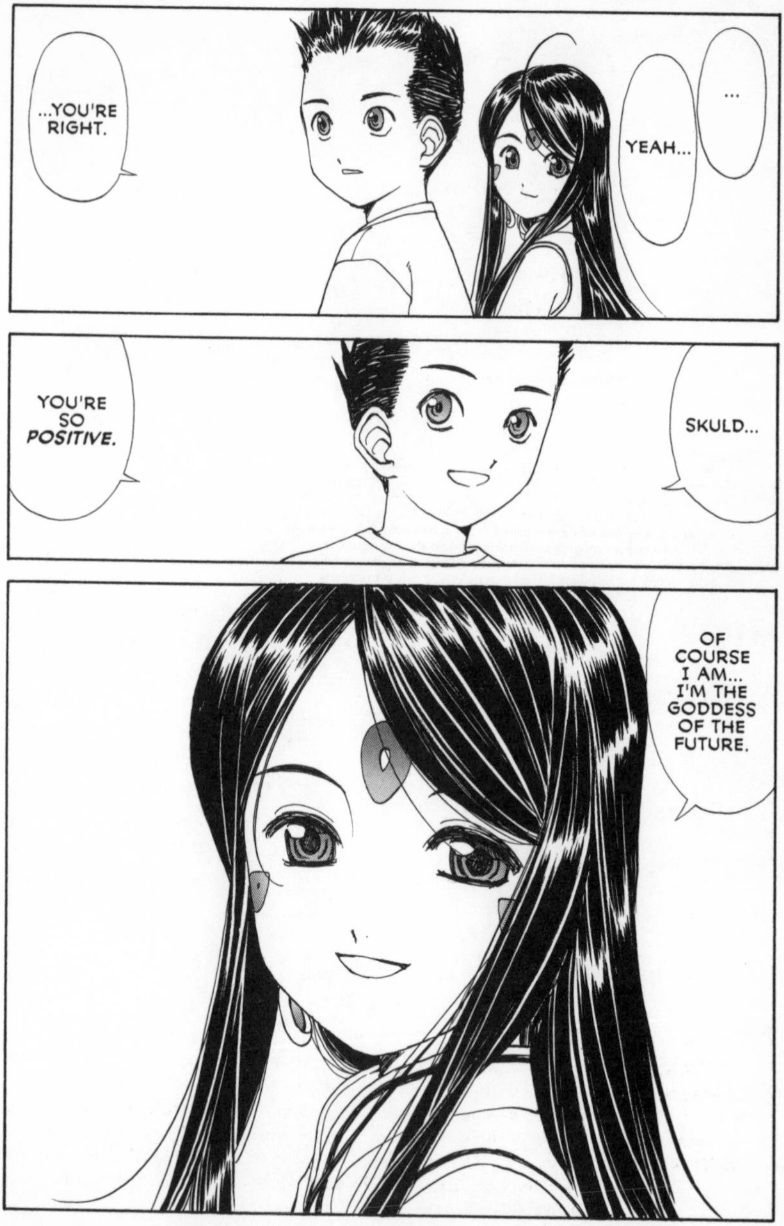
...
YEAH...
...YOU'RE RIGHT.
SKULD...
YOU'RE SO *POSITIVE.*
OF COURSE I AM... I'M THE GODDESS OF THE FUTURE.

## EDITOR
### Carl Gustav Horn

## EDITORIAL ASSISTANT
### Annie Gullion

## DESIGNER
### Scott Cook

## PUBLISHER
### Mike Richardson

English-language version
produced by Dark Horse Comics

OH MY GODDESS! Vol. 34
© 2009 Kosuke Fujishima. All rights reserved. First published in
Japan in 2006 by Kodansha, Ltd., Tokyo. Publication rights for this English
edition arranged through Kodansha, Ltd. All rights reserved. No portion of
this publication may be reproduced or transmitted, in any form or by any
means, without the express written permission of Dark Horse Comics, Inc. Names,
characters, places, and incidents featured in this publication either are the
product of the author's imagination or are used fictitiously. Any resemblance
to actual persons (living or dead), events, institutions, or locales, without
satiric intent, is coincidental. Dark Horse Manga™ is a trademark
of Dark Horse Comics, Inc. All rights reserved.

Published by Dark Horse Manga
A division of Dark Horse Comics, Inc.
10956 SE Main Street
Milwaukie, OR 97222
darkhorse.com

To find a comics shop in your area,
call the Comic Shop Locator Service
toll-free at 1-888-266-4226

First edition: December 2009
ISBN 978-1-59582-448-6

1 3 5 7 9 10 8 6 4 2

Printed at Lebonfon Printing, Inc., Val-d'Or, QC, Canada

# letters to the
# ENCHANTRESS

10956 SE Main Street, Milwaukie, Oregon 97222
omg@darkhorse.com • darkhorse.com

*NOTE: Full addresses and e-mail addresses will not be printed, unless you ask! All fan artwork, letters, and e-mails submitted become the property of Dark Horse Comics.*

Recently (like, vol. 32 recently), the designer of *Oh My Goddess!*, Scott Cook, was kind enough to do a guest commentary and fan art of Urd for Letters to the Enchantress. This inspired a fan letter of its own!

Mr. Scott Cook,

I don't know if you're still working with Dark Horse Comics and still designing the *OMG!* series—I just started, ^_^* Even if you are/aren't (like I said, I'm clueless), the art is incredible! By the way, I have a cousin, and he's hooked on manga. Recently, he told me he wants to create a series of his own and wants me to do the art for him! We're rookies, I guess, but I've never done something like this before. Is there any advice you could give us for creating an original manga? Also, are there some tips that you could give me for the artwork? It would be a big help if you could.

Thanks,
Nick
New Rochelle, NY

P.S. In the *OMG!* universe, all of the people, I mean, almost all the characters seem to be human on some level. Have you ever done a character that was part animal? Like someone with fox ears?

Hi, Nick!

First off, I must say how flattered and surprised I was when your letter arrived at our offices. I am not sure how my measly bit of fan art inspired you to write in, when there are 134 pages of flawlessly executed story pages from *Oh My Goddess!* mastermind Kosuke Fujishima preceding my single contribution, but thank you very much. ^^;

If I were to give any pointers to you and your cousin (or anyone else for that matter) about aspiring to create your own comics, I would simply say, DRAW EVERY DAY. It doesn't matter what you draw, but draw something! If you are in need of some inspiration, I love to peruse the galleries over at creativeuncut.com. While there, check out the awesome character designs Kosuke Fujishima did for Namco's *Tales* series. Just like his characters in *OMG!*, they are incredible!

Although I don't show as much disdain for cat-eared characters as Oku Hiroya does in the bonus section of *Gantz* Vol. 8, I really don't find anything interesting about them. I do enjoy Rumiko Takahashi's design of InuYasha, but that's mostly because of his gigantic sword, Tetsusaiga! *KAZE NO KIZU!*

Designer Scott

And now, it's time for a Letters to the Enchantress super-special feature! As you know, every two months we switch off between "new" volumes of *OMG!* (such as the vol. 34 you're reading right now) and "old" volumes (such as the recent vol. 13) that years ago Dark Horse released in flopped format, but which we're now going back and redoing unflopped.

Anyway, many of these "old" volumes contain a personal message from Kosuke Fujishima—a message that originally appeared in the volume when it first came out in Japan. But before it gets collected into volume format in Japan, each individual chapter of *Oh My Goddess!* appears in its home magazine, *Afternoon*—also the home of the second-longest-running manga in English, *Blade of the Immortal*, as well as *Gunsmith Cats*, *Eden*, and several other titles from Dark Horse and other U.S. manga publishers (*Genshiken!* From Del Rey! And be sure to check out their *Moyasimon*, too, even though it's from *Evening*, not *Afternoon*. Yeah, there's an *Evening*, too. There's also a *Morning*, where Viz's *Vagabond* comes from).

Well, it turns out that not only did Fujishima-sensei write comments for the volumes, he also wrote them for each chapter as they appeared in *Afternoon* over the years. Not only that, he also responded personally to some of the Japanese readers' letters! So, starting in vol. 34 and continuing in future volumes, we're going to translate them all! Let's start where *Oh My Goddess!* itself did—in the fabled land known as "the 1980s." In the immortal words of that eighties prophet, Bill S. Preston, Esq., "YOU guys are gonna go back in TIME!!!"

**Fujishima's comments from the November 1988 issue of *Afternoon—OMG!* Chapter 1:**

*"I first introduced a goddess character in a comic that came with a* You're Under Arrest! *gift T-shirt I did for an issue of* Comic Morning Party Extra. *Everyone said it was so*

*good that I decided I'd use her for my new series. I went to the editorial department for a meeting, and it was decided that we'd go with the goddess story. I'm not sure about the future, but I'll try to make the comic as fun as I can.*

*"The Kerker muffler for my GSX-R arrived, and I've finally succeeded in attaching it. Mmm . . . how cool! I turn on the engine. The idling is surprisingly quiet. I try giving the engine a bit more fuel. Whooa! It's loud!! My bike's become a total street racer."*

The English-language editor comments on the comments. ^_^ Kosuke Fujishima began his career as an assistant to Tatsuya Egawa (creator of *Golden Boy*) on Egawa's manga *Be Free!*, which ran in Kodansha's aforementioned weekly *Morning* magazine. Thus it was not surprising that when Fujishima began his first independent manga in 1986, *You're Under Arrest!*, it was in a *Morning* spinoff magazine, *Comic Morning Party Extra*, where it ran until 1992. In other words, *You're Under Arrest!* began two years before *Oh My Goddess!*, and Fujishima kept doing it during the early years of the *OMG!* series, until about the time of *Oh My Goddess!* Vol. 6.

I wonder if Fujishima's remark "I'm not sure about the future" suggests that, at the time he began *Oh My Goddess!*, he didn't know which series would last longer, *OMG!* or the already running *You're Under Arrest!* In any case, it turned out to be *OMG!*, but that doesn't mean there's anything wrong with *YUA!* In fact, the series has had a whole new life in anime after the manga; since 1994 there have been multiple *You're Under Arrest!* anime movies, OAVs, and TV series, most of which have been licensed in the U.S. through AnimEigo, ADV, and now Sentai Filmworks.

If you don't already know, *You're Under Arrest!* is a buddy cop story set in modern

Tokyo; only, this being a Kosuke Fujishima manga, the buddies are both attractive women, and every chapter seems to involve some crazy or customized vehicle—in fact, one of the two lead characters, Natsumi, has been known to ride a Suzuki GSX-R with Brembo brakes, which possibly prompted Fujishima's matching boast about his Kerker muffler. ^_^ In the midnineties, Dark Horse released eight selected chapters of the *You're Under Arrest!* manga in English that were later collected into two graphic novels: *You're Under Arrest!—The Wild Ones* and *You're Under Arrest!—Lights and Siren!* Note that both were flopped, as was standard for English versions of manga at the time . . .

### Fujishima's comments from the December 1988 issue of *Afternoon—OMG!* Chapter 2:

*"I bought the car I've been wanting for ages. It's a Nissan Silvia. It's brand new. Yay! But my garage is incredibly small. It's a real horror for me, with so little driving experience, to fit that big Silvia into the garage. I still can't park my car by myself."*

Editor's note: In the U.S., the Nissan Silvia was known as the Nissan 240SX.

### Fujishima's comments from the January 1989 issue of *Afternoon—OMG!* Chapter 3:

*"I had my first experience as a model for Morning magazine's mon-collection feature. It's actually quite hard to pose and laugh naturally. We managed to finish the shoot, but the conclusion was that the professionals are really great."*

### Fujishima's comments from the February 1989 issue of *Afternoon—OMG!* Chapters 4 and 5:

*"After several years of not going, I finally went to the dentist. I managed to have a tooth pulled with no problem, but it turned out that the dentist was really into radio-control cars. We had an enjoyable talk while getting my treatment done. Doctor, let's go RC buggying next time."*

### Fujishima's comments from the March 1989 issue of *Afternoon—OMG!* Chapter 6:

*"Namie Iwao from Kiosk Flapper [another manga series] helped me out with this chapter. Thank you for coming to my aid in the midst of so much work. When I told her, 'Please come again,' her face was twitching oddly. But I really meant to come and 'hang out,' so please don't worry."*

Editor's note: Namie Iwao is a now-retired manga artist who was active in the same magazines as Fujishima in the late 1980s and early nineties, although none of her series were ever released in English. Her *Parodius Superb* manga was based on the Konami *Parodius* game, which itself was labeled by *Electronic Gaming Monthly* in 1992 as "Best Game That Never Came Out in the U.S." ^_^

### Fujishima's comments from the April 1989 issue of *Afternoon—OMG!* Chapters 7 and 8:

*"I received a Motocompo from an acquaintance, but it's run-down and doesn't move. I want to fix it up somehow, but I don't have the time right now, so I'll just leave the bones for the time being. Let's wait and see if I can take it apart and put it back together.*

*"Right now I'm going through a reconstruction operation for my teeth. I've had three teeth pulled, and have shiny chogokin metal attachments, wires, springs, and rubber bands installed in my mouth. For a while, my smile's going to be rather scary."*

Editor's note: The Motocompo (short for "motor compact") was a very small scooter sold by Honda in Japan in the early 1980s; when the seat, handlebars, and footrests were folded into the body, it could easily be stored in even a compact car's trunk (which was its purpose), and it weighed only 42 kg unfueled. Fujishima had Natsumi in *You're Under Arrest!* keep a Motocompo stashed in her partner's Honda, useful when a chase involved narrow streets, or to outflank a perpetrator.

*Chogokin* (which means "super alloy") is the mythical metal that the great Go Nagai came up with for his 1972 manga *Mazinger Z*, the first of his "super robot" line that continues today with such works as *Mazinkaiser, New Getter Robo,* and, of course, *Shin Mazinger Shougeki! Z Hen.* It also gives its name to Bandai's Soul of Chogokin high-quality toy series, although this series did not yet exist when Fujishima made the joke about his dental work.

**Fujishima's comments from the May 1989 issue of *Afternoon*—*OMG!* Chapter 9:**

*"I have a parakeet at home. Her name is Raiden. She's a female, but whenever I try to touch her, she bites fiercely. I wonder if it's because I gave her such a manly name? These days I'm wondering if I should've at least named her Sakae or Homare."*

*Reader Shigeaki Noritaka, age 24, an office worker in Osaka Prefecture, wrote in* to *Afternoon* to say, "I was able to get a job 'cuz I cut out *Oh My Goddess!* and carried it around with me. Thank you!" *A 30-year-old fan just signing himself as a "Farm Town Teacher" from Gunma Prefecture wrote to say, "I am a high-school language teacher. I wish the goddess could attend my class!!" Fujishima replied to this second letter, advising him to make sure he stays on top of his subject and doesn't fall "so head over*

*heels in love with Belldandy that she ends up teaching your course instead of you."*

Editor's note: Raiden was the ancient Japanese god of thunder, after whom many manly things have been named over the centuries. It may be Fujishima had in mind specifically the Mitsubishi J2M, the WWII-era Japanese fighter plane also known as the Raiden, because "Sakae" and "Homare" are the names of plane engines from the same period—hence he seems to be suggesting he has a one-track mind when it comes to names he could give his parakeet.

The reader's reference to having "cut out *Oh My Goddess!*" presumably means that he literally cut the chapter pages out of the issues of *Afternoon* magazine they ran in. That would have been the only way to carry just *OMG!* around (that is, without toting a stack of heavy manga magazines) in the spring of 1989, as the manga was so new the first volume of the Japanese collection hadn't yet come out.

Note that the translation of some of the readers' names is uncertain; even Japanese people often have to explain to other Japanese how you say their name aloud when you read it, or, conversely, how you write it if all you know is how it sounds. The only way to know for sure is to ask the person, but, you know, it's been twenty years since these letters to *Afternoon* were written . . . ^_^

**Fujishima's comments from the June 1989 issue of *Afternoon*—*OMG!* Chapter 10:**

*"I moved to a new residence. It's a ten-minute walk or so from the train station, a nice environment with good sunshine. But much to my sorrow, there is no bookstore nearby. Ah!! I wanna see some books!! It's both happy and sad to think that days of*

battling my way to Itoxyoxkadox [Ito-Yokado] Department Store by bicycle are about to begin."

Reader Kenji Obayashi, age 24, unemployed in Fukuoka Prefecture, wrote in to Afternoon to say, "Oh! My Goddess! I fell strangely in love with the sight of a northern European goddess drinking tea with her legs tucked beneath her." A fan signing themselves "Kinko C.P.S.," age 16, a student in Osaka Prefecture, said, "I took a clipping of Belldandy along when I went to cheer for my high-school baseball team, and we won!" Fujishima replied to this second letter, saying, "Belldandy isn't a lucky-charm stone, like lapis lazuli. But at this rate, we might start hearing about how a reader grew five centimeters or lost ten kilos!"

Editor's note: Ito-Yokado is, as indicated, a nationwide department-store chain in Japan that has, in recent years, expanded into China, with stores in Beijing and Chengdu. Regarding the peculiar spelling used, i.e., "Itoxyoxkadox"—the x's were actually circles (*maru*) in the original Japanese, often used to "bleep" out a word in Japanese.

The effect here is a little different, though—more like just adding nulls; the complete name of the store is still there once you remove them. Japanese censorship is often more symbolic than functional. Why it was felt necessary to modify the store's name at all is uncertain—after all, Fujishima mentioned other brand names and models elsewhere in his comments. It may possibly have been due to whatever commercial or advertising relations the publisher had with Ito-Yokado at the time of publication.

**Fujishima's comments from the August 1989 issue of *Afternoon*—OMG! Chapter 12 (note that, apparently, there were no comments in the July 1989 issue):**

"Tokio Kazuka, who helped me out this time, owns an FT400 that's been modded in many ways, and even has a mist device to cool the engine. I became a fan of it after riding it. Maybe the most important issue is how easy a bike is to ride?"

Reader Shinichi Ogishima, age 21, profession unknown, of Kanagawa Prefecture, wrote in to Afternoon to say, "Having the ending of Oh My Goddess! in color last issue was so impressive! Goddess, you were even more lovely than the flowers blooming in the five-kilometer radius around you. ♥♥♥" Fan Katsuhiko Sugiyama, age 16, a student from Yamanashi Prefecture, writes, "I now have a girlfriend just like Belldandy. It would be so nice if flowers bloomed all around when we kissed, too." The Japanese editor of Oh My Goddess! answered this by saying, "When we get a postcard like this one, we get over our envy and just feel jolly." Fujishima, however, went a bit further, commenting happily, "It's a prodigious feat. But I'll have to examine whether or not she really looks like Belldandy, so send me a photo of your girlfriend." The editor then broke in, exhorting, "Let's all enter the Miss Belldandy Contest!"

Editor's note: The Honda FT400 was a 1982 bike designed for dirt tracks. Tokio Kazuka, who was active as a manga artist from the late eighties through the 1990s, has not been published in English to date; his best-known work in Japan was probably *The Ejection Girl Gang!*, which not surprisingly featured a motorcycle-riding heroine; it ran in Fujimi Shobo's former *Monthly Comic Dragon* magazine (which later merged into *Monthly Dragon Age*, home of the *Highschool of the Dead* and *Slayers Evolution-R* manga).

**Fujishima's comments from the September 1989 issue of *Afternoon*—OMG! Chapter 13:**

*"I got a license plate issued for my pokke and started riding it. It's a small bike to begin with, so when I ride it, it really is a pocket bike. I usually ride an 1,100 cc model, and it looks like a 400 cc. To make my bike look like an 1,100 cc, I've probably gotta ride a 3,000 cc."*

Editor's note: By "pokke," Fujishima means the "pocket bike" model that Suzuki made to compete with the Honda Monkey—featured in this volume, of course! Presumably, "1,100 cc" refers to Fujishima's Suzuki GSX-R; it would be a bit unreal for a pocket bike, even by manga standards—although go back to chapter 12 to see just how heavy an engine Keiichi's seniors were able to put on a Supercub. ^_^

**Fujishima's comments from the November 1989 issue of *Afternoon—OMG!* Chapter 15 (note that, apparently, there were no comments in the October 1989 issue):**

*"Recently, I've been listening to old (but not really that old) songs for background music. Momoe Yamaguchi and Masanori Sera and Twist are really hot for me right now. But there are also some songs that haven't been reissued as CDs, and the downside is that they're hard to find. Does somebody have a Hiromi Ota CD?"*

Editor's note: Momoe Yamaguchi was a popular teen singer and actress in the 1970s who retired in 1980 to raise a family. Guitarist Masanori Sera was the frontman of a band called Twist in the late 1970s; today he is a solo artist, and contributed the ending theme "Aoi kage" ("Blue Shadow") to the anime series *Casshern Sins* (out next year in the U.S. from Funimation). Hiromi Ota (her name is also sometimes seen spelled in English as "Hiromi Ohta") is a pop singer who had been in retirement for several years

when Fujishima wrote this, but returned to performing in 1998.

**Fujishima's comments from the December 1989 issue of *Afternoon—OMG!* Chapter 16:**

*"As I do my work, reference material keeps piling up. It'd be convenient if I could always use the material needed at the time I need it, but this time, it was buried below all the other stuff on the desk, and I had to do a wild search for it. Fellow readers, be sure to keep your room organized!"*

The English-language editor of *Oh My Goddess!* recently came to the conclusion that if a piece of paper on his desk is 1) covered with an illegible scrawl, 2) further indecipherable because of coffee spills, and 3) has been sitting there for three years, then it's probably not of great importance and can be thrown away. Using this philosophy, he's been able to rapidly reclaim several feet of space. ^_^

More comments from the history of *Oh My Goddess!* in vol. 35, and, of course, more of *your* letters, too!

**Kosuke Fujishima's Oh My Goddess!**

*Can't wait on the Goddesses? Change directions!*

Just gotten into the new unflopped editions of *Oh My Goddess!*, and found you can't wait to see what happens next? Have no fear! The first **20 volumes** of *Oh My Goddess!* are available **right now** in Western-style editions! Released between 1994 and 2005, our *OMG!* Western-style volumes feature premium paper, and pages 40% larger than those of the unflopped editions! If you've already got some of the unflopped volumes and want to know which Western-style ones to get to catch up, check out http://www.darkhorse.com/Zones/Manga for a complete breakdown of how the editions compare!

*Vol. 1: Wrong Number*
ISBN 1-56971-669-2 / $13.99

*Vol. 2: Leader of the Pack*
ISBN 1-56971-764-8 / $13.99

*Vol. 3: Final Exam*
ISBN 1-56971-765-6 / $13.99

*Vol. 4: Love Potion No. 9*
ISBN 1-56971-252-2 / $14.99

*Vol. 5: Sympathy for the Devil*
ISBN 1-56971-329-4 / $13.99

*Vol. 6: Terrible Master Urd*
ISBN 1-56971-369-3 / $14.99

*Vol. 7: The Queen of Vengeance*
ISBN 1-56971-431-2 / $13.99

*Vol. 8: Mara Strikes Back!*
ISBN 1-56971-449-5 / $14.99

*Vol. 9: Ninja Master*
ISBN 1-56971-474-6 / $13.99

*Vol. 10: Miss Keiichi*
ISBN 1-56971-522-X / $16.99

*Vol. 11: The Devil in Miss Urd*
ISBN 1-56971-540-8 / $14.99

*Vol. 12: The Fourth Goddess*
ISBN 1-56971-551-3 / $18.99

*Vol. 13: Childhood's End*
ISBN 1-56971-685-4/ $15.99

*Vol. 14: Queen Sayoko*
ISBN 1-56971-766-4 / $16.99

*Vol. 15: Hand in Hand*
ISBN 1-56971-921-7 / $17.99

*Vol. 16: Mystery Child*
ISBN 1-56971-950-0 / $18.99

*Vol. 17: Traveler*
ISBN 1-56971-986-1 / $17.99

*Vol. 18: The Phantom Racer*
ISBN 1-59307-217-1 / $17.99

*Vol. 19/20: Sora Unchained*
ISBN 1-59307-316-X / $18.99

*Adventures of the Mini-Goddesses*
ISBN 1-56971-421-5 / $9.99

AVAILABLE AT YOUR LOCAL COMICS SHOP OR BOOKSTORE
*To find a comics shop in your area, call 1-888-266-4226
For more information or to order direct:
•On the web: darkhorse.com
•E-mail: mailorder@darkhorse.com
•Phone: 1-800-862-0052 Mon.-Fri. 9 A.M. to 5 P.M. Pacific Time.